The Doctrine of Double Effect is a mainstay of non-consequentialist moral thinking, yet remains misunderstood, and fundamental doubts about it are widespread. In this splendid and path-breaking book, David Černý does more than has ever been done before to uncover the historical origins of this view, to explore its different formulations, and to defend the reasoning behind it. This is a rare achievement, a genuine contribution to analytic ethical theory and applied moral philosophy, and at the same time an exemplary model of the relevance of the history of ideas to philosophy.

*Saul Smilansky*
*Professor, Department of Philosophy*
*University of Haifa, Israel*

David Černý's monograph is authoritative, imaginative and cutting-edge. It is the only work I know of that sheds light on the intellectual origins of *the principle of double effect* and relates them to the contemporary debate in a manner that dispels misunderstandings and advances our understanding of the principle. The 'Principle of Double Effect' could easy be the standard book on the topic for the next ten or twenty years and both students and specialists will learn much from it.

*George Pavlakos*
*Professor of Law and Philosophy*
*University of Glasgow*

David Černý shows in this book that there are several formulations of *the principle of double effect,* and that they need to be distinguished if we wish to think more carefully about good or possibly good acts that have bad consequences. He presents a novel defense against various objections that have been raised against it. His analysis of the principle's historical context and development allows him to shed new light on the various distinctions presupposed by its correct understanding and use.

*Thomas M. Osborne Jr.*
*Professor, Center for Thomistic Studies*
*Chair, Department of Philosophy*
*University of St. Thomas*

The Doctrine of Double Effect is one of the most important principles in applied ethics yet, at the same time, one of the most puzzling. In his book, David Černý offers a combination of a historical and an analytical analysis in order to clarify and explain it. His book is a compulsory reading for anybody interested in ethical theory and in applied ethics.

*Professor Daniel Statman, Chair*
*Department of Philosophy, University of Haifa*

W0010061

# The Principle of Double Effect

This book offers a comprehensive history of the principle of double effect and its applications in ethics. Written from a non-theological perspective, it makes the case for the centrality of the double effect reasoning in philosophical ethics.

The book is divided into two parts. The first part thoroughly examines the history of double effect reasoning. The author's history spans from Thomas Aquinas's opera omnia to the modern and influential understanding of the principle known as proportionalism. The second part of the book elucidates the principle and addresses various objections that have been raised against it, including those that arise from an in-depth discussion of the trolley problem. Finally, the author examines the role of intentions in ethical thinking and constructs a novel defense of the principle based on fine distinctions between intentions.

*The Principle of Double Effect: A History and Philosophical Defense* will be of interest to scholars and advanced students working in moral philosophy, the history of ethics, bioethics, medical ethics, and the Catholic moral tradition.

**David Černý** studied in Bologna and Rome, received his Ph.D. in Philosophy from Charles University in Prague. He is a Research Fellow at the Institute of State and Law and the Institute of Computer Science of the Czech Academy of Sciences. He has widely published in the Czech and Italian languages.

# Routledge Studies in Ethics and Moral Theory

For more information about this series, please visit: https://www.routledge.com/Routledge-Studies-in-Ethics-and-Moral-Theory/book-series/SE0423

# The Principle of Double Effect

## A History and Philosophical Defense

David Černý

Routledge
Taylor & Francis Group
NEW YORK AND LONDON

First published 2020
by Routledge
605 Third Avenue, New York, NY 10017

and by Routledge
2 Park Square, Milton Park, Abingdon, Oxon OX14 4RN

First issued in paperback 2022

*Routledge is an imprint of the Taylor & Francis Group, an informa business*

Publisher's Note
The publisher has gone to great lengths to ensure the quality of this reprint but points out that some imperfections in the original copies may be apparent.

*Library of Congress Cataloging-in-Publication Data*
A catalog record for this title has been requested

ISBN 13: 978-1-03-240033-4 (pbk)
ISBN 13: 978-0-367-44246-0 (hbk)
ISBN 13: 978-1-003-00952-8 (ebk)

DOI: 10.4324/9781003009528

Typeset in Sabon
by codeMantra

I dedicate this book to my fiancée Alena, who gives meaning and joy to my work.

# Contents

# Acknowledgments

My wholehearted thanks go to Danny Statman (University of Haifa), who read the entire manuscript and did not find it as terrible as I had feared; he even agreed to write a foreword for my book. I am also thankful to David Enoch (The Hebrew University of Jerusalem), who, despite his workload, read the theoretical part of my book and provided important feedback on it. At times I took an obdurate stance, which, of course, is no fault of David's. Tom Osborne (University of St. Thomas, Houston) rigorously read and commented on the whole manuscript, for which I am very thankful to him; I am also thankful for the fact that he liked the book and was not afraid to show it. George Pavlakos (University of Glasgow) was the first to recommend that I offer this book to some good publishing house; without him it might still be uselessly taking up space on my computer's hard disk. And the best comes last, as the saying goes. My greatest thanks go to Saul Smilansky (University of Haifa). Saul read through the entire manuscript, helped me improve it (of course, in such a way that I could not blame him for possible shortcomings) and supported me in my work throughout. But I am most grateful to him for the friendship that developed between us along the way, for the debates over good food and wine (in Israel) or beer (in the Czech Republic) and for the projects we share. I am also indebted to three anonymous reviewers for Routledge; their fair and encouraging comments helped me to improve my manuscript.

# Foreword

*Daniel Statman*

For consequentialists, all that matters in determining the morality of some action is its consequences. If the overall consequences are good, the action is right. If the overall consequences are bad, it is wrong. This view would entail a simple, straightforward way of resolving dilemmas involving life and death. Other things being equal, if doing A is predicted to result in more deaths than doing B, then B is the required moral action. To refer to the well-known trolley problem, if you divert a running trolley to a different track in order to save the lives of five workers who would otherwise be killed, then you ought to do that, even if, as a result of the diversion, you would be bringing about the death of a different worker standing on the other track.

Although there is something very appealing about this consequentialist approach, some of its implications are hard to swallow. In particular, if all we should ultimately care about is the number of bodies (so to say) that might result from our action (or inaction), then killing a healthy person in order to use her organs to save ten patients who would otherwise die would be morally permissible – would actually be *mandatory* – a conclusion which seems unacceptable. Hence the attraction of *deontology*, according to which one may never use people as means to the realization of social or moral ends, valuable as these ends might be.

Yet deontology has its own objectionable implications. If knowingly bringing about the death of some (innocent) person is unconditionally prohibited, then attacks on legitimate military targets predicted to bring about the death of civilians would be barred, which would significantly undermine the ability of armies to fight effectively against enemy bases or soldiers located in close proximity to residential areas. Similarly, medical treatment aimed at relieving the pain of a dying patient would be morally forbidden if it is predicted to hasten her death.

In neither of these approaches does consequentialism or deontology seem morally satisfactory. What is needed is some kind of a middle ground position which would retain parts of each, and this is precisely where The Doctrine of Double Effect (DDE) enters the scene. DDE starts by rejecting the consequentialist assumption that consequences are all that matter but also rejects the idea that the only alternative is one that implies a sweeping prohibition on knowingly bringing about the deaths of innocent people. According to DDE, while *intentionally* doing so is (almost) unconditionally forbidden, *knowingly* doing so is not, provided that the anticipated bad results are not disproportionate to the anticipated good ones. While attacking enemy headquarters is morally permissible, even if it is expected to lead to the deaths of two civilians living nearby, it is impermissible if it is expected to lead to the deaths of one thousand civilians in a big, neighbouring hospital.

DDE can thus be seen as a moderated version of deontology. It rejects the consequentialist assumption that, in decisions regarding life and death, we should care only about numbers, but it also rejects the understanding of deontology, according to which we may never select a course of action that is predicted to cause the deaths of innocent people. The key notion of DDE is *intentionality*. DDE accepts the deontological view that killing (innocent) people intentionally is almost absolutely forbidden. It adds, however, that unintentionally, albeit foreseeably, bringing about their deaths as a side effect of some justified action might be permissible.

How the intention of the agent can make such a moral difference, however, is perplexing and is the focus of a long philosophical debate. Some contemporary writers completely ignore the genealogy of DDE in its various historical versions, while others deal only with the historical aspects of DDE and bracket questions concerning its current use. In the book before you, David Černý does a great job of combining these two points of view, the historical and the analytical, in an attempt to clarify the meaning of DDE and justify its central assumption that unintentionally killing people might be morally permitted. His combination offers readers a unique perspective on DDE and makes a significant contribution to understanding how it might be justified. Whether or not Černý succeeded in articulating a defensible version of DDE is now for the readers to judge.

# 1 Introduction

Human action is not black and white: it can have good and bad consequences, which together give rise to the moral dilemmas of everyday life. A father rushing his ill son to hospital does not observe the prescribed speed and increases the risk that he will run over a pedestrian or cause an accident. A physician considers an operation which will save his patient's life but kill her unborn child. A dentist, while operating, causes his patient pain. A man decides to visit his friend in hospital, although he knows that he will make his wife angry. Soldiers must bomb the enemy's ammunition deposit, but they know that innocent civilians will be killed. Life constantly places us in situations when we must consider an action that does not have only good consequences. In the many hundred years of tradition of moral reflection a doctrine has crystalized determining the conditions on which an action that has good and bad consequences can be actualized: we speak of the principle or doctrine of double effect or practical deliberation based on double effect.

According to the principle of double effect an act with good and bad effects can be actualized if certain conditions are met; mostly four are stated:

1   The act itself, regardless of its consequences, is at least morally indifferent (it is morally good or indifferent).
2   Only the good effect is intended, the bad effect must not be intended.
3   The bad effect is not a means of attaining the good effect.
4   There is a grave reason to actualize the act that has both types of effects (good and bad).

The doctrine of double effect originated in the context of Catholic moral theology. It first appeared, at least according to some historians, in the work of the medieval philosopher and theologian Thomas Aquinas. It was further developed by other Catholic authors such as Tommaso de Vio, Francisco de Vitoria, Domingo de Sta Teresa and in the 19th century by the Jesuit moral theologian Jean Pierre Gury in his influential work *Compendium theologiae moralis*. The principle of double effect received the highest status in the work of Peter Knauer, the founder of a modern strand of moral theology – proportionalism, who made it a hermeneutic principle in the light of which all basic concepts of moral theology are defined and all human action evaluated.

But it would be wrong to believe that the principle of double effect is strictly associated with Catholic moral theology. In the recent decades it has received the attention of authors not adhering to this tradition, whether affiliated to another religious tradition or without religious creed. Most often this moral principle is encountered in the works of modern applied ethicists who discuss its validity and possibilities of application in the context of contemporary ethical discussions.

Let us take a look at just a few examples from contemporary applied ethics.

**1. Just War.** One of the central moral rules of *ius in bello* is the principle of civilian immunity, which forbids killing innocent civilians. However, as Steven P. Lee has observed, if this principle were taken literally, we would be morally bound to unconditional pacifism arising from the tension between the following two statements[1]:

i   Killing civilians in war is morally totally inadmissible.
ii  War cannot be conducted without civilian casualties.

The first statement expresses an important moral norm, which for many is undoubtable, while the other is a realistic evaluation of the possibilities of conducting war: regardless of efforts to avoid civilian casualties there will always be some, and they are even highly probably linked to certain types of attacks, e.g. bombing. The principle of double effect can[2] provide a way out of this tension. In the context of just-war theories it is often formulated as follows: civilian casualties must not be intended, they must be merely foreseen, and there must be a proportional reason for carrying out a certain kind of military action. The expression "proportional reason" is intended to convey that the planned strategic military outcome of the action must be so important (for example, destabilizing the enemy army's headquarters) that it outweighs the unintended civilian casualties.

**2. Palliative Care.** Palliative care strives to accompany (not only) dying patients on their path through their disease, to alleviate their pain and other symptoms, to improve their psychological and mental state, and to ease their existential or spiritual anxiety. In the context of modern palliative care the double effect principle is most commonly mentioned in connection with administering opioids at the end of life when they can affect the patient's respiratory drive and thus have the potential to shorten her life. When the palliator in alleviating serious pain or other symptoms with which the patient finds it difficult to cope (i) intends to alleviate the pain or other symptoms (ii) in order to improve the patient's quality of life or facilitate an easier death for her, (iii) alleviating the pain or other symptoms is the action's intended effect, (iv) accelerating the process of dying is an unintended negative consequence of the physician's action, (v) there is a proportional reason to actualize the action regardless of the negative consequence associated with it.[3] Today many authors are stressing that the fear regarding opioids is unjustified as, correctly administered, opioids do not make life shorter; quite the contrary – they prolong it. But the reasoning structure laid out above in connection with end-of-life measures can also be applied to more complex situations. For example, some patients are highly agitated towards the ends of their lives and calm down when they are administered a drug such as Diazepam. But a consequence of that is that they are sleepy, do not drink enough, do not move sufficiently and thus run a higher risk of developing pneumonia. In other cases some patients are assisted in breathing by a centesis in the abdomen, but draining several litres of fluids in ill patients can result in shock and death. In all these cases the principle of double effect can be applied.[4]

**3. Roboethics.** Different versions of the trolley problem have played an important role in roboethics, a modern branch of applied ethics. They appear, for example, in discussions of the ethical rules that ought to govern autonomous vehicles in case of imminent collisions. Some authors hold that the principle of double effect (possibly together with the principle of triple effect) can systematically explain the various moral intuitions evoked by the numerous versions of this problem's traditional formulation. It is even fairly easy to model moral decision-making that conforms to the principle of double effect by means of prospective logical programming in the ACORDA[5] language. Thus, the principle of double effect could also play an important role beyond the context of trolley problems: for example in ethically regulating the behaviour of medical, nursing, caring, rescuing or military robots.

But the principle of double effect remains a controversial principle: there is no agreement whether the principle is valid (its validity is rejected mostly by authors adhering to the consequentialist tradition) and there is even no agreement as to what form it should in fact take. In contemporary bioethical literature two claims most commonly appear: (i) the principle of double effect takes the form I have stated above and (ii) the history of the principle of double effect begins among authors belonging to the famous school in the Spanish Salamanca. In other words, it is assumed that there is precisely one principle of double effect (perhaps in different formulations), which first appears in the works of philosophers and theologians of the Salamanca school.

In my work I would like to dispute both claims and defend the following three theses:

1   It is impossible to speak of one principle of double effect. In history
    we encounter various formulations, which are not merely different

expressions of the same principle. All formulations are set in a certain ethical context, in which they can play and often do play a different role. To speak of "the principle of double effect" is, from the historical point of view, inadequate.

2    The first formulation of deliberation based on a principle of double effect – on weighing the moral permissibility of actualizing an action that has good and bad consequences – appears in the work of the Dominican philosopher and theologian Thomas Aquinas.

3    The principle of double effect in the form I give it in the last chapter of my work remains a controversial moral principle, where its presuppositions (especially ethics taking into account the intentions of actors in ethical evaluation of their acts) are especially controversial. When these presuppositions are accepted, the principle of double effect appears to be a rational way of justifying a certain act.

In the second chapter, titled *A Brief History of the Principle: Thomas Aquinas*, I focus on the medieval philosopher and theologian Thomas Aquinas. In the *Secunda Secundae* of his *Summa Theologiae Doctor Angelicus*, as he is called, discusses the admissibility of killing the aggressor in an act of self-defence in the context of discussing commutative justice. Here Thomas explicitly says that one human act can have two consequences: (i) one is good (saving one's life), and (ii) the other is bad (aggressor's death). The moral evaluation of self-defence is set in the broader framework of Thomas's perfectionist conception of morality and starts from the premise that maintaining own life is natural to every being. If killing the aggressor is not included in the agent's intention (according to Aquinas's terminology *praeter intentionem*) and is further appropriate to the act's end (self-defence), it is not impermissible from the moral point of view. In the same chapter he further gives a detailed account of the theory of *fontes moralitatis* (moral evaluation of human action is determined by three sources: object, end and circumstances) and distinguishes between human action *in genere moris* and *in genere naturae*.

But not all authors have regarded Thomas's treatise as the first formulation of a certain version of the principle of double effect. Interpretative disputes have focussed on the meaning of the phrases *in intentione* and *praeter intentionem* and also *per accidens* and *quandoque*. That is why I analyze the individual interpretations, in turn – ones penned by Joseph T. Mangan, the first historian of the principle of double effect, Leonard Lessius, author of the 17th-century treatise *De iustitia et iure*, Steven A. Long, T. A. Cavanaugh, Gareth B. Matthews and Joseph Boyle. My analyses result in the claim that Thomas Aquinas in fact presents his version of the principle of double effect, which is, however, an application of already existing principles of moral evaluation of human action to the particular example of self-defence. Thomas's version of the principle of double effect therefore plays a fairly marginal role in his thought. But I have succeeded in defending the first thesis of my work: Thomas Aquinas is the founding father of the ethical tradition employing the principle of double effect.

In the third chapter, called *A Brief History of the Principle: Cajetan to J. P. Gury*, I attempt to remove some deficiencies of historical overviews of the development of the principle of double effect. Although these overviews mention all the important authors, they do so often very briefly and do not provide the reader with the original Latin texts and their interpretation. For this reason I have selected the authors I regard as most important – Tommaso de Vio, called Cajetan, Francisco de Vitoria, Domingo de Sta Teresa and Jean Pierre Gury – and the key passages of their works, which I have translated. I analyze the selected texts in detail, comment on them and structure their arguments and formulations of the principle of double effect as intelligibly as possible, to some extent formally. I leave the question whether all the authors mentioned presented the same version of the principle of double effect open until the conclusion of the following chapter.

In the 20th century the climate among Catholic moral theologians changed and they began to raise questions that were impermissible for the preceding moral tradition. These theologians increasingly emphasized the importance of moral description of human action, which was in their view quite inadequately determined only in terms of its physical description. A growing number of experts in moral theology also disputed the infallibility of the moral teaching of the Catholic Church, expressed e.g. in Pope Paul VI's controversial encyclical *Humanae vitae*, especially in connection with means of artificial birth control (contraception). These events prepared the ground for a new direction in moral theology, which obtained the name proportionalism and spread especially in the United States of America. But the (perhaps inadvertent) founder of proportionalism was the young German Jesuit theologian Peter Knauer.

The fourth chapter focusses primarily on two spheres: (i) presenting the hermeneutic function of the principle of double effect according to Peter Knauer and (ii) comparing his conception and formulation of the principle of double effect with those from the preceding chapters. With Peter Knauer I focus on his new formulation of the principle of double effect and the role it plays in his entire moral system. This principle speaks not only on a limited number of acts but also on the whole of morality. In light of the principle of double effect Knauer tries to define all the basic concepts of morality, such as the concept of bad and good action. I show how in distinguishing between psychological and moral intentions the author redefines the concept of intention and how he construes the concept of moral causality. In the concluding part of the section devoted to Knauer I try to illustrate his somewhat vaguely defined concept of proportional reason, to which the principle of double effect itself and thereby in fact all of morality is ultimately reduced.

In a further section of the fourth chapter I prove my second thesis: I summarize the individual formulation of the principle of double effect and demonstrate that they are set in different ethical systems in which they often play very different roles. In the concluding part of the chapter I briefly deal with the proportionalism of the American theologian G. L. Hallett and show how in his work the principle of double effect was transformed into a criterion of value maximization.

In the fifth chapter I direct attention to four important authors: the British theorist and philosopher of law Herbert L. A. Hart, the British moral philosopher Philippa Foot, her American colleague Judith J. Thomson and Francis Kamm. I lay out Hart's theory of intentions and its application in criminal law, but I specially focus on the author's criticism of moral asymmetry between hysterectomy and craniotomy. Advocates of the principle of double effect usually regard hysterectomy as licit, but they reject the possibility of craniotomy, since the physician's intention in this medical procedure is killing the foetus (crushing its head). Hart, on the other hand, claims that the physician's intention need not be to kill the foetus: the physician may intend crushing the foetus's head without the object of his intention being killing it. I show that Hart's criticism is incorrect.

In the following part of the chapter I focus on the British moral philosopher Philippa Foot. The author does not reject the validity of the principle of double effect; she acknowledges that it is an important moral principle which explains some of our intuitions. Foot, therefore, believes that it is insufficient to criticize the principle of double effect: it is necessary to present a theory that will accommodate moral intuitions equally well or better than the principle of double effect does. The author presents a series of thought experiments which include morally asymmetrical situations (in one scenario the action is morally licit, in the other it is illicit); this moral asymmetry is well explained precisely by the principle of double effect. She then formulates her theory of positive and negative obligations, which on her view explains the moral asymmetry of the scenarios discussed equally well as the principle of double effect. Foot also touches on the most problematic point of the principle of double effect and assigns it a label: the closeness problem (I discuss it in the sixth chapter). In her paper *The Problem of Abortion and the Doctrine of Double Effect* of 1967 a runaway tram rushing along rails to a switch behind which five persons are working on one rail and only one on the other is mentioned for the first time. From this an extensive sphere of contemporary ethical and experimental research called trolleyology was born.

Foot laid the foundations of trolleyology, but the discussion developed primarily thanks to the American philosopher and theorist of rights Judith Jarvis Thomson. In my book I focus on three thought scenarios Thomson presents to demonstrate the inadequacy of Foot's solution: I have called them The Casual Passer-by, The Fat Man on the Bridge and The Loop. The principle of double effect is very well able to explain the moral asymmetry between The Casual Passer-by and The Fat Man on the Bridge, but the last scenario, The Loop, is problematic for it. I discuss this scenario in detail and try to show that advocates of the principle of double effect can apply it to this difficult scenario as well.

These first chapters of more or less historical character do not serve merely as a means to elucidate the historical development and context of the principle of double effect: their finality is also a discussion of difficult moral dilemmas and gradual elucidation of the conditions of applying the principle of double effect. I also believe, and try to persuade my readers, that some historical distinctions, namely these between different kinds of *finis* (*operis* and *operantis*) and intentions, can shed a new light on the ongoing discussion about the doctrine of double effect and thereby find its firm place in intention-based applied ethics.

In the sixth and longest chapter, entitled *Defence of the Principle of Double Effect*, I prove the last thesis of my book: the principle of double effect is a valid, although controversial, moral principle in the context of a moral theory which grants the important role of intentions in ethical evaluation of human action.

In the first part of the sixth chapter I consider the possibility of reducing the number of components of the principle of double effect, I introduce the concept of extensional and intensional means and define the concept of intensional means and relationship between "to be a means" and "to be intended" in greater detail. I determine the character of the principle of double effect as a principle of moral justification and retain all four conditions in its formulation for didactic reasons. The final version of the principle of double effect thus attains the classical modern form:

1   **Principle of double effect:**

    i   **Character of the act.** The action must be good or at least morally indifferent (independently of its consequences).

    ii   **Intention of actor.** The actor intends only the good effect. The bad effect may be foreseen, tolerated and admitted, but it must not be intended.

    iii   **Distinction between means and consequences.** A bad effect must not be a means to attaining a good effect.

iv **Proportion between good and bad effect**. The good effect must outweigh the bad.

In the next section of the chapter I return to the morally asymmetric scenarios of hysterectomy and craniotomy and attempt to criticize Hart's conception, according to which a physician performing craniotomy need not intend the foetus's death. The following subchapter aims to critically evaluate Rachels's argument, according to which intentions do not play an important role in moral evaluation. I criticize Rachels's instrumental conception of human action, introduce the concept of c- and f-intention and show their role in moral evaluation of human action. Next I address the objections levelled by Thomas Scanlon against the direct relevance of intentions and, by answering them, I further elucidate the role of intention in moral discourse. Then I focus my attention on Francis Kamm's criticism of the doctrine of double effect and her proposed doctrine of triple effect intended to replace the former. I address her objections in detail and try to show that the actions presented by Kamm in different scenarios as morally permissible in fact turn out to be illicit.

I further present Bratman's influential theory of intentions and focus on his three roles of intentions, discuss two important thought scenarios (strategic bomber and terror bomber) and show how Bratman's theory of the three roles of intentions helps to distinguish between intended consequences and merely admitted ones. The last part of the sixth chapter attempts to come to terms with the closeness problem by means of the concepts of c- and f-intention introduced earlier, whereby the entire chapter and effort to defend the principle of double effect is concluded. I believe that I have succeeded in proving the third thesis of my work: in a certain context (an ethics accounting for intentions) the principle of double effect can be defended and applied to solving difficult moral dilemmas. The conclusion of the chapter summarizes the four conditions of the principle of double effect and offers general rules for applying the last condition: the good effect must outweigh the bad effect.

## Notes

1  Steven P. Lee, *Ethics and War: An Introduction* (Cambridge: Cambridge University Press, 2012), 173–181.
2  I intentionally write "can" since some authors reject the principle of double effect as invalid and seek other solutions to the tension between ethics and the actual options of waging war. For example, Stephen Nathanson claims that the principle of double effect justifies too much, including even terrorist attacks. And Uwe Steinhoff rejects the absolutist view according to which civilians have an absolute right to immunity over the course of a war, so that their right not to be killed can be outweighed in some situations, if there is a sufficiently grave proportional reason for it. Cf. Stephen Nathanson,

*Terrorism and Ethics of War* (Cambridge: Cambridge University Press, 2010), 96–103; Uwe Steinhoff, *On the Ethics of War and Terrorism* (New York: Oxford University Press, 2007), 33–59.
3 Robert C. Macauley, *Ethics in Palliative Care: A Complete Guide* (New York: Oxford University Press, 2018), 209–210.
4 Fiona Randall and Robin S. Downie, *The Philosophy of Palliative Care: Critique and Reconstruction* (New York: Oxford University Press, 2006), 113. But at the same time the authors add that many specialists in palliative care are not aware of all the conditions of applying the principle of double effect and often don't understand them, which precludes its broader application in practice.
5 Luís M. Pereira and Ari Saptawijaya, *Programming Machine Ethics* (Dordrecht: Springer, 2016), 109–118.

# 2 A Brief History of the Principle
## Thomas Aquinas

## Introduction

In its simplest formulation the principle of double effect says that under certain conditions it is morally licit to perform an action with good and bad consequences. Most historical analyses agree that an explicit formulation and application of the principle of double effect is first to be found in the important Dominican thinker of high scholasticism, Thomas Aquinas. However, some authors point out that in an implicit form this principle is apparently encountered much earlier. Joseph T. Mangan recalls the *Old Testament* story of Eleazar, of whom the sixth chapter of the First Book of Maccabees says[1]:

Eleazar, called Avaran, saw that one of the animals was taller than all the others and was equipped with royal armour. He figured that the king must be on it. So, he gave his life to save his people and to secure an everlasting name for himself. He ran courageously into the midst of a group of soldiers to reach it, killing men right and left so that they had to give way to him on both sides. He got under the elephant and stabbed it from underneath. He killed it, but it fell to the ground on top of him, and he died there.[2]

The Old Testament text speaks of Eleazar who decided to sacrifice himself for his people (an action that is of itself morally good) by jumping under an elephant carrying the king of the enemy and killing it by stabbing it from underneath. Eleazar did not wish to die (it was not part of his intention), he wanted to kill the enemy and merely foresaw that he will not be able to escape from underneath the elephant and will die. His own death was not intended, it was merely foreseen as a necessary component of a moral act (self-sacrifice for his people).

As I have already stated, most authors agree that the first explicit formulation of the principle of double effect is found in the work of the Italian Dominican Thomas Aquinas, born in 1124 or 1225 in the Italian town of Roccasecca, a few years after the founder of the Dominican order St. Dominic died and possibly in the same year when the University in Naples was founded.[3] Thomas was an extraordinarily prolific writer, writing commentaries on Aristotle, theologians and the Bible, small theological and philosophical expositions, systematic theological works, a special place among which belongs to *Summa Theologiae* divided into three parts, the second of which consist of two parts (*Pars prima, Pars secunda, Pars tertia*; *Pars secunda* consists of *Prima secundae partis* and *Secunda secundae partis*[4]). The first part, speaking of God insofar as he is in himself (*secundum quod in se est*, qq. 2–43) and of God as the principle and end of all reality (*secundum quod est principium rerum et finis earum*, qq. 44–119), was written in 1265–1267 while Aquinas was staying in Rome. *Prima secundae* was completed in summer 1270, work on *Secunda secundae* began immediately afterwards and was completed in December of the following year. Aquinas probably began writing *Tertia pars* in Paris in winter 1271–1272 and proceeded with it in Naples in the following year, when after a mystical experience on June 12th, 1273 he terminated his writing activity.[5]

The core of Aquinas's moral expositions in the *Summa Theologiae* is not, as was long claimed, natural law, the commandments or the virtues, but **human action** (*actus humanus*, stemming from the human being as a person, which Aquinas contrasts with *actus hominis*, not having its origin in reason and free will).[6] Aquinas devotes questions 6–89 of *Prima secundae* to human action; the external principles of human action are discussed by questions 90–108 (law) and 109–114 (grace). The first part of *Secunda secundae* (questions 1–46) deals with the theologal virtues (faith, hope and love), there follows an exposition of the cardinal virtues (prudence, temperance, justice and courage) in questions 47–170.[7]

## Self-Defence and the Principle of Double Effect

A *locus classicus* of the history of the principle of double effect is found in *Secunda secundae* (abbreviated II-II, or IIaIIae) in *quaestio* 64, situated in the context of discussing offenses against commutative justice (*de vitiis oppositis commutative iustitiae*). In the seventh article Aquinas asks whether it is allowed to kill an aggressor in self-defence (*utrum alicui liceat occidere aliquem se defendendo*) and answers:

> Respondeo dicendum quod nihil prohibet unius actus esse duos effectus, quorum alter solum sit in intentione, alius vero sit praeter intentionem. Morales autem actus recipiunt speciem secundum quod intenditur, non autem ab eo quod est praeter intentionem, cum sit per accidens, ut ex supradictis patet. Ex actu igitur alicuius seipsum defendentis duplex effectus sequi potest: unus quidem conservatio propriae vitae; alius autem occisio invadentis. Actus igitur huiusmodi ex hoc quod intenditur conservatio propriae vitae, non habet rationem illiciti: cum hoc sit cuilibet naturale quod se conservet in esse quantum potest. Potest tamen aliquis actus ex bona intentione proveniens illicitus reddi si non sit proportionatus fini. Et ideo si

aliquis ad defendendum propriam vitam utatur maiori violentia quam oporteat, erit illicitum. Si vero moderate violentiam repellat, erit licita defensio: nam secundum iura, vim vi repellere licet cum moderamine inculpatae tutelae. Nec est necessarium ad salutem ut homo actum moderatae tutelae praetermittat ad evitandum occisionem alterius: quia plus tenetur homo vitae suae providere quam vitae alienae.

Sed quia occidere hominem non licet nisi publica auctoritatae propter bonum commune, ut ex supradictis patet; illicitum est quod homo intendat occidere hominem ut seipsum defendat, nisi ei qui habet publicam auctoritatem, qui, intendens hominem occidere ad sui defensionem, refert hoc ad publicum bonum: ut patet in milite pugnante contra hostes, et in ministro iudicis pugnante contra latrones. Quavis et isti etiam peccent si privata libidine moveantur.[8]

Aquinas's text, believed to be historically the first application of an ethical deliberation based on the principle of double effect, is situated in the context of his **perfectionist conception of morality**[9]: human life is one of the perfections required for the actualization of all other goods and as such is the object of natural inclinations.[10] Human action aimed at conserving the good of life (*conservatio propriae vitae*) is not ethically illicit (*non habet rationem illiciti*), for it is natural for a human (and within Aquinas's metaphysics not only for a human) to want to continue his own existence as long as possible (*hoc sit cuilibet naturale quod se conservet in esse quantum potest*). Although the inclination to life as a good is natural, it does not follow that every manner of conserving one's life is morally justified, as indicated by the very title of the seventh question *Whether it is permitted to kill a man in defending oneself* (*Utrum liceat alicui occidere hominem se defendendo*).

In his *respondeo* Aquinas first on the general level of theory of human action claims that a certain act $\varphi$ can have two effects (*unius actus esse duos effectus*), one of which is intended (*in intentione*), while the other one is not (*praeter intentionem*). Aquinas, as we shall see later, endorsed a doctrine according to which the moral character of human action is specified by its object, which determines the type (kind) of act (*morales autem actus recipiunt speciem secundum quod intenditur*).[11] The object of the act – also called rather misleadingly[12] *finis operis, materia circa quam, finis proximus* – formally determines the intrinsic finality of the human act and impresses a moral specification on it. Let us imagine two persons, $P_1$ and $P_2$, performing the same action with respect to a merely "physical" description: both $P_1$ and $P_2$ perform a series of corporeal acts which comprises taking hold of a certain amount of money, placing that amount in the pocket and returning home. Their action in its "physical" form has some extrinsic unity (taking an amount of money), which structures and orders the sequence of the individual actions and bestows the character of human action on it. This ordered sequence of actions can be conceived as matter, for we consider it only in its physical manifestation (a human body moves in a certain way, causally affects its surroundings, a certain sum of money is transferred into a pocket, etc.). Only if we consider the object of the act in a moral sense do we imprint a certain moral character on this matter (identical in the case of $P_1$ and $P_2$). In other words, scholastically speaking, the matter is **in-formed** by a certain specifying principle and constitutes a specific moral act. Let us say that $P_1$ decided to steal a thousand crowns from his neighbour, while $P_2$ receives from the neighbour a thousand crowns the neighbour owed him. $P_1$ commits a theft (a kind of action specified by its object), which is an immoral kind of act, while $P_2$ merely receives back his own money which the neighbour is returning to him according to an arrangement the two have made.[13] When we speak of the object of an action from the moral point of view, we speak of a formal principle determining the kind of action (theft, murder, alms, etc.).[14]

Christopher Kaczor mentions another example of explaining the difference between action considered "physically" (*in genere naturae*) and from the moral point of view (*in genere moris*).[15] In Shakespeare's well known plays *King Lear* and *Romeo and Juliet* there are scenes in which drinking of poison occurs (drinking poison is – from the "physical" point of view – an identical type of action, or more precisely, the drinking of poison in *King Lear* and in *Romeo and Juliet* are instances (*tokens*) of the same kind (*type*) of action). In the former the poison is drunk by Regan, in whose case it is not a suicide as Regan does not drink the poison as poison, with a suicidal intention: from the moral point of view her act of drinking poison cannot be characterized as suicide (her sister Goneril is to be blamed for her death). Romeo, on the other hand, has bought the poison from an apothecary in Mantua and on seeing Juliet in the Capulet tomb drinks it with the intention of ending his life: from the moral point of view his drinking the poison was an act of suicide.

From the general reflection on the moral qualification of human action Aquinas proceeds to the act of self-defence itself, which can have (*sequi potest*) two effects: (i) conserving one's own life (*conservatio propriae vitae*) and (ii) killing the aggressor (*occisio invadentis*). Although conserving one's own life is morally licit (*non habet rationem illiciti*), a human act guided by a good intention can become morally illicit if it is not proportionate to its end (*proportionatus fini*). Aquinas wants to say that if in the act of defending his own life the defender employs more force than is necessary (proportionate to the end, i.e., to defence of life), his act will become morally illicit, while if the use of force is proportionate to the act's end the moral evaluation of the act of self-defence remains the same.

In his exposition on the admissibility of self-defence Aquinas, as is his habit, synthesizes the preceding tradition, especially representatives of early scholasticism, the Cistercian monk Alan of Lille (1128–1200/3) and Alexander of Hales (1185–1245). Alan of Lille in his *De Fide Catholica* (written in 1185–1200) writes that a defender can fend off the aggressor by force even if he dies as a result, if his death is not intended (*non intendendo eum occidere*), while Alexander of Hales in his *Summa theologica* focusses on the intention to conserve one's own life (*intentio conservationis propriae salutis*).

Aquinas's grasp of the problem of killing the aggressor in self-defence can also be viewed in the context of his general exposition of the ethical character of human action (*de bonitate et malitia humanorum actuum in generali*) in *Prima secundae*, q. 18.[16] Here Aquinas speaks of the conditions determining the moral evaluation (*fontes moralitatis*)[17] of human deeds against the backdrop of the general metaphysical assumption that every thing (i.e., human action too) has as much good as it has being, which pertains to it from its essence.[18] Only God is absolute being, fullness of being (*plenitudo essendi*) and as *esse ipsum subsistens* he is also the absolute good, absolute subsisting perfection. Of its nature human action (as action) cannot be an absolute good, but it can attain such fullness of being as pertains to it *in quantum* human action, and in the measure in which this relative fullness of being pertains to it, it is also good. Conversely it holds that in the measure in which it does not attain the fullness of being that pertains to it, it is bad.[19]

Every thing first of all has fullness of its being based on its form, due to which it is, as in-formed, situated is a certain particular kind; e.g. a human can have the fullness of human being only thanks to his substantial form, which contentually determines the kind of thing a human is, and from the logical point of view the fact that each particular human falls under the general kind "human." Analogically a human action receives its primary specification of fullness of being – specification according to natural species – from its object (*ex obiecto*), i.e., the primary moral specification of human action comes from its object, which on the moral level specifies human action and imprints on it the primary moral charge (of its object an act can be good – giving alms, or bad – murder, theft).[20]

A human being is human based on the substantial form which, however, does not immediately and fully determine all the perfection (fullness) a human being can attain (*plenitudo perfectionis*); a human being is bearer of accidental determinations (accidents) which contribute to the full specification of being human (e.g., being of a certain weight is accidental to a human being, but "good" weight, i.e., weight corresponding to and appropriate for a healthy human organism, contributes to human perfection). It is similar in the case of a human action to whose (moral) perfection extrinsic, accidental factors also contribute – the circumstances (*circumstantiae*) of the action.[21] Let us consider e.g. an action which from a disinterested "physical" point of view can be described as transferring a certain sum of money to own pocket. If it is someone else's money and it is transferred to the pocket without authorization, then from the moral point of view (*ex obiecto*) it is a theft. In one case the thief is an unknown person, in another case it is the administrator of the robbed person's property. The fact that the thief is once an unknown person and another time a person entrusted with financial administration of the robbed person's property does not enter the essential determination of the act (its moral specification), but it is a circumstance (*circumstantia*) making the theft on the part of the administrator (at least on many authors' view) a morally graver offense.[22]

The last source of the morality of human action according to Thomas Aquinas is its end (*finis*), for action is not determined only by its object (what kind of action it is – the act's end, *finis proximus, finis operis*), but also by the agent's end (*finis remotus, finis operantis*), since rational agents' actions *qua* actions are always directed to some end.[23] The relationship between *finis operis* and *finis operantis* in Aquinas is again rather complicated by the fact that the Angelic Doctor conceives *finis operantis* as more formal than *finis operis*, so that it can imprint a new character on an act already formally determined by its object.[24] Aquinas gives a simple example: Let us imagine that someone steals money in order to seduce a woman with it and so commit an act of adultery. From the point of view of specification by the act's object it is a theft, but with respect to the agent's more formal end (*finis operantis*) it is adultery. It is therefore a case of an adulterer who committed theft: he stole money **in order to** be able to commit adultery.[25]

An important part of the doctrine of *fontes moralitatis* is the conviction that human action is morally determined by all three factors: object, circumstances and end. Morally proper action is such that is proper from the point of view of object, circumstances and end (*bonum ex integra causa*), while a defect in one of these sources of morality suffices to render the action improper (*malum ex quocumque defectu*).[26] Let us introduce the doctrine with a simple example: let us say that a good surgeon is characterized by three capacities: (i) outstanding theoretical knowledge and practical skill, (ii) self-possession and (iii) sobriety. A good surgeon is one who makes use of his theoretical knowledge over the course of operations and has excellent operating technique at his disposal, reacts calmly and prudently even in difficult circumstances and of course is sober. If one of these components is "deficient," the surgeon cannot be regarded, in the given situation,[27] as a good surgeon. Human action in its moral dimension is like a work of art: one defect decreases its value.

Let us now return to the text where Aquinas discusses killing an aggressor over the course of defending one's own life. The object of the action is good (conservation of life), so is the agent's end (he defends himself **in order to** save his life); Aquinas defines the circumstances as using means adequate to the end and, in accordance with the doctrine generally outlined in *Prima Secundae*, q. 18, stipulates that if the means are proportionate to the end then the action is morally licit, but if they are not then the action, which is proper *ex obiecto*, is illicit by reason of circumstances.

## Interpretations of Aquinas's Text

### *Joseph T. Mangan*

Although reading Aquinas's text seems to suggest that it speaks of an application of an ethical deliberation based on the principle of double effect – and therefore some authors regard Aquinas, historically speaking, as the founder of the tradition incorporating this practical ethical principle – interpreters do not agree as to whether this appearance will stand the test in light of a critical interpretation of Aquinas's *oeuvre complete*. It is possible to say that at present four different interpretations of the exposition of the admissibility of killing an aggressor in self-defence exist.

One of them is found in an important historical-critical analysis of the principle of double effect written by the Catholic moral theologian and member of the Society of Jesus Joseph T. Mangan *An Historical Analysis of the Principle of Double Effect.*[28] Mangan specifies the principle of double effect in the following way:

Person $S$ can perform action $\varphi$, in which he foresees the actualization of a good and a bad effect, if the following four conditions are simultaneously met:

1   The action itself is of the nature of its object good or at least indifferent;
2   Only the good effect is intended, the bad one is not;
3   The good effect is not reached by means of the bad effect;
4   There is a proportionally grave reason for $S$ to perform $\varphi$ and thereby consent to the production of the bad effect.

Mangan interprets Aquinas's text in the following way: it is morally illicit for someone (in this case someone defending his own life) to intend the aggressor's death (i) as the final end of his action or (ii) as an intermediate end preceding the final end, which is defence of own life. But if the aggressor's death is not intended, either as end or as a means, and if using the given means is proportionate to the end (defence of life), then it is possible to act so that one of the effects of the action is the aggressor's death. Mangan views Aquinas's text as an expression of the principle of double effect and construes its logical structure as follows:

1   First Aquinas on a general ethical level specifies that there is nothing to prevent some action having two effects, one good and one bad, provided that only the good effect falls in the agent's intention, not the bad one.

2   He further explains that human action receives moral character from what the agent intends, not from what he does not.

3   Finally, the mere fact that an action is good of its object and end does not imply that it is good in the final evaluation: it can be rendered morally illicit if the selected means are not proportionate to the end.

Mangan correctly states that the key to a correct interpretation of Aquinas's text from *IaIIae*, a. 64, q. 7 is correct grasp of the meaning of the terms *intendere* and *non intendere*, *ex intentione* (or as Aquinas says *in intentione*) and *praeter intentionem*. In Aquinas's thought the noun *intentio* has a broad semantic field of application; etymologically it means "being directed (in-tending) to something" (*Intentio... significat in aliquid tendere*[29]) and can acquire gnoseological or ethical connotations.[30] From the ethical point of view *intentio* is an act of will presupposing an act of reason ordering things with respect to their end (*intentio nominat actum voluntatis, praesupposita ordinatione rationis ordinantis aliquid in finem*[31]). Aquinas underlines that there is no intention without a choice of means; the will relates to its ends in various ways:

1   absolutely (when we naturally wish to be healthy – *voluntas*),

2   as reachable by means of something else (we want to be healthy, therefore we eat healthy food and exercise).[32]

Mangan grounds the plausibility of interpreting Aquinas's text on the admissibility of self-defence as an application of the principle of double effect on an extensional definition of what falls under the intention (what is *in intentione* or, scholastically, what is the object of the intention) of the will, or as we would say today (and Aquinas would definitely not protest), of the acting person. If only the **final end** (*finis ultimus*) of a certain action (in our case self-defence) can be the object of the intention, or more modernly speaking, if the acting person can intend only the final end of his action in his action, with the exclusion of means directed to reaching this end, then Aquinas's text cannot be construed as an application of the principle of double effect. For in such case, says Mangan, Aquinas would be saying that:

1   The defending person must not intend killing the aggressor as the final end of his action (defence of own life);

2   But the defending person can wish the aggressor's death as a means to reaching the final end of his action.

Though the Jesuit theologian does not specify that in such case the means to actualizing the final end could be characterized as *praeter intentionem*, it follows from the context of his discussion of the difference between what is *in intentione* (defence of own life) as the final end of the action and what is not *in intentione* but is wished for by the defending person as a means to the final end. Understandably, such interpretation of the phrase "*in intentione*" excludes the possibility that in his exposition of the admissibility of self-defence resulting in the aggressor's death Aquinas resorts to the principle of double effect: the third condition in Mangan's formulation clearly states that the good effect (defence of own life) must not be reached by means of the bad effect (on this interpretation killing the aggressor would be a means to reaching the good effect).

### Lessius and Long

The Jesuit moral theologian Leonardus Lessius (in the original Dutch language Lenaert Leys), who lived in 1554–1623, was the author of an influential moral theological treatise entitled *De iustitia et iure* (first published in 1605), reedited more than 20 times only over the course of the 17th century. In the second book of his *opus magnum* in *caput nonum* the Dutch theologian deals with altogether 26 problems (which he calls *dubitationes*), which in their content follow Thomas Aquinas's exposition in IIaIIae of his *Summa Theologiae*, q. 64 and 65. The eighth *dubitatio* entitled *Whether it is allowed to kill another in defending one's own life* (*Utrum liceat alterum occidere in vitae suae defensionem*) explicitly deals with the problem whether killing the aggressor can be intended as a means to the final end (defence of own life) and answers:

> Dico secundo, licitum est in actu defensionis intendere omne id, quod iudicatur ad vitae membrorumque defensionem necessarium: ac proinde interdum etiam laesionem mortiferam, et consequenter ipsam mortem [...] Ratio est; quia nisi liceret eam sic intendere, defensio fuit saepe rederretur impossibilis [...] Quod autem D. Th. insinuat, privatae personae non licere occidere invasorem nisi per accidens [...] sensus est, personae privatae non esse licitum, absolute desiderare ut invasor moriatur [...].[33]

Lessius can be regarded as advocating an interpretation according to which Aquinas's text denies that killing the aggressor could become the intended final end, but nothing prevents it from being intended as a means to attaining this end.[34] He clearly states that in an act of defending one's own life one can intend all one judges to be necessary, including inflicting a lethal injury (*laesione mortifera*) resulting in the aggressor's death. But it is necessary to keep in mind that on this interpretation intending the aggressor's death is possible only as a means, not as the final end.[35] A modern author endorsing this other interpretation of Aquinas's text is Steven A. Long. In his work *The Teleological Grammar of the Moral Act*[36] Long insists that the concept of "intention" refers only to the action's final end, not to its means. If the final end of the action is defence of own life, whereby the means to this end is killing the aggressor, his death can be regarded as *praeter intentionem*. Hence the author infers that Aquinas is in fact saying that the defender can legitimately choose and desire lethal means of self-defence as means of effectively defending his own life.

### T. A. Cavanaugh

A third possible interpretation of Aquinas's text is presented by T. A. Cavanaugh in his monograph *Double-Effect Reasoning. Doing Good and Avoiding Evil*.[37] The author focusses on interpreting the phrase *praeter intentionem*, which Aquinas explicitly links with the expression *per accidens*: what is not part of the agent's intention (*praeter intentionem*) is accidental (*per accidens*). Aquinas links *praeter intentionem* and *per accidens* in IaIIae, q. 43, a. 3, focussing on the sin of scandal (*scandalum*) as follows:

> Per accidens quidem, quando est praeter intentionem agentis, ut puta cum aliquis suo factu vel verbo inordinato non intendit alteri dare occasionem ruinae, sed solum suae satisfacere voluntati.[38]

*Per accidens* is therefore not in the agent's intention, it can be an unintended and accidental consequence of his action, as when someone (without knowing it) serves his guests bad oysters and unintentionally poisons them? Or when someone pushes a co-player over the course of a game, resulting in fall and injury? This interpretation of the link between *praeter intentionem* and *per accidens* does not accord with Aquinas's conviction that we are not responsible for the accidental consequences of our actions, as evident from his solution to the question whether one who accidentally killed a human is responsible for the offense of homicide (*videtur quod aliquis casualiter occidens hominem incurrat homicidii reatum*). In his answer Aquinas underlines that chance (*casus*) is beyond the agent's intention (*praeter intentionem*) and *ipso facto* is neither intended, nor willed: a person is not morally responsible for an accidental killing. From that Cavanaugh infers that *praeter intentionem* does not refer to the accidental consequences of human action; what does it refer to, then? The author recalls Aquinas's doctrine, already mentioned above, according to which the moral character of human action is determined by the "sources of morality": object, circumstances, and end: if all the conditions are met then the action is correct, a defect in any of them changes the moral character of the act (*bonum ex integra causa, malum ex quocumque defectu*). *Praeter intentionem* are the circumstances of the action that do not immediately – as *fontes moralitatis* – enter the action's moral characterization.

Let us now again focus on defence of own life. On Cavanaugh's interpretation Aquinas is saying that in the instant when the defender decides to defend his life against attack, he consciously and willingly risks the aggressor's life, so that his death can be a conscious, though unintended consequence. In other words, between consciously killing the aggressor (the defender's intention is to end the aggressor's life) and accidentally killing the aggressor (his death is an accidental consequence of self-defence) there is a third possibility: defence of life comprising the conscious risk of killing the aggressor. Killing intentionally differs from consciously risking own life or the life of another: police persons consciously risk their lives, which does not mean, however, that they either intend their death or that their death is altogether accidental. Similarly it is possible to assume the risk of an action that may result in death without the death being altogether accidental or intended.

According to his modern interpreter in q. 64, a. 7 the Angelic Doctor restricts use of the phrase *praeter intentionem* to what happens *quandoque* (sometimes): the defender consciously risks the aggressor's life and sometimes the consequence of self-defence is the aggressor's death; however, it is not regarded as a foreseen consequence of the action.[39] But if this interpretation is correct, it is impossible to say that Aquinas is presenting the first form of the principle of double effect. A simple example will illustrate why that is so. Let us say that a large marine ship has crushed into an iceberg, which has torn the rear part of its left side; water is entering the ship very quickly. The captain does not have much time to think and must save the passengers and crew. He decides to close a watertight barrier separating the damaged part from the rest of the ship, though he knows very well that not all the crew will be able to reach the safe side in time. This scenario is a classical situation in which an ethical deliberation based on the principle of double effect is applied: (i) the captain has the damaged part of the ship separated (action), (ii) the positive consequence of this action is saving a great part (majority) of the passengers and crew, (iii) its negative consequence is the death of several crew members who are unable to reach safety in time, and (iv) there is a proportionate reason for the action which outweighs the negative consequences (if he does not close the watertight barriers, all will perish in the icy waters of the ocean). An important aspect of the ethical analysis of this situation is the relationship between the action (closing the barrier) and its negative consequences (death of some crew members): the captain does not merely risk them, within his deliberation he views the negative consequences as something that will obtain, cannot be avoided, but he nonetheless must act in order to prevent a great catastrophe. In other words, the negative consequence is a necessary component of the entire complex of action + intention + causal consequences. In the case of Cavanaugh's interpretation of *praeter intentionem* as concerning that which obtains only *quandoque* there is merely an accidental relationship between the act of self-defence and the negative consequence (death of aggressor), although the defender consciously undertakes the risk that the negative consequence will obtain.

Nonetheless, in Aquinas's text Cavanaugh finds the core of ethical deliberations associated with the principle of double effect, which he summarizes in the following three points:

1   There are moral norms not admitting of any exception (one of these norms is: "you will not end an innocent human life"). But these norms lead to difficult problems (*hard cases*), e.g. "is it licit to kill the aggressor in an act of righteous self-defence?"
2   The acting persons' intentions play a key part in the moral evaluation of their deeds.
3   It is possible to extract four conditions from Aquinas's text stating the admissibility of an action apparently banned by a moral norm:

   a   The action is proportionate to the end *(proportionatus fini)*.
   b   The action itself, considered without respect to the bad consequence, is morally licit.
   c   The acting person is morally more bound to follow a good (defence of own life) than avoid an evil (death of aggressor).
   d   The acting person intends the good consequence; he does not intend the bad one either as a means, or as the final end of the action.

### Gareth B. Mathews

The recently deceased American philosopher Gareth B. Matthews also refuses to interpret Aquinas's text as containing, explicitly or *in nuce*, the principle of double effect.[40] However, his reasoning strategy is somewhat different. The author does not reflect on the meaning of the phrases *in intentione* or *praeter intentionem* (only indirectly, when he very briefly rejects Joseph Boyle's interpretation, of which I will speak later). Instead he presents two modern formulations of the principle of double effect and shows that neither can be found in Aquinas's text, at the same time offering a *précis* of Aquinas's reasoning and inferring two moral principles.

The first formulation (labelled A) states that if a certain action has two consequences, one bad and one good (which evokes a situation of moral conflict), then it is possible to actualize that action if the following four conditions are met[41]:

1   The action itself must be morally indifferent or good.
2   The bad consequence must not be a means to attaining the good consequence.

3   The motive must be only attaining the good consequence.
4   The good consequence must be equivalent in importance to the bad
    consequence.

Is this formulation to be found in Thomas Aquinas? Let us imagine
that an aggressor is attacking us without reason. There is a large stone
lying at our feet, we pick it up and throw it at the aggressor, who drops
down dead upon being hit in the head. According to Aquinas's text
our action would be morally justified if the following three conditions
are met:

1   Our intention was defence against the aggressor.
2   Our intention was not, on the other hand, to kill the aggressor.
3   Hitting the aggressor with the stone was proportionate to the end,
    which was defence of our life.

But according to Matthews these three conditions do not correspond to
the four conditions of formulation A of the principle of double effect,
since prerequisite no. 2 is not satisfied. The American philosopher believes that the action itself can be characterized as "throwing a stone
at the aggressor," with two consequences: a good one (defending own
life) and a bad one (aggressor's death). Although the bad effect is not
intended, it is nonetheless a means to attaining the good effect.

Another formulation of the principle of double effect is found in the
work of the American moral theologian Germain Grisez; Alan Donagan
gives it roughly the following form (formulation B)[42]: an action with a
good and a bad consequence can be actualized when the following conditions are met:

1   The intention is to actualize the good effect, not the bad effect.
2   The actualization of the good effect is a proportionally grave reason
    for admitting the bad consequence.

Formulations A and B are presented as two **different** formulations of
the **same** principle, which cannot be correct. On a general level it holds
that if two ethical principles provide different answers in the case of an
identical situation, then they cannot be identical. Formulation B allows
for performing foetal craniotomy (directly killing a foetus as a means to
attaining an end), if it is the only means to save the mother's life, but the
possibility of this operation is fully closed for proponents of formulation
A. What the two formulations of the principle of double effect have in
common is that they are not found in the work of Thomas Aquinas;
*Doctor angelicus* includes the means in the agent's intention, and if craniotomy is a means to attaining an end, it is killing an innocent human
being and as such illicit (which excludes formulation B).

Matthews concludes his *exposé* of the expositions in Aquinas's article on self-defence with what he says is a simpler and more trustworthy interpretation, summarized in the following six points:

1    Some human action has a good consequence and a bad consequence, only one of which is intended (*aimed at*).
2    Human action receives its moral character only from that which is intended (*aimed at*).
3    An act of self-defence can have two consequences: (a) conservation of own life and (b) death of aggressor.
4    An act of self-defence can have a morally correct purpose, for it is natural to conserve one's own life, insofar as it is possible.
5    But even action directed to a good end can be incorrect, if it is not proportionate to that end: e.g. using more force in defending own life than necessary.
6    It is (*prima facie*) incorrect to kill a human being, unless it is done by a person appointed by a public authority with respect to the common good (soldier, executioner). For all others the intention to kill a human being is illicit.

According to Matthews this interpretation of Aquinas's exposition on the admissibility of killing the aggressor in an act of self-defence allows one to infer two ethical rules concerning the admissibility of killing a human (I have made minor adjustments):

1    Person S must not intend to kill a human being, unless S is appointed to do that by a public authority (the sovereign, the state...) with respect to the common good.
2    Person S may kill another human being only if the following three conditions are met:

     a    S's life is threatened;
     b    S intends to defend his own life, not kill the aggressor;
     c    The means selected by S for self-defence are proportionate to the end.

## Critical Evaluation

We have had the opportunity to get acquainted with four different interpretations of Aquinas's key text from *Secunda secundae* of the *Summa Theologiae*. According to the first one Aquinas requests that the aggressor's death not be intended (*praeter intentionem*), whether as the action's final end or as a means to attain it. The agent's intention (*in intentione*) therefore comprises the structure means-end (ordered by the final end). Within this interpretation authors such as the Jesuit moral theologian Joseph T. Mangan hold that Aquinas is presenting the historically first version of the principle of double effect and applying it to the case of self-defence.

According to the second interpretation the term *intentio* applies only to the action's final end, not to the selected means, so that nothing prevents the defender from consciously and intentionally choosing lethal means and killing the aggressor in an act of self-defence. Within this interpretation, endorsed in the modern period by the Spanish Jesuit Vincentius M. Alonso or the American theologian Steven A. Long, Aquinas's treatise on the moral admissibility of self-defence cannot be construed as an application of the principle of double effect in the form we most frequently give it today.

Gareth B. Matthews also refuses to view Aquinas's text as the first formulation and application of the principle of double effect.

Finally the last interpretation is presented by the American philosopher T. A. Cavanaugh, who interprets Aquinas's phrase *praeter intentionem* as relating to that which is not necessarily linked with the action under consideration. Cavanaugh regards his interpretation as the middle way between intentional killing and altogether accidental and unintended putting to death: According to him Aquinas is speaking of the moral admissibility of consciously risking the aggressor's life, which can sometimes result in his death. Although *Doctor angelicus* does not present a modern version of the principle of double effect, the author does find a certain core of ethical deliberations associated with it in his work.

## Intention and the Final end

Which of these interpretations is correct, or perhaps better, which is more correct? The second interpretation assumes that Aquinas is advocating a doctrine according to which intention concerns only the action's final end and the means as such are not the intention's objects (intended). Some passages of Aquinas's work support this interpretation. For example in *De Veritate* Aquinas distinguishes between two acts of the will: *intentio* (intention) and *electio* (choice) and states that intention is an act of the will linked to the intellect ordering the means (*ea quae sunt ad finem*) to the end, while *electio* is an act of the will ordering the means among one another (*ad invicem*).[43] Nonetheless, as a number of other texts show, this interpretation is incorrect. The entire question 12 of *Prima Secundae* is devoted to intention, which is an act of the will; in the second article the Dominican theologian explicitly asks whether intention concerns only the final end (*Utrum sit tantum ultimi finis*) and answers:

> [...] intentio respicit finem secundum quod est terminus motus voluntatis. In motu autem potest accipi terminus dupliciter, uno modo, ipse terminus ultimus, in quo quiescitur, qui est terminus totius motus; alio modo, aliquod medium, quod est principium unius partis

motus, et finis vel terminus alterius. Sicut in motu quo itur de a in c per b, c est terminus ultimus, b autem est terminus, sed non ultimus. Et utriusque potet esse intentio. Unde etsi semper sit finis, non tamen oportet quod semper sit ultimi finis.[44]

Aquinas's interpretation is very intuitive: every change, let us say local motion, has some final end, the last point in which the change (motion) terminates. Let us say that person S goes from point A to point D but over the course of the journey also passes through points B and C. From the point of view of the movement as a whole the final terminus of the motion is point D, but insofar as S passes through points B and C in the direction of the final end these points are also partial ends, or perhaps better, intermediate ends. The will also undergoes some change (*motus*), which in a global perspective is determined by the final end (*finis remotus*), intended as such by the acting person. Nonetheless, the actualization of this final end proceeds by means of means, which are structurally related to the final end (they are ordered with respect to this end) and as such are the intention's objects; if a physician wants to remove a tumour infected with cancer, he must perform a certain series of operations which are directed to the action's end and as part of the means-end structure determine its ethical evaluation. The physician, simply speaking, must not choose arbitrary means to attain the end of his action: he must proceed *lege artis*, with respect to the patient's autonomy, her mental state and state of health, choose the most considerate operation method, secure good pre-operation and post-operation care and pain management.

In the quoted passage Aquinas speaks of the final end (*finis ultimus*), but end is also divided into end of action (*finis operis, finis proximus*) and agent's end (*finis remotus, finis operantis*). A human action finds its final end, in which it as a certain particular action comes to a rest (*in quo quiescitur*), in the fulfilment of the agent's end, which happens as a result of the actualization of a certain action (fulfilment of the action's object), which is a means with respect to *finis operantis*, although in the context of the action-means structure (*finis operis*) it is an end ordering the means. How are we to understand this? Let us say that Peter decided to give Jane money (object of action – gift of money, extrinsic act) for some reason (why? *finis operantis*). Both ends are objects of Peter's intention; in one case it is possible to speak of **proximate intention** (intention of the object of action), in the other of **remote intention** (agent's intention). Peter's action – handing over a certain sum of money to Jane – is terminated in the instant of transfer; the proximate intention is fulfilled, and the action can be characterized as gift of money. That does not mean, however, that Peter's remote intention is also fulfilled: he may have given Jane the money so that she could go to college and Jane bought a new car with it instead. So, the proximate intention is fulfilled by the action itself, while the remote intention need not. Let us take a look at the following table[45]:

*Table 2.1* Proximate and remote intention

| Physical action | Proximate intention | Remote intention |
| --- | --- | --- |
| Passing sum X to another | Bribery | Obtaining a contract |
| Passing sum X to another | Loan | Making the recipient indebted |
| Passing sum X to another | Gift of money | Expressing love |

Three instances of the same type of physical action (passing a certain sum of money to another) may represent three morally different types of action (bribery, loan and gift of money). The proximate intention is fulfilled in the instant the money is transferred; the action (bribery, lending, and giving money) is completed. But fulfilment of the remote intention is still open, for it does not follow from the act of giving a bribe that the bribing person will obtain the contract he wishes to secure by means of the bribe.

If I understand Aquinas correctly, he is explicitly saying that the intention's objects are both the means and the action's final end, to whose fulfilment these means were chosen. His theory will be more evident when I expound it in the context of Aquinas's doctrine of the structural moments of human action. Human action can be characterized as willing imbued with reason, the willing of a human person gifted with the cooperating capacities of will and intellect. Aquinas distinguishes among several structural moments of human action.[46] At the beginning there is an understanding (*intellectus*), prospective in character, not retrospective (it focusses on what could be attained by means of the action). For example, a physician considers alleviating the pain in a terminally ill oncological patient. But he does not consider it as a mere sequence of operations with a certain consequence, but as something good (*sub ratione boni*): *intellectus* proceeds to willing (*velle* or *velleitas*). Alleviation of pain becomes the object of the physician's intention (*intentio*), but the problem of means remains open. Let us say that the physician has three different ways of pain alleviation at her disposal; after consulting the patient and with regard to his state of health, to the patient's idea of the result of pain alleviation, and to her professional knowledge she considers all three (*consilium*), affirms one of them (*consensus*), and then chooses it (*electio*). There follows a rational determination of the action direction (*imperium*) and the action itself (*usus*), e.g. applying a certain medicine in the patient's circulation.[47]

Distinguishing among the structural moments of human action (which can be divided into intrinsic – *intellectus* through *imperium*, and extrinsic – *usus*) does not mean that these are different types of acts of the will; it is rather a formal distinction within one act depending on the will's relationship to the end and the means. Also, Aquinas's doctrine of the structure of human action cannot be construed so that all the elements are **always** actualized consciously, in the manner of some conscious, reflexive analysis. Note that the Italian Dominican reserves the term *intentio* for the action's end, while *electio* refers to the means; these, however, are moments of the same act distinguished only according to relationship to the final end (*intentio*) and the means (*electio*).[48] Although Aquinas distinguishes between intention and choice within the structural moments of human action, these are not different types of acts of the will, but a mere formal distinction of the will's relationship with respect to the means and the end.[49] Let us imagine that the final end of an action is D and there are three means to reach it: A, B and C. An act of the will directed to choice (*electio*) of the means is formally distinct from the intention D, but only in that D is the final end of the action, while the choice of, let us say, B is a choice of a means directed to D. Since B is a means with respect to D, it must become the intention's object as that which is to be actualized, but not as the final end.

There are other texts in Aquinas's extensive work confirming the interpretation according to which the intention's object is not only the final end. In his exposition of intention Aquinas says:

> Est enim intentio non solum finis ultimi, ut dictum est, sed etiam finis medii. Simul autem intendit aliquis et finem proximum, et ultimum; sicut confectionem medicinae, et sanitatem.[50]

Here Aquinas clearly repeats his conviction that an intention's object need not be only the final end, but also mediate ends. He gives the example of health (final end) and medicine (means). We want to be healthy (agent's final end), so we have an appropriate medicine prescribed and take it accordingly (the end of the action is fulfilled in the instance of taking the medicine). With respect to the agent's end taking the pill is a means (we take the medicine **in order to** be healthy), but it is also an end (end of action) and as such is the object of intention (proximate intention).

From these analyses of Aquinas's texts two conclusions can be inferred:

1  The object of an intention need not be only the last end, but also the means. A certain act chosen as a means to attaining an end is often also an end and as such is therefore intended (= is the intention's object).

2  The object of an act of choice (*electio*) cannot be *praeter intentionem*, since an intention concerns a certain end only as attainable by certain means. *Electio* is impossible without *intentio*.[51]

Long's interpretation of Aquinas's treatise on the legitimacy of killing the aggressor in an act of self-defence is therefore incorrect: the intention's object is the entire ordered means-end structure, which rules out that an action ethically legitimate by the nature of its end can be attained with immoral means. Besides, returning to the physician who considers alleviating her patient's pain: would Long designate killing the patient as *praeter intentionem* if the end of the action was alleviating pain (that could not be alleviated by other means)? If so – and it seems to me that he ought to grant that – then he would also have to grant that physicians may kill their patients if it is not the final end of their action. However, that does not accord with the doctrine of the sacred character of innocent human life and the ethical system in whose framework the principle of double effect is most commonly set.

## Cavanaugh and per accidens

Cavanaugh's interpretation of Aquinas's treatise on the legitimacy of killing the aggressor in an act of self-defence grants that the expression "*praeter intentionem*" does not refer to ends and means, but – as opposed to Mangan or Boyle – the author claims that it also does not refer to consequences that the agent prospectively cognizes as necessary, unintended but foreseeable consequences of his action. This interpretation is based on Aquinas's use of the adverb "*quandoque*" (sometimes) in the *respondeo* to the fourth objection, according to which homicide is a graver sin than fornication or adultery. But no one is allowed to commit fornication or adultery in order to save his life. Therefore, the objection concludes, it is also not allowed to kill the aggressor while defending one's life. Aquinas answers:

> [...] actus fornicationis vel adulterii non ordinatur ad conservationem propriae vitae ex necessitate, sicut actus ex quo quandoque sequitur homicidum.[52]

But Aquinas's answer does not mention whether killing the aggressor is foreseen as inevitable: it does not say that it is, nor does it say that it is not. It simply does not speak on the problem at all. The objection was of a simple dialectical structure: from the ethical point of view killing a human being is a graver offence (Aquinas would say sin) than fornication or adultery. It is illicit to commit those two sexual acts to save our life, *a fortiori* it is therefore illicit to kill an aggressor endangering our life. In his answer the Italian theologian distinguishes the individual types of action according to their intrinsic ordering to the end, which is conservation of own life. If I understand Aquinas correctly, he is saying that an act of adultery or fornication is not intrinsically (*ex necessitate*) ordered to conserving human life, which is why it must not be used for this purpose. On the other hand an act of self-defence does have a necessary relationship to conserving human life, which is why it is possible to further consider the conditions when it is legitimate from the ethical point of view and when it is not.

Joseph Boyle characterizes the negative consequence of an act of self-defence as a foreseen consequence of the type of action that self-defence is.[53] His interpretation therefore agrees with Mangan's exposition and contradicts Cavanaugh's exposition of Aquinas's text. Nonetheless, one passage of Aquinas's commentary on Aristotle's *Physics* seems to contradict this interpretation. There the Angelic Doctor says:

> [...] quod enim vel semper vel ut frequenter coniungitur effectui, cadit sub eadem intentione. Stultum est enim dicere quod aliquis intendat aliquid, et non velit illud quod ut frequenter vel semper adiungitur.[54]

Aquinas's reflection seems to take the following form: some events (or their consequences) are always or frequently linked with the corresponding action. If that is so, it is impossible to claim that they do not fall under the intention with which the action occurs, as it is foolish to claim that someone walks barefoot through a stream and does not want to get his feet wet.[55] Similarly, returning to the principle of double effect, it would not be possible to claim that killing the aggressor is *praeter intentionem* if it is always or at least frequently the consequence of an act of self-defence.

But Joseph Boyle has convincingly shown that the text quoted above does not imply that all that is *praeter intentionem* must be linked with the action in question accidentally or rarely. Aquinas's commentary, from which the passage comes, focusses on explaining the difference between a cause which is *per se* and one which is *per accidens* and explains the meaning of the phrase *"per accidens"* in connection with human persons *qua* rational agents. The whole passage goes:

> [...] effectus causae agentis a proposito est illud quod accidit ex intentione agentis: unde quidquid provenit in effectu praeter intentionem, est per accidens. Et hoc dico si id quod est praeter intentionem ut in paucioribus consequatur: quod enim vel semper vel ut frequenter coniungitur effectui, cadit sub eadem intentione.[56]

Here Aquinas explicitly links what is *praeter intentionem* and *per accidens*, but clearly adds a condition (*et hoc dico*): *praeter intentionem* is *per accidens* only when it occurs rarely (*in paucioribus consequatur*). This is confirmed by Aquinas's other texts, e.g. in *Summa contra gentiles* he writes:

> [...] sciendum est quod non omne quod est praeter intentionem oportet esse fortuitum vel casuale [...]. Se enim quod est praeter intentionem sit consequens ad id quod est intentum vel semper vel frequenter [...] non erit fortuitum nec casuale; esset enim casuale, si sequeretur ut in paucioribus.[57]

Here Aquinas is clearly saying that if something is *praeter intentionem*, it is not necessarily the result of chance or luck: if it is always (*semper*) or frequently (*frequenter*) linked with the action, it cannot be regarded as product of chance or luck. Nonetheless, the question remains in what way those consequences of human action that are *praeter intentionem* and are not accidental or consequence of chance are linked with the intention (intentions), i.e., with what the agent is trying to achieve with his action by fulfilling the object of this intention (intentions). In *De Malo* Aquinas says:

> [...] aliquando accidens alicuius effectus coniungitur ei ut in paucioribus et raro; et tunc agens dum intendit effectum per se non oportet quod aliquo modo intendat effectum per accidens. Aliquando vero huiusmodi accidens concomitatur effectum principaliter intentum semper, vel ut in pluribus; et tunc accidens non separatur ab intentione agentis.[58]

In the quoted passage the Angelic Doctor distinguishes between two types of accidental consequences of action:

1   consequences that occur only rarely (*ut in paucioribus et raro*);
2   consequences that occur always or sometimes (*semper vel ut in pluribus*).

Consequences that occur only rarely are not intended in any way. Today we would say that they are not intentional: when a lumberjack cuts down a tree which upon falling kills a casual passer-by, it is an unexpected, unplanned and unintended consequence that is only rarely linked with cutting down trees. Killing the passer-by was not a consequence of intentional action. But if some unintended consequence is linked with an action that occurs always or frequently, then – though it is not an object of the intention – it nonetheless falls under this intention (*cadit sub eadem intentionem*). This consequence is not intended *per se* (Joseph Boyle proposes to speak of it as intended *per accidens*[59]). Two possible situations can therefore be distinguished in all:

1   X are consequences that occur rarely (*ut in paucioribus et raro*). These consequences are not intended in any way, whether *per se* or *per accidens*.
2   X are consequences that occur always or frequently (*semper vel ut in pluribus*). These consequences are not intended *per se*, which is why they can be designated as *praeter intentionem*, but they cannot be separated from the intention's object.

What does it mean that they cannot be separated from the intention's object? The lumberjack felling a tree intends (intention of action) to cut down a tree and uses various means to do so (an axe, power saw, etc.). He fells it for some reason (agent's intention). In the instant when the tree falls a casual tourist walks under it and the tree kills him. Something like that happens very rarely and killing the tourist is not intended by the lumberjack (it is neither his proximate nor remote intention); it is not intended whether *per se* or *per accidens*. The matter is different when a certain consequence is frequently linked with the action in question, e.g. in the case of defence of own life, which often results in killing the aggressor. In such case this consequence (aggressor's death) cannot be altogether separated from the intention of the action and agent's intention, though not in the sense that it would become part of the respective intention's object. In the commentary on Aristotle's *Physics* mentioned above Aquinas says: "For it is foolish to say that someone intends something and does not want that which is frequently or always associated with it." Let us well note the words employed: Aquinas is not saying that when someone intends something it would be foolish if he claimed that he does not intend that which is frequently or always associated with the thing intended. Instead he uses the phrase *"non velit,"* meaning "does not want." I understand him as follows: the consequences of our action which are not intended and frequently or always accompany our actions fall under the prospective deliberation of the intellect considering possible action. To give an example: if someone is considering defending his life he realizes that one of the consequences of this type of action is the aggressor's death. Though this is not intended (it is not an object of any of the intentions), the defender nonetheless foresees, even with certainty, that it will occur. It is therefore inseparable from the intention, for it is a foreseeable consequence of an action whose finality is determined by the proximate and remote intention. It is therefore possible to say that the aggressor's death is *praeter intentionem*, though as such it is a consequence more closely linked to the action then the death of the tourist caused by the falling tree is. While killing the tourist is not a consequence of intentional action, killing the aggressor is, for though it is not intended, it is foreseen by the agent and, which is important, accepted.

## Conclusion

These reflections indicate that when Thomas Aquinas says that a bad consequence of an act of self-defence is *praeter intentionem*, it does not imply that it is accidental. E. C. Brugger summarizes this conclusion with the following words:

> Since he [Thomas Aquinas] clearly denies that foreseeable effects are necessarily intended, he cannot reasonably be read as holding that they are necessarily intended in the context of self-defence. Boyle is therefore correct in concluding strongly that Aquinas should be read as asserting

that though an aggressor's death can be foreseen with certainty to fol-low from one's act of self-defence, it is not *per se* intended.[60]

I have rejected Cavanaugh's, Lessius's and Long's interpretation of Aquinas's text. Does it mean – as the Jesuit theologian Joseph Mangan claims – that Aquinas endorsed the principle of double effect as we un-derstand it today? I will only propose an answer to this question in the fourth chapter, where I will compare three different formulations of the principle of double effect known from history and attempt to show whether they have something in common or not.

## Notes

1 Joseph T. Mangan, "An Historical Analysis of the Principle of Double Ef-fect." *Theological Studies* 10, no. 1 (1949): 41–61, 42.
2 1 Macc. 6 (Common English Bible).
3 The University in Naples was founded in 1224, St. Dominic died in Bologne on August 6th, 1221. The Dominican order was founded in 1215.
4 When Aquinas died the *Summa* was not copied as a whole; *Secunda secun-dae* was copied most often. Cf. Mark D. Jordan. "The Summa's Reform of Moral Teaching," in *Contemplating Aquinas. On the Varieties of Interpre-tation*, ed. Fergus Kerr (London: SCM Press, 2003), 41–54.
5 Jean-Pierre Torrell, *Initiation à Saint Thomas d'Aquin. Sa personne et son oeuvre* (Fribourg: Editiones Universitaires, 1993).
6 Jean Porter, "Recent Studies in Aquinas's Virtue Ethics." *Journal of Reli-gious Ethics* 26, no. 1 (1998): 191–215. The same stance is taken e.g. by Ralph McInerny, cf. Ralph McInerny, "Ethics," in *The Cambridge Com-panion to Aquinas*, eds. Norman Kretzman and Eleonore Stump (Cam-bridge: Cambridge University Press, 1993), 196–216.
7 Concerning unity of contents and logic of division, the French theologian M. D. Chenu proposed reading the *Summa* in light of the Neoplatonic scheme *ex-itus-reditus*: *Prima pars* discusses the emanation of all reality from God as its principle, *Secunda Pars* deals with the return to God as the final end. Some au-thors think this scheme is not adequate since it does not comprise *Tertia pars*, others note that *Secunda* and *Tertia pars* speak of the return of man created in the image of God, who attains the fulfilment of this return in communion with God through Christ (*qui secundum quod homo via est nobis tenendi ad Deum*, Prol., *Tertia pars*). Cf. Torrell, *"Initiation à Saint Thomas d'Aquin."*
8 Thomas Aquinas, *Summa Theologiae*. IIaIIae, q. 64, a. 7. Unless otherwise stated the translations from Latin are my own:

> I respond that nothing permits one action to have two consequences, only one of which is intended, while the other one is unintended (literally "be-yond intention"). Moral deeds receive specification according to what they intend, not of what is beyond intention, since that is accidental, as evident from what has been said above. Two effects can issue from defense of own life: one is conserving own life, the other is killing the aggressor. Such ac-tion is not illicit, since it intends conserving own life: it is natural for every being to conserve its own existence as much as it can. But action issuing from a good intention can become illicit when it is not proportionate to its end. So if someone used disproportionate force to defend his life, his action would be improper. But if he fends off violence in a moderate manner, his

defence is licit, since the law says 'it is permitted to fend force off with force within limits of legitimate defense.' For salvation it is not necessary that one gives up legitimate defence in order that the aggressor not be killed: he is bound to greater responsibility for his own life than to the life of another.

However, since only a public authority acting with respect to the common good is allowed to kill a man, as evident from what has been said above, a man is not allowed to intend killing a man in order to defend himself, with the exception of those holding public authority, who in their intention to kill a man in self-defense relate to the common good, as evident in the case of a soldier facing an enemy and a guard fighting against burglars. But even they would sin if they were guided by personal desire.

9  **Value perfectionism** in ethics is an idea according to which the good of something (in our case of a human being) is a matter of full development of the functions essential to the given thing (human). **Moral perfectionism** is an ethical theory placing value perfectionism in the focus of its interest. In his work Thomas Aquinas harmonically develops value and moral perfectionism. Cf. Mark Timmons, *Moral Theory. An Introduction* (Lanham: Rowman & Littlefield Publishers, 2013), 75.

10  The concept of natural inclinations plays an important part not only in Aquinas's work, but also in the work of two modern representatives of the renaissance of ius-naturalism, one of whom – the French philosopher Jacques Maritain – belongs in the post-war period and classical school of natural law, while the other – John M. Finnis – is the founder of the neo-classical school of natural law. In the first author cf. Jean Maritain, "La loi naturelle ou loi non écrite," in *Œuvres complètes*. Vol. XVI., eds. Jean Maritan and Raïssa Maritain (Paris, Fribourg: Éditions Universitaires, Éditions Saint-Paul, 1999), 695–918. For Finnis cf. John M. Finnis, *Natural Law and Natural Rights*. 2nd ed. (Oxford: Clarendon, 2011). Inclinations as such as the ontological and gnoseological foundation of natural law are the subject of the extensive study Steven J. Jensen, *Knowing the Natural Law. From Precepts and Inclinations to Deriving Oughts* (Washington, DC: The Catholic University of America Press, 2015).

11  Cf. Ralph McInerny, *Aquinas on Human Action. A Theory of Practice* (Washington, DC: The Catholic University of America Press, 1992), 80–81; Ralph McInerny, *Ethica Thomistica: The Moral Philosophy of Thomas Aquinas*. Revisited edition. (Washington, DC: The Catholic University of America Press, 1997), 159–182.

12  Aquinas distinguishes between intrinsic and extrinsic human acts. The structure of an intrinsic act is fairly complex, comprising prospective cognition, volition, intention, choice of means, etc.; an extrinsic act is the performance, realization of the end of an intrinsic act. If someone e.g. plans a robbery, chooses the means and decides to take action, he has realized an intrinsic act of robbery, although he can be prevented from it e.g. by falling down the stairs and breaking his leg. The object is called *materia circa quam* with respect to the extrinsic act, with respect to the intrinsic act it is called *end*. Cf. Steven J. Jensen, *Good & Evil Actions. A Journey through Saint Thomas Aquinas* (Washington, DC: The Catholic University of America Press, 2010).

13  Cf. a Thomistic exposition of moral specification of human action in Yves R. Simon, *Morale* (Paris: Beauchesne et Ses Fils, 1961).

14  Cf. Joseph de Finance, *Éthique Générale* (Roma: Presses de l'Université Grégorienne, 1967), section 225; Angel R. Luño, *Etica General* (Pamplona: Ediciones Universidad de Navarra, S. A., 1991).

15  Cf. Christopher Kaczor, *Proportionalism and the Natural Law Tradition* (Washington, DC: The Catholic University of America Press, 2002), 48.

16  Cf. Thomas Aquinas, *Summa Theologiae*. IaIIae, q. 18.

17  The doctrine of the three sources of morality (object, end, circumstances) originates in the medieval discussion of the circumstances of action that confessors should ask about over the course of administering the sacrament of penance (the 4th Lateran Council of 1215 explicitly states that confessors ought to consider the circumstances of actions with penitents; the most popular list of seven circumstances stems from Boëthius). Another source of this doctrine is discussion as to whether there are intrinsically bad actions. As is well known, in the Middle Ages Pierre Abélard was interpreted as advocating a doctrine according to which human behaviour is good or bad only based on its intention or end. This view was sharply attacked by Peter of Lombardy, who inclined to the view that some deeds are bad regardless of the fact that they are directed to a good end. Cf. Thomas M. Osborne Jr., *Human Action in Thomas Aquinas, John Duns Scotus & William of Ockham* (Washington, DC: The Catholic University of America Press, 2014), 149–152. However, the expression "*fontes moralitatis*" comes from the 19th century.

18  Cf. John F. Wippel, *The Metaphysical Thought of Thomas Aquinas. From Finite Being to Uncreated Being* (Washington, DC: The Catholic University of America Press, 2000). Aquinas's basic metaethical thesis says: "being" and "good" refer to the same (*idem secundum rem*), they differ only in meaning (*differunt secundum rationem tantum*). Cf. Eleonore Stump, *Aquinas* (New York: Routledge, 2005), 62.

19  Cf. Thomas Aquinas, *Summa Theologiae*. IaIIae, q. 18, a. 1. A human action can be designated as good in a premoral, metaphysical, and moral sense of the word. In the metaphysical sense it is good insofar as it is an action, i.e., insofar as it is a being (*quantum habet de actione et entitate, tamtum habet de bonitate*). The moral character (action as good or bad) is determined by **object** (*secundum speciem*), **circumstances** (*secundum circumstantias*), and **end** (*secundum finem*). Cf. Aquinas, *Summa Theologiae*. IaIIae, q. 18, a. 4.

20  Cf. Thomas Aquinas, *Summa Theologiae*. IaIIae, q. 18, a. 2. Aquinas's doctrine of object as the specifying principle of human action is fairly complex. The object can be a thing, but also human action. E.g., in the case of theft Aquinas once says that the object of a theft is a thing belonging to another (*res aliena, De Malo*, q. 2, a. 7, ad 8), another time he defines the object as taking a thing belonging to another (*suscipere aliena, Summa Theologiae*, IaIIae, q. 20, a. 1, ad 1). Generally speaking, the object specifying an intrinsic act can be an extrinsic act. It is essential that an object cannot be considered in itself, but always only **with respect to the order of reason**: the object of a theft is not money as a certain physical object (a handful of banknotes) but money as belonging to someone else who has not consented to taking it. Part of Aquinas's doctrine is also the already mentioned distinction between object *in genere naturae* and *in genere moris*, which makes it possible to state that materially *(in genere naturae)* identical acts (more precisely: tokens of the same type of action) can be different objects from the moral point of view: a sexual act can in one case be a marital act, in another case an act of adultery. Detailed analysis of Aquinas's doctrine of the specification of human actions is found in Joseph Pilsner, *The Specification of Human Actions in St Thomas Aquinas* (Oxford: Oxford University Press, 2006).

21  The following seven are most often mentioned as circumstances: *quis, quid, ubi, quibus auxiliis, cur, quomodo, quando*. Aquinas's doctrine is fairly complex also in the case of circumstances, for circumstances sometimes enter the object of the action itself and modify its kind. In the case of theft the

amount of the money stolen is a factor increasing the theft's gravity which, however, does not change the type of action it is (the theft of ten million is a graver offense than the theft of a thousand crowns, but in both cases it is a theft). However, if the theft is of a sacred object, this circumstance enters the object of the action and changes its kind: it is not a theft but a sacrilege (*sacrilegium*).

22 Cf. Thomas Aquinas, *Summa Theologiae*. IaIIae, q. 18, a. 3. In *De Malo*, q. 2, a. 7, ad. 8 Aquinas explicitly states that *finis remotus* is the circumstance *cur* (why), while *finis proximus* is the action's object. So, the noun *finis* has two meanings in this context: (i) *finis proximus*, the object of the action, (ii) *finis remotus*, the circumstance *cur*, the third source of moral evaluation of human action. Aquinas also endorses the traditional division of end (*finis*) into intrinsic end of action (*finis operis*) – object, and end of agent (*finis operantis* or *finis remotus*). When we say that human action is morally specified by its end, we mean *finis operis* or *finis proximus* (*finis dat speciem actui*). Cf. Thomas Aquinas, 4 *Sent.*, d. 16, q. 3, a. 1. Here Aquinas speaks of *finis operis* and *finis agentis*. Circumstances can enter the moral evaluation of human action in three ways (the examples come from David S. Oderberg, *Moral Theory: A Non-Consequentialist Approach* [Malden, MA: Blackwell Publishers, 2000a]): (i) an act morally indifferent of its object can be good or bad due to its circumstances (I go for a walk – I go for a walk when I should be taking an exam); (ii) an act morally good of its object can become bad due to its circumstances (it is good to exercise regularly, doing it contrary to the doctor's recommendation is bad); (iii) an action good or bad of its object can acquire an "added good" of a different kind due to circumstances (not buying superfluous luxury goods as an act of abstemiousness is good, not buying superfluous luxury goods at a time when I am in debt is better as an act of abstemiousness and prudence); and (iv) circumstances can make a good or bad act into a better or worse act (stealing money from someone is bad, stealing money with the use of violence is worse). Note that circumstances cannot make an action which is bad of its object morally good.

23 Cf. Thomas Aquinas, *Summa Theologiae*. IaIIae, q. 18, a. 4.

24 "*Ad secundum dicendum quod finis, etsi non sit de substantia actus, est tamen causa actus principalissima, inquantum movet ad agendum. Unde et maxime actus moralis speciem habet ex fine.*" Thomas Aquinas, *Summa Theologiae*. IaIIae, q. 7, a. 4, ad 2. Translation:

> To the second it is necessary to say that although the end does not belong to the nature of the act, it is nonetheless its principal cause, since it motivates to action. That is why a moral act is specified as to its kind primarily by its end.

25 Cf. Janet E. Smith, *Humanae Vitae: A Generation Later* (Washington, DC: The Catholic University of America Press, 1991), 217.

26 Cf. John M. Finnis, *Moral Absolutes. Tradition, Revision, and Truth* (Washington, DC: The Catholic University of America Press, 1991), 16–17.

27 I add "in the given situation" because human action is evaluated *in concreto*, as particular human deeds. In this way the analogy with *fontes moralitatis* is better preserved.

28 Cf. Joseph T. Mangan, "An Historical Analysis," 41–61.

29 Thomas Aquinas, *Summa Theologiae*. IaIIae, q. 12, a. 1.

30 Cf. Battista Mondin, *Dizionario enciclopedico del pensiero di San Tommaso d'Aquino* (Bologna: ESD, 1991), 336. A detailed analysis of Aquinas's conception of intentionality, including the distinction among various

meanings of the concept *intentio*, is found in André Hayen, *L'Intentionnel selon saint Thomas*. Deuxième édition (Bruges: Desclée de Brouwer, 1954), 47–51.

31 Thomas Aquinas, *Summa Theologiae*, IaIIae, q. 12, a. 1, ad 3.

32 "*Non enim solum ex hoc intendere dicimur sanitatem, quia volumus eam, sed quia volumus ad eam per aliquid aliud pervenire.*" Thomas Aquinas, *Summa Theologiae*. IaIIae, q. 12, a. 1, ad 4. Translation: "For we do not say that we intend health because we want it, but because we want to attain it by some means."

33 Leonardus Lessius S. J., *De iustitia et iure*. Editio secunda, auctior et castigatior (Antverpiae: Ex officina plantiniana, 1609), l. 2, c. 9, dub. 8, n. 53. Translation:

> Secondly I say that in an act of defense it is licit to intend everything that is regarded as necessary for defense of life and bodily integrity, and therefore sometimes also a lethal injury and resulting from it death itself. [...] The reason is that if it was not possible to intend in this way, defense would often be impossible. [...] St. Thomas also stresses that private persons may kill aggressors only *per accidens* [...] which means that for private persons it is illicit that they totally desire the aggressor to die [...].

34 According to Mangan a similar interpretation is presented by the Spanish Dominican and scholastic theologian Domingo de Soto in his *De justitia et jure* and by the Spanish Jesuit theologian Gabriel Vásquez in his *Opuscula moralia*.

35 The Spanish Jesuit Vincentius M. Alonso reaches a similar conclusion in his dissertation, where he says that the seventh article of question 64 of the *Summa Theologiae* does not treat of the principle of double effect as we understand it today ("el articulo septimo de la cuestion 64 de la Secunda Secundae, no se trata de uno caso de doble efecto en la signification que modernamente damos a estos terminus"). Quoted according to Joseph T. Mangan, "An Historical Analysis," 46.

36 I have not been able to access the author's work and draw on the work of E. Christian Brugger, cf. Christian E. Brugger, "*Praeter Intentionem* in Aquinas and Issues in Bioethics," in *Bioethics with Liberty and Justice. Themes in the Work of Joseph M. Boyle*, ed. Christopher Tollefsen (Dordrecht: Springer Science Business Media, 2011), 97–111.

37 Cf. Thomas A. Cavanaugh, *Double-Effect Reasoning. Doing Good and Avoiding Evil* (Oxford: Clarendon Press, 2006), 1–14.

38 Thomas Aquinas, *Summa Theologiae*. IIaIIae, q. 43, a. 3, *respondeo*. Translation: "For accidentally, if it is not in the agent's intention, as when someone does not intend to give another an occasion to fall [into sin] with his inordinate word or action, but only to satisfy his own will."

39 This interpretation is based on Aquinas's answer to the fourth argument against the admissibility of killing the aggressor in self-defence, having the following structure: (i) killing a human (*homicidium*) is a graver sin than simple fornication or adultery, (ii) from the ethical point of view it is illicit to commit fornication of adultery in order to save one's life (Aquinas holds that fornication and adultery are mortal sins and spiritual life has higher priority than corporeal life), and (iii) therefore it is illicit to kill a human in order to save one's life. In his *ad quartum* Aquinas distinguishes between fornication and adultery which are not necessarily (*ex necessitate*) directed to saving one's life and an act of self-defence – which is necessarily, of its own nature, directed to saving one's life – but from which killing the aggressor does not follow necessarily, but only sometimes (*actus ex quo quandoque sequitur homicidium*).

40 Gareth B. Matthews, "Saint Thomas and the Principle of Double Effect," in *Aquinas's Moral Theory: Essays in Honor of Norman Kretzmann*, eds. Scott MacDonald and Eleonore Stump (Ithaca, NY: Cornell University Press, 2008), 63–78.

41 This formulation, rather non-typical, comes from Ronald Munson, *Intervention and Reflection: Basic Issues in Medical Ethics* (Belmont, CA: Wadsworth, 1979), 27.

42 Cf. Alan Donagan, *The Theory of Morality* (Chicago, IL: University of Chicago Press, 1977), 161.

43 "[...] dicendum quod intentio est actus voluntatis in ordine ad rationem ordinantem ea quae sunt ad finem in finem ipsum; sed electio est actus voluntatis in ordine ad rationem comparantem eq quae sunt ad finem ad invicem." Thomas Aquinas, *De Veritate*, q. 22, a. 13, ad 16.

44 Thomas Aquinas, *Summa Theologiae*. IaIIae, q. 12, a. 2, *respondeo*. Translation:

> [...] intention regards the end as a *terminus* of the movement of the will. A *terminus* of movement can be taken in two ways: i) as the very last terminus, in which the movement comes to an end, which is the terminus of the entire movement, ii) as some point midway which is the beginning of one part of the movement and end or terminus of another part. So in the movement from A to C though B, C is the last terminus, B is also a terminus but not the last. Both can be the object of intention. So although the object of an intention is always an end, it need not always be the final end.

45 Cf. Christopher Kaczor, *"Proportionalism and the Natural Law Tradition,"* 96–97.

46 Thomas Aquinas, *Summa Theologiae*. IaIIae, qq. 6–17.

47 The so-called neoscholastic scheme of structural moments of human action rigorously distinguishes between operations of the intellect and operations of the will, which is interesting and important from the analytical point of view; however, we should keep in mind that the acting person is a unity of intellect and will. Interpreters do not agree on the precise identification and order of the structural moments of human action. Basic information is to be found in Kevil L. Flannery, "John Finnis on Thomas Aquinas on Human Action," in *Reason, Morality, and Law. The Philosophy of John Finnis*, eds. John Keown and Robert P. George (Oxford: Oxford University Press, 2013), 132.

48 Cf. Thomas Aquinas, *Summa Theologiae*. IaIIae, q. 12, a. 1.

49 Cf. Christian E. Brugger, *"Praeter Intentionem* in Aquinas," 101.

50 Thomas Aquinas, *Summa Theologiae*. IaIIae, q. 12, a. 3. Translation: "The object of the intention, as has already been said, is not only the final end, but also a middle end. Someone can intend simultaneously a proximate end and the final end, as e.g. a medicine and health."

51 Let us say that the final end is D. A, B and C are means and as such are objects of choice. However, they are only objects of choice – as means – because the final end is D, since A, B and C become means *qua* means only with respect to the object of the intention, i.e., to D. For the conclusions above cf. Joseph M. Boyle, "Praeter Intentionem in Aquinas." *The Thomist: A Speculative Quarterly Review* 42, no. 4 (1978): 649–665. At p. 657 Boyle writes:

> [...] the agent intends the end of his action; he does not intend the means as such. But in many human acts that which is chosen as a means is also intended as an end. Moreover, the means are intimately connected with the intended ends in such a way that one's chosen means cannot be *praeter intentionem*. Both ends of actions and means to these ends are within the agent's intention.

52  Thomas Aquinas, *Summa Theologiae*. IaIIae, q. 64, a. 7, ad 4. Translation: "An act of fornication or adultery is not necessarily directed to conserving one's life, as is an act which sometimes results in homicide."

53  Joseph M. Boyle, "Praeter Intentionem in Aquinas," 658.

54  Thomas Aquinas, *In Libros Physicorum*. L. II, lect. VIII. Translation: "[...] for what is always or often associated with an effect falls under the same intention. For it is foolish to say that someone intends something and does not want that which is often or always associated with it."

55  Cf. Sergio Parenti, "Legge ed eccezione." *Sacra Doctrina* 1 (2015): 197–291, 279.

56  Thomas Aquinas, *In Libros Physicorum*. L. II, lect. VIII. Translation:

> [...] the effect of a cause acting with some intention is what obtains in accordance with the agent's intention: i.e., all that comes to being in effect *praeter intentionem* is *per accidens*. And I say this if that which is *praeter intentionem* obtains only rarely; for what is always or often associated with an effect falls under the same intention. For it is foolish to say that someone intends something and does not want that which is often or always associated with it.

57  Thomas Aquinas, *Summa Contra Gentiles*. L. 3, c. 6. Translation:

> [...] one must know that not all that is beyond intention (*praeter intentionem*) must be a matter of luck or chance. [...]. If that which is beyond intention always or often followed that which is intended [...] it would be a matter of neither luck nor chance; it would be a matter of chance if it occurred only rarely.

58  Thomas Aquinas, *De Malo*. L. 1, a. 3, ad 15. Translation:

> [...] sometimes an accident is associated with a certain effect in few cases and rarely; the agent then need in no way intend the effect *per accidens*, although he intends the effect *per se*. But sometimes this accident is associated with a primarily intended consequence always or in many cases; this accident then cannot be separated from the agent's intention.

59  Cf. Joseph M. Boyle, "Praeter Intentionem in Aquinas," 660.

60  Christian E. Brugger, "*Praeter Intentionem* in Aquinas," 105.

# 3 A Brief History of the Principle

## Cajetan to J. P. Gury

## Introduction

Aquinas's exposition of the admissibility of killing the aggressor in an act of self-defence contained in *Secunda secundae* of *Summa theologiae* is difficult to interpret and interpreters have as yet not reached agreement as to whether Aquinas is in fact presenting the first version of the principle of double effect or not. But with Mangan we can say that with the Angelic Doctor its history (or more precisely, as we will see in the following chapter, the history of different formulations of the principle of double effect in different theoretical contexts) begins, and has as yet not reached its conclusion.

According to Mangan nothing to elaborate the understanding of the principle of double effect was written in the two centuries following Aquinas's death in 1274. But the situation changed at the beginning of the 16th century thanks to interpreters of Aquinas's work such as Tommaso de Vio, called Cajetan, and especially members of the Spanish Salamanca school (*Escuela de Salamanca*) founded by the Spanish Dominican Francisco de Vitoria on his return from studying in Paris.

Overviews of the history of the principle of double effect written by the Jesuit theologian Joseph Mangan or T. A. Cavanaugh follow the most important authors whose work contributed to a more profound understanding of the principle of double effect and possibilities of its application, first to several cases and later to the entire sphere of moral theology. But their expositions do not contain sufficient detail, do not cite most of the important original texts and do not discuss the principle of double effect set in a sufficiently broad context. For this reason I have selected authors whom I consider most important (Tommaso de Vio, Francisco de Vitoria, Domingo de Sta Teresa, and Jean Pierre Gury) and have tried to amend that shortcoming. The entire chapter culminates in the presentation of the principle of double effect in the *Compendium of Moral Theology* by the French Jesuit Jean Pierre Gury, believed by many to be the author of the first modern formulation of the principle.

## Tommaso de Vio

One of the most important figures of the history of Thomism was the Italian philosopher and theologian Tommaso de Vio, also called Cajetan (or in Latin Gaetano, i.e., "from Gaeta"). He was born in 1469 (some sources say 1465 or 1468) in the port town of Gaeta in central Italy in the region of Lazio. At 16 he entered the Dominican order and became Superior General in 1508–1518. In 1517 he was elected Cardinal, from the following year on he was active as papal legate in Germany (as delegate and representative of Pope Leo X he met Luther in 1518).[1]

Cajetan was a prolific and original author and teacher, who became famous already thanks to his brilliant public discussion with the Italian humanist and philosopher Pico della Mirandola in Ferrara in 1494. In 1497–1499 he stayed in the Italian Pavia, where he became the first in Italy to base his teaching on reading Aquinas's *Summa*.[2] Pope Pius V ordered him to publish his exposition of *Summa theologiae* in the first complete edition of Aquinas's work, known as *Piana* (after Pius V) and published in Rome in 1570.[3]

In his exposition of the history of the principle of double effect Mangan claims that Cajetan's interpretation of Aquinas's text in IIaIIae, q. 64, a. 7 construes Aquinas's treatise on the admissibility of killing the aggressor in an act of self-defence as a formulation and application of the principle of double effect as we understand it today.[4] In his commentary Cajetan writes:

> [...] dupliciter potest referri occisio alterius ad conservationem vitae propriae: primo, ut medium ad finem; secundo, ut consequens ex necessitate finis. [...] Nam et finis et medium ad finem cadunt sub intentione: ut patet in medico, qui intendit sanitatem per potionem vel diaetam. Id autem quod consequitur ex necessitate finis non cadit sub intentione, sed praeter intentionem existens emergit: ut patet de debilitatione aegroti quae sequitur ex medicina sanante. Et iuxta duos hos modos diversimode occidere potest licite persona publica, et privata. Nam persona publica, ut miles, ordinat occisionem hostis ut medium ad finem subordinatum bono commmuni, ut in littera dicitur: persona autem privata non intendit occidere ut seipsum salvet, sed intendit salvare seipsum, non destiturus a sui defensione etiam si alterius mortem ex sua defensione oporteat sequi. Et sic iste non occidit nisi per accidens: ille autem per se occidit. Et propterea ad illud requiritur publica auctoritas, ad hoc non.[5]

Cajetan's text is extraordinarily important, since the native of Gaeta was and still is an acknowledged commentator of Aquinas's *Summa* who influenced further generations of Thomists and authors referring to Aquinas as the author in whose work the principle of double effect first appears and is applied to solving some moral dilemmas. In his text Cardinal Cajetan elucidates some important concepts (killing *per se* and killing *per accidens*), determines the relationship between intention, means and ends, and also (retrospectively) confirms the interpretation of J. Boyle (and some other authors) according to which the consequences of an action that are necessarily implied by the given action need not fall under the agent's intention. According to the Italian theologian killing the aggressor while protecting one's own life can be viewed in two ways: as a means to an end (*ut medium ad finem*), or as a consequence stemming from the necessity of the end (*ut consequens ex necessitate finis*). Cajetan clearly states that both the end and the means to the end fall under the intention (*sub intentione*) and gives an intelligible example: the intention of a physician (we could say his remote intention) is his patient's health; in order to attain his end (*finis operantis*), he gives the patient some potion or prescribes a diet. He prescribes a diet (*finis operis*) **in order to** cure the patient (*finis operantis*). Although prescribing the diet is the end of the action (*finis operis*), the entire action complex does not comprise only the action as such, but the action finalized by some intention (motive): from the point of view of the final end, which is the agent's end (*finis operantis*), prescribing the diet is a means. Both the end and the means are intended by the physician, though each in a rather different way (the patient's health is the physician's final end, prescribing the diet is a means to attain this end).

The Italian Thomist further specifies the relationship between an action and its necessary consequences associated with the end: if something is necessarily associated with a certain end (*consequitur ex necessitate finis*), but is not an end in itself (today we would say that it is a necessary, unintended, but predictable consequence of the action), it is not intended (is *praeter intentionem*). Cajetan gives the example of administering a medicine to an ill person: the end is curing the patient (administering the medicine is a means); both the end and the means are part of the agent's intention. There is a negative effect associated with administering the medicine, which is weakening of the ill person's organism. It is not a means to attain the final end (that is administering the medicine), it is not the final end (that is curing the patient), but it is associated with administering the medicine and its effects in such a way that the finality of the physician's action (curing the patient by means of administering the medicine) cannot be fulfilled otherwise than by administering the potion and accepting the negative effect. The negative effect is therefore necessitated by the end (*ex necessitate finis*). We can easily find a modern example: chemotherapy is still one of the most frequent means of fighting malignant tumours. The procedure is unpleasant for the patient, causes nausea, weakness, hair loss, damages the organism. These side effects are not intended by the physician; they are merely predicted and accepted as inseparable effects associated with a morally good action, viz. curing the patient.[6]

Finally the Italian Dominican theologian applies the clarified distinctions to the case of killing the aggressor by a private person (self-defence) and a public person (soldier). The soldier pursues killing the enemy as a means which is together with its end subordinate to a common good (peace in society as a condition of full-fledged development of human beings *qua* social creatures), while a private person in an act of self-defence does not intend to kill the aggressor in order to save his life. The end of his action is defense of his life, even if its consequence is killing the aggressor. Cajetan says that a soldier intending the enemy's death killed him *per se* (intentionally), while a person defending his life killed the aggressor *per accidens* (accidentally or as a consequence of the accepted risk; the killing was not part of the structure means-end). Homicide committed by a soldier and by a person defending his life therefore differs with respect to intention, so there must exist an element justifying the soldier's action at the moral level: he must be authorized to the action by a public authority.

## Francisco de Vitoria

Another remarkable figure of the scholastic and Thomistic tradition was the Spanish Renaissance philosopher and theologian, the Dominican Francisco de Vitoria (about 1492–1546),[7] founder of the renown Salamanca school. De Vitoria studied in Paris (1508–1513) under Jean du Feynier and Pierre Crockaert, who entrusted him with the first printed edition of *Summa Theologiae* in Paris, more precisely of *Secunda secundae* (1512), to which he wrote the foreword.[8] On his return to Salamanca[9] a group of philosophers and theologians formed around Francisco, such as Domingo de Soto, Vitoria's successor Melchior Cano or Domingo Bañez (who spoke of Francisco as of the second Socrates). Francisco de Vitoria is regarded as the founder of modern international law who had marked influence on great figures of theory and philosophy of law such as Hugo Grotius (1583–1645) and Alberico Gentili (1552–1608).

In Salamanca Francisco de Vitoria introduced *dictatum*, a new teaching practice, which he got to know in Paris and regarded as very valuable. It consisted in slowly dictating a text, so that students could write down every word of the lecture. As a result, the preserved student notes can be taken for a sound source of knowledge concerning the content of his lectures, which has not been preserved in another form.[10]

De Vitoria deals with the problem of the moral admissibility of killing the aggressor in self-defence in his *relectio De Homicide*. The term *relectio* (again-reading, from the Latin *relego, relegere, relectus*) is used to denote a practice when professors at the University in Salamanca presented a topic of their lectures to the wide public. *Relectio* followed up on the

medieval *quaestio quodlibetalis*, but unlike the practice of public discussion it was a continuous lecture, normally read from a pre-prepared
manuscript for the duration of two hours, measured by a water-clock.
Over the course of his university career Vitoria delivered altogether 15
*relectiones*, 13 of which were published in print based on his students'
notes. The first edition is from 1557 from the printing house of Jacques
Boyer and *De Homicide* is the tenth of the 13, although chronologically
it was Vitoria's third lecture.[11]

Vitoria's commentary on Aquinas's treatise on the moral admissibility
of killing the aggressor in an act of self-defence is interesting not only in
that Francisco is part of the long Dominican Thomistic tradition reading
Aquinas's text and interpreting it very much like the Jesuit theologian
Joseph Mangan did in the 20th century. In his *relectio* Vitoria also discusses the interpretation a form of which we have already met e.g. in the
case of the Dutch moral theologian Leonardo Lessius, who in his treatise
*De iustitia et iure* of 1605 claimed that in an act of self-defence one can
intend all that is necessary for it, including causing a fatal injury and
thereby the aggressor's death.

The seventh article of *De Homicide* asks a question identical to the
one Thomas Aquinas asks in IaIIae, q. 64, a. 7: whether it is permitted
to kill someone in defending one's own life (*utrum aliqui liceat occidere
aliquem se defendendo*). Vitoria answers:

> Occidere invadentem non est illicitum. Ad probationem hujus con-
> clusionis, praesupponit sanctus Thomas quod ex una operatione
> possunt provenire duo effectus, quorum unus est ex intentione
> operantis, alius praeter intentionem operantis. Sic ex defensione
> mea sequitur unus effectus per se intentus, scilicet defensio mea, et
> alius effectus est vulneratio invadentis, sed est praeter intentionem.
> Unde hic effectus, quia praeter intentionem, nec imputatur nec est
> culpabilis.[12]

While Aquinas speaks of an act (*actus*), Vitoria uses the term operation
(*operatio*). Two consequences result from an operation of self-defence:
one is intended (literally: of the agent's intention), it is therefore intended
*per se*, while the other is unintended (*praeter intentionem*). Since injuring the aggressor is not intended by the defender, it cannot be imputed to him as moral guilt. Vitoria, rigorously following Aquinas's
exposition, adds that the self-defence must be conducted by adequate
means (be conducted within the limits of legitimate defence, *cum moderamine inculpatae tutelae*) and gives an example: if it is possible to
defend oneself with a mere shield, one must not use a sword or any other
weapon. He also stresses that killing the aggressor must never become
the defender's intention, e.g. in an effort at revenge during the act of
self-defence (*tamquam in vindictam ut seipsum defendat*). Leaving aside

minor terminological differences, the Spanish Dominican's interpretation of Aquinas's text does not diverge from the original in any way. His answers to the doubts (*dubia*) associated with the moral treatment of an act of self-defence are of more interest. The first of these asks whether one can intend the aggressor's death in case there is no other effective way of defending one's own life (*utrum liceat intendere mortem invasoris quando alias non potest quis se defendere*).[13] Contemporary authors (*moderni*)[14] affirm this: yes, in defending one's life one can intend the aggressor's death, if there is no other possibility of fulfilling the end of one's action. Their main argument in the form Vitoria gives it is very simple:

> [...] licet velle occidere invasorem: ergo licet intendere, quia non est aliud volitio quam intentio, quia intentio est actus voluntatis.[15]

The argument is intelligible: on the general level it states that it is permitted to want to kill the aggressor and from the fact that intending (intention) is an act of the will, as wanting is, the legitimacy of intending the aggressor's death is inferred. Vitoria also explains the reasons for accepting the argument's non-obvious assumption, expressed with the words *licet velle occidere invasorem* (it is permitted to want to kill the aggressor):

> Quia cuicumque licet velle finem, licet velle medium necessarium ad finem; si enim licet velle navigare, licet conducere navim tamquam medium necessarium. Sed licet velle defendere me et servare vitam meam. Iste est finis; et iudico quod non possum servare et defendere vitam mea nisi occidendo istum, quia hoc est medium necessarium ut suppono. Ergo licet velle interficere illum, quia alias occidet me nisi occidam illum.[16]

This argument takes a rather different form than it will later acquire in Lessius: the Dutch theologian does not derive the possibility to intend the aggressor's death from the fact that we are entitled to want it (*velle*), but from the fact that it is a necessary means of effective self-defence.[17] *Moderni*, as their views are presented by Francisco, argue as follows:

1   If *S* can want an end, he can also want the means necessary to reach it.
2   *S* can want (= it is morally licit) to save his life.
3   *S* regards killing the aggressor as a necessary means to reach his own end.
4   Therefore *S* can want to kill the aggressor.
5   An intention is an act of the will just as wanting is.
6   Intention (*intentio*) and wanting (*velle*) are the same act.
7   It is therefore possible to intend killing the aggressor.

Thomas Aquinas would probably reply to this argument that mere wanting (which really is an act of the will, a human person's first reaction to the prospective rational grasping of a certain possible end) does not yet proceed to an effort to actualize some action. Let us imagine that we are mentally entertaining the idea of going swimming. This can entice us to want to go swimming, but the wanting itself can easily pass and is not a strong commitment to action. Intention, on the other hand, is an act of the will directed to a certain end (going swimming acquires the character of an end) with an implicit choice of means (the choice of means itself is an object of selection (*electio*)) and as such is a stronger commitment to action than mere wanting. In the structure of human action wanting and intention are both acts of the will, but they are formally distinct, as we distinguished between intention and choice based on relationship to the relevant objects in the previous chapter.

But Francisco de Vitoria chooses a different strategy and rejects the universal validity of the argument's assumption: if *S* may want an end, he may also want the means necessary to reach it. The first step of his reasoning strategy is to reject the claim that it is licit to want to kill the aggressor:

- *S* can want (= it is morally licit) to kill the aggressor *X*, if the death of *X* is a necessary means to reach *S*'s end. But the death of *X* is not a necessary means to reach *S*'s end, therefore *S* must not want *X*'s death.[18]

The objection formulated later by Lessius quite naturally suggests itself: if I say that the aggressor's death is (sometimes or even frequently) not a necessary means to defense of one's life, does it not mean that self-defence will often be quite ineffective? But let us note that Vitoria is not denying that killing the aggressor can sometimes be a consequence of an act of self-defence. He is rather denying that in self-defence it is necessary to want the aggressor's death; in his view it is enough if one wants to defend his life, e.g. by getting hold of a shield and fighting. We may not want to kill (it is not necessary for an act of self-defence), but we may want to take up a shield and fight (*velle ponere clypeum et pugnare*). But even if we accept the identification of wanting (*velle*) and intention (*intentio*), it does not follow that we are allowed to intend the aggressor's death, for it is illicit to want his death.

## The Salamanca School

In his exposition of the history of the principle of double effect Joseph Mangan states that it became a universally accepted moral principle, at least implicitly, at the end of the 16th century.[19] However, at that time it was not understood as a general moral principle applicable in the entire sphere of moral theology; this step was taken by authors of the monumental work *Cursus theologicus* belonging to the **School of Salamanca** (*Escuela de Salamanca*), founded by the Spanish Dominican Francisco de Vitoria at the university in Salamanca on his return from France. *Cursus theologicus* contains the treatise *De peccatis*, authored by Domingo de Sta Teresa, according to Mangan dating from 1647. While Aquinas formulates a certain version of the principle of double effect in the context of discussing offences against commutative justice, in particular within the eight *quaestiones* that can be summarized as a treatise on homicide (*De homicido*), Domingo de Sta Teresa discusses the principle of double effect as applicable to the problem of the admissibility of illicit sexual pleasure. Mangan believes, however, that Domingo's interpretation and application of the principle makes it possible to understand it as applicable in all spheres of moral theology. This is also confirmed by the subsequent tradition, which presented the principle of double effect ever more frequently in the general part of moral theology and referred to it also when solving particular moral problems.

In his *Cursus theologicus, tractatus* XIII, *disputatio* 10, *dubium* 6 Domingo de Sta Teresa first explains the difference between causes *per se* and causes *per accidens*.[20] Causes *per se* are ones that are of their nature and directly oriented to the production of a certain effect. For example poison is *per se* the cause of someone's death; because of its nature it is directed to the effect at hand: killing the one who takes it. An example of a cause *per accidens* can be the sinking of a ship as a result of the helmsman's carelessness. The carelessness is not the cause of the ship's sinking in the same way as the poison is the cause of the death (the ship could have been sunk perhaps by striking an underwater reef), but if the helmsman had been more careful, the ship would not have sunk.

Over the course of elucidating the character of cause *per se* in the context of moral discourse the principle of double effect is formulated as follows:

> [...] quoties causa influens per se etiam notabiliter in aliquem effectum malum, aeque immediate, vel per prius habet alium effectum bonum, isque sufficienter necessarius censetur juxta materiae gravitatem et qualitatem, potest talis causa licite applicari ad hunc effectum posteriorem [...] dummodo licet praevisus, non tamen sit intentus, neque expresse volitus, neque medium per se ad finem intentum.[21]

Let us notice a minor terminological difference, occurring also in Gury's *Compendium of Moral Theology*, which according to many authors contains the first modern formulation of the principle of double effect: where Thomas Aquinas speaks of human act (*actus*) and Francisco de

Vitoria of operation (*operatio*), there now appears the term "cause" (*causa*). In my view Domingo's formulation of the principle of double effect can be formulated as follows[22]: if $\varphi$ is a human action having two consequences $C_1$ and $C_2$, of which $C_1$ is a good consequence, and $C_2$ is a bad consequence, then it is possible to actualize $\varphi$ if the following three conditions are satisfied:

1   $\varphi$ is the cause of a proportionally (with respect to $C_2$) weighty good effect;

2   a   $C_1$ precedes $C_2$, or
    b   $C_1$ follows from $\varphi$ as immediately as $C_2$;

3   The bad effect $C_2$ is merely foreseen (*praevisus*), but it is not intended (*intentus*) or directly wanted, and it is not a means to the intended end.

In modern formulations of the principle of double effect the important condition usually appears that action $\varphi$ itself is at least morally neutral, i.e., it is either good or neutral. But in explicating his principle Domingo states the traditional doctrine according to which moral acts derive their specification only from what is intended (*actus humani species non sumitur nisi ab eo quod est per se in intentione agentis*), not from what is not intended (*praeter intentionem*).

## Jean Pierre Gury

In his historical exposition of the principle of double effect Mangan states that it is not easy to determine how the detailed and sophisticated explication and application of the principle of double effect in the collective work of the members of the Salamanca school influenced the following generations of moral theologian.[23] It is interesting that the work *Salmanticenses morales* (first published in 1665) contains no general treatment of the principle of double effect. In the years following the publication of *Cursus Theologicus* moral theologians were becoming more aware of the general character of the principle of double effect as a moral principle, though many reserved no special treatment to it at the general level (as a principle, not as part of its particular applications). According to Mangan this holds e.g. for Buseubaum (1600–1668), Gobat (1600–1679), or La Croix (1652–1714). Other authors did so, though without referring to the *Salmanticenses* (e.g. Reiffenstuel (1641–1703), Roncaglia (1677–1737), Billuart (1685–1757), or Gury himself (1801–1866). Mangan brands the grasp of the principle of double effect at the general level in most of these authors as inadequate and incomparable with the depth and breadth of the discussion encountered in *Cursus theologicus*. But the situation changed upon the publication of a popular compendium of moral theology penned by the French Jesuit moral theologian Jean Pierre Gury, first published in 1850 under the title *Compendium theologiae moralis*. Mangan writes:

It is only beginning with the various editions of Gury's admirable and repeatedly reedited *Compendium Theologiae Moralis* in the 19th century that the moral theologians universally give an adequate, thorough explication of the principle of the double effect as a general principle applicable to the whole field of moral theology.[24]

Gury's treatise differs radically from Thomas Aquinas's exposition.[25] While Thomas devotes minute attention to explicating human action in all its structural moments, from intrinsic to extrinsic act, and reserves dozens of *questiones* in *Prima secundae* to it, Gury only discusses some aspects of human action in the limited space of several pages. The intrinsic aspect of action is almost entirely left out from his compendium. The entire first treatise (*tractatus*) is devoted to human action (*De actibus humanis*) and divided into three chapters (*capita*):

1   On the notion of human acts (*De notione actuum humanorum*);
2   On the principles of human acts (*De principiis actuum humanorum*);
3   On the moral character of human acts (*De moralitate actuum humanorum*).

Just a little under three pages of the text of the first chapter is devoted to clarifying the nature of human action. Gury first defines act at the general level as the actualization (*determinatio*) of some potency or putting the potency to act (*facultas agendi*) to action, or the process of actualizing (*exercitium*) this potency. The human being is capable of acting in a certain way and action consists in actualizing this potency, as e.g. drinking a glass of water (an act) is the actualization of the potency to drink a glass of water. The potency itself is also known as the first act (*actus primus*), while its actualization is the second act (*actus secundus*). Human action, human deeds or acts are such that proceed from the human being *qua* human being, they are actualized with the participation of the essential abilities of human persons – their ability to think, want and freely decide.

The division of human acts into good, bad, and indifferent, found at the end of the first chapter, is important from the moral point of view. According to Gury it holds that a certain deed $\varphi$ is:

1   **Good** (*bonus*), if $\varphi$ corresponds to right reason (*recta ratio*), i.e., accords with some moral norm. $\varphi$ is also called **licit** (*licitus*).
2   **Bad** (*malus*), if $\varphi$ does not correspond to right reason, i.e., does not accord with some moral norm. $\varphi$ is also called **illicit** (*ilicitus*).
3   **Indifferent** (*indifferens*), if $\varphi$ does not accord with some moral norm, but at the same time does not contradict any norm.

Gury's formulation of the principle of double effect appears very early on in the second chapter devoted to the principles of human action, where he deals especially with its voluntariness and the form it takes. When he has clarified the character of voluntary (*voluntarius*) action and its consequences and the difference between two important forms of what is voluntary (*voluntarium directum*, which is *per se* the object of an intention, and *voluntarium indirectum*, which is not wanted *in se*, but merely *in alio*, as e.g. the consequence of some cause),[26] the Jesuit theologian introduces two important principles. The first principle determines by three conditions in what circumstances the consequence of an action can be morally imputed to agents,[27] while the other is already fully devoted to the formulation and explication of the principle of double effect. Gury introduces it with the following words:

> Licet ponere causam bonam aut indiferentem ex qua immediate sequitur duplex effectus, unus bonus, alter vero malus, si adsit causa gravis, et finis agentis sit honestus.[28]

The reason for postulating this principle Gury states is that if it did not hold, then by actualizing a given cause (by the action) the acting person $S$ would be committing an immoral deed (literally sin) for three possible reasons:

1  $S$ intends a bad consequence;
2  $S$ actualizes the cause;
3  $S$ foresees a bad consequence.

But the principle of double effect excludes all three possibilities, since:

1  It cannot be for the reason of the intended goal, because it is assumed to be honest;
2  It cannot be for the reason of actualizing the given cause, because it is assumed to be good or indifferent;
3  It cannot be for the reason of anticipating (*praevisione*) the bad consequence, because it is compensated for by the good consequence.

According to Gury all the four conditions presented in his formulation of the principle of double effect are essential. It can be adapted in the following way: person $S$ is allowed to actualize an action $\varphi$ from which two consequences $C_1$ and $C_2$ follow, of which $C_1$ is good and $C_2$ is bad, if the following four conditions are satisfied:

1  $S$'s end is honest (*honestus*);
2  $\varphi$ is good or at least indifferent;
3  $C_1$ is an immediate consequence of $\varphi$;

4   There is a grave reason (*ratio gravis*) to actualize $\varphi$ and there is no other reason preventing the actualization of $\varphi$ (e.g. some preceding obligation not to act).

The French theologian also devotes space to explicating the validity of all four conditions, which is sufficiently intelligible:

1   $S$'s end must be good, otherwise $S$ would intend something bad and would commit an immoral action (= sin);
2   $\varphi$ must be good or at least indifferent, which means that $\varphi$ must not contradict a moral norm.
3   $C_1$ must follow from $\varphi$ just as immediately (*aeque immediate*) as $C_2$, for if $C_2$ were the immediate effect of $\varphi$ and $C_1$ were achievable by means of $C_2$, the good would be attained by wanting evil (*bonum ex malo quaereretur*).[29]
4   There must be a proportionately grave reason for actualizing the action and the agent must not be under an obligation (*obligatio*) preventing this actualization.[30]

Let us take a look at conditions 1 and 3 of my reformulation of Gury's principle of double effect. The first condition states that the agent's end must be honest, i.e., moral, or $S$ would be intending something bad, which is morally illicit (we are not allowed to want to steal, cheat, murder, or rape). $S$ intends as an end (= the end is the object of his intention) both the end of the action (in the second chapter we designated such intention as proximate) and the agent's end (remote intention), or the action's motive. If some $X$ is a means to actualizing the end $S$, then it enters the means-end structure to which the intention is directed. In other words, if $X$ is a means, then $X$ is intended as a means to some end and as such is part of $S$'s intention. From that it follows that if $Y$ is not part of the intention $S$, it cannot be a means to actualizing a certain end that $S$ has. The first condition of Gury's formulation of the principle of double effect excludes the possibility that the bad effect $X$ could be a means to attaining the good effect, for $S$ must not intend anything bad and if $X$ is a bad consequence, it must not enter $S$'s practical deliberation of the ends and means to attain them. The third condition stating that $C_1$ must be an immediate consequence of the action $\varphi$ (it must not follow from the bad effect) is therefore redundant and can be left out.

The final form of Gury's version of the principle of double effect in my formulation therefore runs as follows: person $S$ is allowed to actualize an action $\varphi$ from which two consequences $C_1$ and $C_2$ follow, of which $C_1$ is good and $C_2$ is bad, if the following three conditions are satisfied:

1   $S$'s end is honest (*honestus*);
2   $\varphi$ is good or at least indifferent;

3 There is a grave reason (*ratio gravis*) to actualize $\varphi$ and there is no other reason preventing the actualization of $\varphi$ (e.g. some preceding obligation not to act).

It is an interesting question whether the principle of double effect is a principle of justifying action (in certain conditions we are entitled to act so and so, although our action will bring about not only a good effect, but also a bad one), or a principle limiting the moral imputability of a certain action to its author. Gury speaks of the licitness of action (a licit action is one that is moral), but some other authors speak as if the action – or more precisely, its bad consequence – could not be imputed to the agents.[31] In my view this interpretation is erroneous, since although the bad effect is not intended, it is nonetheless foreseen, i.e., the agent acts with the awareness that his deed will have not only a good consequence, but also a bad one. The production of the bad consequence is therefore an intentional consequence of the action and as such must be imputed to the agent. Nonetheless, if we understand the principle of double effect as a principle of justification, then, if the relevant conditions are satisfied, we are entitled to act (our action is morally justifiable).

## Conclusion

In this chapter we have dealt with some of the important figures of the history of the principle of double effect. The important Thomistic philosopher, theologian and Cardinal of the Catholic Church Tommaso de Vio or Cajetan interprets Aquinas's formulation of the principle of double effect in IIaIIae, q. 64, a. 7 in the way in which this principle – at least according to Mangan – is understood today. According to Cajetan both the ends (*finis operis* and *finis operantis*) and the means to attain these ends are part of the intention (fall under the intention). If the intention (motive) of a physician's action is to cure the patient, then both the action itself (administering the potion), which from the point of view of motive is a means, and the means to attaining the end of the action (administering the potion, e.g. choice of ingredients, their preparation, etc.) fall under his intention. Human action is often accompanied by consequences necessitated by the end of the action (*consequitur ex necessitate finis*), which, however, are not intended, whether as ends or as means. A physician applying chemotherapy does not intend nausea, weakness and hair loss in his patient, but if the patient is to be cured of the cancer (or his state is to improve so that he can be operated on), then he must undergo the chemotherapy and from the necessity of this end follows also the fact that the treatment will be accompanied by undesirable effects.

Another important figure in the history of the principle of double effect is Francisco de Vitoria, Renaissance philosopher and theologian and founder of the famous school at the Spanish university in Salamanca. In his *relectio* Francisco faithfully follows Aquinas's line of interpretation and claims (as Aquinas does) that killing the aggressor in an act of self-defence is not intended. But the self-defence must be conducted with adequate means: if we can defend ourselves with a mere shield, we must not use a sword. The adequacy of means is context-dependent: sometimes running away is sufficient to save one's life, at other times it is necessary to fight without weapons (if we are more adept fighters than the aggressor is), at other times it will be necessary to use a weapon. A highly interesting part of De Vitoria's treatment of self-defence are the answers to certain objections (*dubia*), especially the one according to which it is possible to intend killing the aggressor if his death is a necessary means to attaining the action's end. Francisco's answer focusses on whether over the course of defending one's life the aggressor's death is a necessary means and states that it is not: the means of self-defence is fight, not death. The aggresor's death can be a consequence of the fight, but it is not in itself a necessary means.

Another important moment in the history of formulations of the principle of double effect was the publication of the treatise *De peccatis* authored by another theologian of the Salamanca school Domingo de Sta Teresa. According to Mangan this treatise, which is a part of the collective work *Cursus theologicus*, presents the principle of double effect as a general moral principle applicable to the entire sphere of moral theology for the first time in the principle's history. Domingo de Sta Teresa gives the principle of double effect the following form (in my formulation): if $\varphi$ is a human action having two consequences $C_1$ and $C_2$, of which $C_1$ is a good consequence and $C_2$ is a bad one, then it is possible to actualize $\varphi$ if the following three conditions are satisfied:

1    $\varphi$ is the cause of a proportionally (with respect to $C_2$) weighty good effect;

2    a    $C_1$ precedes $C_2$, or
    b    $C$ follows as immediately from $\varphi$ as $C_2$ does;

3    The bad effect $C_2$ is merely foreseen (*praevisus*), but it is not intended (*intentus*) or directly wanted, nor is it a means to the intended end.

The last author I engaged with, and the most important one, is the Jesuit theologian Jean Pierre Gury. In his *Compendium of Moral Theology* Gury presents the principle of double effect already in the first treatise *Of Human Action* as a general principle, applicable not only in a limited number of cases but in all of moral theology. Gury is often regarded as the author who first presented the modern formulation of the principle of double effect. When the redundant third condition of when it is licit to actualize an action having a good and a bad consequence is left out, the principle of double effect takes the following form: it is licit for person $S$ to actualize action $\varphi$, from which two consequences $C_1$ and $C$ follow, of which $C_1$ is good and $C_2$ is bad, if the following three conditions are satisfied:

1  $S$'s end is honest (*honestus*);
2  $\varphi$ is good or at least indifferent;
3  There is a grave reason (*ratio gravis*) to actualize $\varphi$ and there is no other reason preventing the actualization of $\varphi$ (e.g. some preceding obligation not to act).

An open question, on which we will focus in the conclusion of the following chapter, is whether Gury's formulation of the principle of double effect is equivalent to Thomas Aquinas's formulation.

## Notes

1  Basic information on the life and work of Cardinal Cajetan is found in Frederick Coplestone, *A History of Philosophy. Vol. III: Late Medieval and Renaissance Philosophy* (New York: Doubleday, 1993), 337–340.
2  Some Dominicans of the Roman province based their teaching on Aquinas's *Summa* already at the beginning of the 14th century, but a year later they were reprimanded by the chapter in Perugia and were ordered to return to the *Sentences* by Peter of Lombardy. This ordinance was confirmed by the general chapter in Metz in 1313. But at approximately the same time a summary of the *Summa* was written by Giovanni Dominici at the request of Pope John XXII, which became a predecessor of the later great commentaries. Aquinas's *Summa* did not get to the forefront in the university milieu through Aquinas's confréres, but through the Dutch theologian and professor at the University in Cologne Henric de Gorichem (about 1386–1431), who taught at that university according to the *Summa* and even wrote *Quaestiones in Summam Sancti Thomae (Compendium Summae Theologiae)*, published in print more than 40 years after his death. The recommendation to study all of Aquinas's work first appeared in the *studia* of the members of the Dominican order in 1424 and was supported by the order's general superior Salva Casetta in Cologne in 1483. In 1512 the first published commentary on *Prima secundae* appeared, written by Conrad Köllin, originally professor at the German Heidelberg and later at the University of Cologne. In Paris the *Summa* was taught by Peter Crockaert since 1509, while at the University in Leuven the *Summa* replaced Lombard's *Sententiarum* only in 1596. Cf. Jean-Pierre Torrell, *Aquinas's Summa. Background, Structure, & Reception* (Washington, DC: The Catholic University of America Press, 2005), 94–96.
3  Other editions are known as *Parma* (after the Italian town Parma, published in 1852–1873) and *Vivès* (after the publisher, published in Paris in 1871–1872). Cajetan's commentary is part of the critical edition of Aquinas's work whose publication began following an incentive of Pope Leo XIII, which is why it is called *Editio Leonina*.
4  Cf. Joseph T. Mangan, "An Historical Analysis of the Principle of Double Effect." *Theological Studies* 10, no. 1 (1949): 41–61. 52.

5 Cajetan's commentary (*Commentarium in Summa S. Thomae*) is quoted from *Sancti Thomae Aquinatis Doctoris Angelici Opera Omnia* (Iussu impensaque Leonis XIII P. M. edita). Tomus Nonus. Romae: Ex typographia Polyglotta, 1897 (commentary on IIaIIae, q. 64, a. 7). Translation:

> Killing another person can be related to saving one's own life in two ways: first as a means to an end, second as stemming from the necessity of the end. Both the end and the means fall under the intention, as is evident in a physician who intends the health [of a patient] by means of a potion or a diet. But what comes from the necessity of the end does not fall under the intention, but obtains beyond intention, as evident in the case of the weakening of an ill person which is a consequence of administering a medicine. In accordance with these two ways a public or a private person can kill someone in a licit way. A public person – e.g. a soldier – pursues killing the enemy as a means subordinate to the common good, as the commented-on text says. A private person does not intend to kill in order to save himself, but intends to conserve his own life and will not cease to defend himself, even if the aggressor's death had to be a consequence of his action. Therefore a private person kills *per accidens*, a public person kills *per se*. That is why public authority is necessary for that, while it is not necessary for self-defence.

6 Cf. Thomas A. Cavanaugh, *Double-Effect Reasoning. Doing Good and Avoiding Evil* (Oxford: Clarendon Press, 2006), 17.

7 Some authors state 1483, 1486, 1492 and 1493 as date of birth. A date of death sometimes cited is also 1546.

8 Cf. Jean-Pierre Torrell, "*Aquinas's Summa*," 98–101.

9 Vitoria returned to Spain in 1523. First he taught theology at the Dominican school Sant Gregorio in the town of Valladolid, a centre of Spanish scholastic philosophy. Two years later his confréres nominated him as a candidate to hold the chair of theology (*Cátedra de Prima*) at the University in Salamanca and he obtained the position by a majority vote. His first lecture was on *Secunda secundae* of Aquinas's *Summa Theologiae*. Thereby Peter of Lombardy's *Sententiarum libri quattuor* were replaced by the *Summa* in Salamanca.

10 Francisco de Vitoria and John P. Doyle, *Reflection on Homicide & Commentary on Summa Theologiae IIa-IIae Q. 64 (Thomas Aquinas)* (Milwaukee, WI: Marquette University Press, 1997), 13.

11 Francisco de Vitoria and John P. Doyle, "*Reflection on Homicide*," 14–16.

12 Ibid., 192. Translation:

> Killing the aggressor is illicit. To prove that conclusion St. Thomas assumes that one operation can give rise to two effects, one of which is intended by the agent, the other is unintended (*praeter intentionem*). Thus of my self-defense there follows one consequence intended *per se* – my defense itself – the other consequence is injury of the aggressor, which, however, is unintended (*praeter intentionem*). Since this consequence is unintended, it is not imputed to me and does not imply guilt.

13 Lessius, as we know from the preceding chapter, believed that in defending one's own life one can intend all that is necessary to that end (*licitum est in actu defensionis intendere omne id, quod iudicatur ad vitae membrorumque defensionem necessarium*).

14 These are probably the nominalistic proponents of *via moderna*, since Vitoria labels authors such as Gabriel Biel, Jacob Almain or Peter of Ailly as *modern*.

15 Francisco de Vitoria and John P. Doyle, *"Reflection on Homicide,"* 192. Translation: "It is permitted to want to kill the aggressor: therefore it is permitted to intend it, since wanting is nothing other than intending, as intention is an act of will."

16 Ibid. Translation:

> Since all are permitted to want the end, they are also permitted to want the means necessary to reach the end: if a sea voyage is permitted, it is also permitted to use a ship as a necessary means. But I am permitted to want to defend myself and save my own life. That is the end and I judge that I cannot save and defend my life, unless I kill the aggressor, for I assume that it is a necessary means. It is therefore permitted to kill him, for if I do not do so, he will kill me.

17 In his treatise *De iustitia et iure* the Spanish Dominican, Thomistic philosopher and theologian and member of the Salamanca school Domingo de Soto offers yet another conception of the licitness of killing the aggressor in an act of self-defence. Like Aquinas and other authors he distinguishes between two consequences of one act: one is good (conservation of own life), the other is bad (aggressor's death). De Soto also specifies that the first consequence is intended (*ex intentione agentis proferatur*), while the other obtains beyond the agent's intention (*accidat praeter eis intentionem*). Human action acquires its moral character from what is intended, therefore self-defence is morally licit, since based on natural law everyone may defend their own life. But unlike Aquinas and also Lessius or his confrére Francisco de Vitoria, Domingo de Soto says that killing the aggressor is possible when it is a necessary means to defending one's life (*nemini licet aggressorem occidere nisi id fuerit necessarium medium*). Domingo differs from Aquinas in that he admits killing the aggressor as a means to reaching an end; he differs from Lessius in that he does not claim that killing the aggressor as a means is part of the agent's intention. Cf. Domingo de Soto, *De iustitia et iure*. L. 5, q. 1, a. 8.

18 Francisco formulates his argument in the first person and says that it is not necessary for my self-defence that I want to kill the aggressor (*non est necessarium ad defensionem meam quod velim interficere*). Cf. Vitoria and Doyle, *"Reflection on Homicide,"* 192–194.

19 Cf. Joseph T. Mangan, "An Historical Analysis," 56.

20 Salmanticenses, *Cursus theologicus*. Tomus quartus (Lugduni: Joannis Antonii Huguetan, 1697). Tr. 13, disp. 10, dub. 6.

21 Ibid. Translation:

> [...] although a certain *per se* cause also has a bad consequence, it is licit to realize the cause of this bad consequence, if a proportionally weighty good effect just as immediately follows from it or comes beforehand. [...] although the bad effect can be foreseen, it must not be intended (*intentus*) or directly wanted or be a means to the intended end.

22 Cf. also Thomas A. Cavanaugh, *"Double-Effect Reasoning,"* 22. However, my reformulation of the principle of double effect differs from Cavanaugh's.

23 Cf. Joseph T. Mangan, "An Historical Analysis," 58.

24 Ibid., 59.

25 I used Joanne P. Gury, *Compendium theologiae moralis. Editio decima septima*. Tomus primus (Romae: Typis civilitatis catholicae, 1866). Cf. also Christopher Kaczor, "Double-Effect Reasoning from Jean Pierre Gury to Peter Knauer." *Theological Studies* 59, no. 2 (1998): 297–316 and Christopher Kaczor, *Proportionalism and the Natural Law Tradition* (Washington, DC: The Catholic University of America Press, 2002), 27–29.

26 The difference between *voluntarium directum* and *indirectum* is illustrated by a simple example: I can want to get drunk on wine, in which case the consequence of excessive drinking is the object of intention and *per se* wanted. But I can just want to enjoy a bottle of good wine and the result is that I get drunk. In both cases the intoxication is a consequence of intentional action, but only in the first case is it a consequence that is intended and wanted.

27 These three rules within the first principle serve to maintain the voluntariness of the action. The first rule e.g. stipulates that the agent must foresee the consequence, however vaguely. For the axiom holds that nothing can be wanted unless it has first been cognized (*nihil volitum quin fuerit praecognitum*).

28 Joanne P. Gury, "*Compendium*," caput II. Here Gury explicitly appeals to Thomas Aquinas, *Summa Theologiae*. IIaIIae, q. 64, a. 7. Translation: "It is allowed to actualize a good or indifferent cause from which two consequences immediately follow: one good, the other one bad, if there are grave reasons for it and the agent's end is honest."

29 Cf. Joseph M. Boyle, "Toward Understanding the Principle of Double Effect." *Ethics* 90, no. 4 (1980): 527–538.

30 In his translation Mangan uses the phrase "the author of the action is not bound by some virtue not to act." This translation is taken over by all other authors, such as C. Kaczor, J. Boyle, and T. A. Cavanaugh (cf. their works cited in the preceding footnotes). Mangan states that he is engaging the fifth German edition of Gury's *Compendium of Moral Theology*. In the edition that was available to me we find "*nec teneatur agens ex alia obligatione eam omittere.*" It does not speak of virtue, but of duty or obligation (*obligatio*). I understand this requirement as follows: a pregnant woman learns that her uterus is afflicted by cancer. The only possibility for her to save her life is to undergo hysterectomy (extracting the uterus with the foetus). Hysterectomy is a classic example of applying the principle of double effect. But if the woman expresses a clear, autonomous wish that she does not want the operation (because there is a chance of carrying the child to a state when it can live outside the uterus), although it will mean that she will eventually succumb to the disease, the physician is obliged not to carry out the operation.

31 The Jesuit A. Vermeersch, one of the most important moral theologian of the first decades of the 20th century, writes in his *Moral Theology* (*Theologia moralis: Principia, responsa, consilia*) that a bad consequence of an action for which we have grave reasons is not imputed (*non imputatur*) to the agent. Quoted according to Joseph M. Boyle, "Toward Understanding," note 11.

# 4   Peter Knauer and Proportionalism

## Introduction

In the preceding two chapters I strove to briefly present the historical development of the principle of double effect from Thomas Aquinas up to the Jesuit theologian Jean Pierre Gury, who in his successful and abundantly published work *Compendium theologiae moralis* presented, at least according to some authors, the first modern formulation of the principle of double effect and set it in the context of a treatise on human action. All the authors I discussed belong to the Catholic tradition and their ethics can be characterized as religious ethics. But in the 20th and 21st centuries, the principle of double effect also plays an important part in non-religious ethical system and has found advocates among authors adhering to no religious tradition. I will focus on them in the following chapter; in this chapter I will focus on one of the greatest transformations the principle of double effect has undergone. It was not only its formulation that underwent a transformation but the position it acquired within the whole of moral theology. Thomas Aquinas presents his version of the principle of double effect in the second book of the second part of his *Summa theologiae*, where he discusses the application of general moral principles to particular cases (*singula in speciali*): we have seen that in application to the moral admissibility of killing the aggressor in an act of self-defence the principle of double effect can be interpreted as an application of general moral principles to a particular case. Several centuries later the principle of double effect attains the final character of a general moral rule in Gury's *Compendium of Moral Theology*, though it is one of the moral rules that does not affect the whole of morality, including the understanding of its basic concepts, such as the concept of good (licit) or bad (illicit) behaviour.

The situation changed radically when the young German Jesuit theologian Peter Knauer published a paper that was first published in the French language in 1965 under the eloquent title *La détermination du bien et du mal moral par le principe du double effet* (*Determination of Moral Good and Evil according to the Principle of Double Effect*).[1] Since the article was written in the French language, it was not widely received among English speaking moral theologians, though its basic ideas were made accessible in the USA by the American theologian Richard A. McCormick. But two years later a somewhat adapted English version of the same paper appeared in *Natural Law Forum* and Knauer's ideas came to be widely discussed, distinctly influenced especially American moral theology and prompted the emergence of an active and in the USA widespread stream known as **proportionalism**.[2]

The ground for a broad reception of Knauer's conception of the principle of double effect and its role in moral theology was prepared by certain events and discussions taking place among moral theologians already since the 1960s.[3] One of them was the Church's reaction to the growing liberalization of abortion regulating laws. The Catholic Church strongly opposed the admissibility of abortions, as far as so-called therapeutic abortion was concerned, i.e., abortion carried out for reasons of health. An important condition of the admissibility of therapeutic abortion, grounded in the hundreds of years of Catholic Church tradition, was that putting the foetus to death must not be a case of direct killing. Such situation obtains e.g. over the course of the widely discussed hysterectomy, when the entire uterus of a pregnant woman is removed together with the tumour. The result of hysterectomy is on the one hand saving the woman's life (good effect), on the other hand it is putting the foetus to death (bad effect). The Church through its representatives repeated the doctrine according to which killing the child is a case of indirect killing, because it is not the object of intention (intended). Very similar deliberations were also applied to cases of extrauterine pregnancy, when the blastocyst is implanted outside the uterus, most frequently in *tuba uterina* (in 95% of the cases). This situation is often solved by means of salpingectomy (surgical excision of a fallopian tube), which results in death of the foetus and poses a risk to the possibility of further pregnancy.[4] Some theologians began to pose a question doubting the distinction between directly and indirectly killing the foetus: if excision of a fallopian tube kills the child and at the same time poses a risk to the possibility of a further pregnancy, would not a more logical (and more correct) solution be to remove the foetus and retain the fallopian tube (salpingotomy)? Is it ethically right for a physician to choose a procedure with a higher number of negative effects? Many theologians came to answer the question in the negative.

A similar controversial example is introduced by the German moral theologian Bernard Häring.[5] A gynaecologist was carrying out an operation on a pregnant woman whose uterus was affected with a benign tumour. Over the course of the operation one of the blood vessels in the uterus started bleeding strongly, so in order to save the woman the physician extracted the foetus, removed the uterus and then stopped the bleeding. But later a well-known moral theologian told him that he had committed an objectively bad action (killing the foetus could not be characterized as indirect). Of course, the physician was much surprised: if he had extracted the whole bleeding uterus with the foetus, the theologian would not have objected, although as a result of the action not only the foetus would have been killed, but the woman could not become pregnant again. The whole case is controversial precisely because the distinction between directly and indirectly killing the foetus in some situations means that we are obliged to choose an action having a greater number of negative consequences (death of the child, infertility – excision of uterus, or risk of infertility – excision of fallopian tube) than an alternative action resulting "merely" in killing the foetus.

But the discussion was not limited to abortion. Some authors were pointing out that some (in their view) analogical situations are morally evaluated in different ways. Let us take a look at the following two scenarios[6]:

1   **Lifeboat**: A lifeboat can safely carry only four persons, but over the course of a shipwreck five passengers have got on board. One of them decides to jump in the sea and swim away (to save the other four), although he is certain to die.
2   **Prisoner of war**: X is a prisoner of war who knows where 50 of his co-fighters are hiding. X knows that if the enemy will torture him, he will give away his comrades' hiding place and thereby sentence them to death. That is why X decides to make use of the guards' lack of attention and commit suicide.

Theologians such as Cornelius Van der Poel wonder why, although the two scenarios seem analogical, according to the moral teaching of the Catholic Church only the first one is a case of morally licit action (apparently because the swimmer did not decide to commit suicide, merely to make place in the boat, though it will ultimately result in his death). In the second scenario X directly chooses his death, which is why his action is illicit regardless of the good consequences it might have (saving 50 human lives). Van der Poel views this as an inconsistency, which he believes to be due to the fact that human action is morally evaluated only based on its physical structure. This thesis (distinguishing between a physical act and a moral act) is widespread among the proportionalists: they criticize the tradition for pronouncing moral judgments (X committed suicide) merely based on the physical description of the action (X made a rope out of shoelaces and hanged himself on it) and defines intrinsically bad actions, licit in no circumstances (suicide is always immoral).

The ground for widespread acceptance of proportionalism was prepared not only by the new problems and challenges moral theology was facing in the last quarter of the 20th century but also by efforts at their solution. W. Van der Marck attempted to approach the problem of artificial means preventing pregnancy, use of which was being banned by the

Church, in a new way.[7] He believed that contraception can be a means of cultivating a mutual bond of love and respect between the spouses, without the risk of an unwanted pregnancy. Van der Marck emphasized that materially identical acts can in fact represent two different and morally distinct cases of human action.[8] The defining characteristic of human action is its intersubjective character: humans are social beings and develop in society. Their action can be – in an interpersonal perspective – either community creative, or community destructive. The nature of the action at the level of its significance and immanent finality is determined precisely by the overlap to the sphere of the whole human community. Let us imagine that X is holding a dissector in his hand and excising a human kidney. The description of X's action is a physical description: X is holding a dissector, cutting a human body, excising a kidney. But the action itself is not as yet specified; we do not know whether it is an act of excising an organ for the purpose of transplantation, done with the donor's conscious and informed consent, or a brutal act of physical mutilation. What determines the case is reference to intersubjectivity: excision of a kidney for the purpose of transplantation is a community creating act, while mutilation is not. It is not important here whether Van der Marck's analysis is correct, but that he refuses to classify and morally evaluate human action only based on its physical description. The proportionalists emphasize this element of analysis of human action very much and employ the concept of commensurate reason. A simple example will again illustrate their thinking. Let us have three situations:

1   X points a weapon at Y, pull the trigger, the weapon fires and kills Y.
2   X points a weapon at Y, pull the trigger, the weapon fires and kills Y.
3   X points a weapon at Y, pull the trigger, the weapon fires and kills Y.

In all three cases the description of X's action is identical (the actions are materially identical): X points a weapon at Y, jerks the trigger, the weapon fires and kills Y. But as yet we have not determined what X has in fact done. In the first case Y is an aggressor, against whom X cannot defend himself except with a gun. In the second case Y is an innocent passer-by who falls victim to the aggression and frustration of X. In the last case X is an executioner who executes criminals according to the laws of his country. Although proportionalists do not agree as to whether the death penalty is moral, all agree that it is only possible to specify what action X in fact actualized and then morally evaluate it with reference to other information not included in the physical description of X's action.

An interesting aspect of Van der Marck's analysis is his conviction that in morally describing human action the distinction between good and bad consequences becomes meaningless: only the action itself is good or bad. *A fortiori* therefore the principle of double effect itself becomes meaningless.

Another author whose thinking prepared the way for the reception of Knauer's conception of the principle of double effect and its defining relationship to the whole of morality is Peter Chirico.[9] Chirico assumed that in particular, everyday human life we are often obliged to choose in situations when our choice breaks some general moral rule (norm). In such situations it is necessary to choose so that our choice takes all the values concerned in the action into account and strives for their greatest actualization, even if it implied breaking some absolute moral norm. In his defence of proportionalism Garth L. Hallett later spoke in a very similar way.[10]

Suitable terrain for the reception and massive spread of proportionalism in the USA was also prepared by other phenomena, which I will briefly mention here.[11]

One of them was the change of theologians' attitude to the infallible teaching of the *magisterium* of the Catholic Church, made possible by the Second Vatican Council, kindled especially in connection with the publication of the encyclical *Humanae vitae*.[12] Among moral theologians the encyclical became a source of ceaseless polemics and disagreement with the official Vatican line strictly banning the use of contraception. Many authors were reinforced in their views by the fact that they saw the Second Vatican Council – in some of its pronouncements – as a break from the preceding tradition (e.g. in the teaching on religious freedom), and therefore did not hesitate to claim that also encyclicals, papal circulatory letters addressed at present to all the faithful, could contain error.

Moral theologians were also becoming increasingly aware that although moral theology is specific in some ways (it deals with the human being directed by his action to his creator – God), in formulating moral norms it strives to regulate human action as human (and not specifically Christian) action oriented to fulfilling the values that are common to all humans regardless of their religious faith. Moral theology can therefore proceed autonomously to a great extent, even with respect to the pronouncements of the teaching authority of the Church.

The last factor affecting moral theologians' debate since the 1970s was the re-evaluation of natural law theory, which came to be viewed as old-fashioned and erroneously grounded in a metaphysical, static concept of human nature. The forefront came to be occupied by a historical conception of human beings, who must be morally guided by an ethical system accounting for their historical character. In this way the concept of nature was gradually displaced by the concept of right reason (*recta ratio*), which accounts for human beings in the totality of their existence.

## Peter Knauer and the Hermeneutic Function of the Principle of Double Effect

### Introduction

The radically innovative character of Knauer's conception of the principle of double effect and its role in moral theology is evident already from the introduction to the English version of his paper, which does not appear in the original French version.[13] The German Jesuit first states that in moral theological manuals the principle of double effect plays only a marginal part. But he does not want merely to assign a higher role to it: he elevates it to the basic principle of the whole of morality. In Thomas Aquinas the principle of double effect plays a very limited role and represents an application of already existing ways of determining the moral admissibility of actions (*fontes moralitatis*) to the particular case of defence of own life. Later development attributed increasing significance to the principle of double effect and eventually Jean Pierre Gury made it a universal moral principle, though it is only applicable to certain cases, clearly specified by the conditions of its validity and applicability. But Knauer does not apply the principle of double effect only to a certain defined group of cases, but to the whole of morality, to all of human action. And it is not just a matter of application: the principle of double effect has an important hermeneutic function, for compared to traditional ethics it is better able to explain basic moral concepts and determine the conditions on which it is morally licit to do harm to someone (including oneself).

### New Formulation of the Principle of Double Effect

Every moral theory tries to answer the question what the criteria of correct human behaviour are, what makes it possible to say that certain behaviour is good or bad. Thomas Aquinas, as we have seen in the second chapter, determines the moral character of human deeds (good-bad) against the background of a general metaphysical theory of perfection grounded in the fullness of being. If a certain action is "perfect," i.e., it satisfies all the requirements (object, end, circumstances), it is called good (*bonum ex integra causa*), while if it lacks the required perfection, it is bad (*malum ex quocumque defectu*). In his paper Knauer very briefly, and in my view inadequately, discusses three ways of determining the moral quality of human action: an action is morally good if it[14]:

1   orients the human being to his last end, i.e., to God;
2   conforms to human nature;
3   is simply good.

The German Jesuit rejects the first two options as too abstract (the first one more so, the second one less) and inclines to a rather surprising solution: the morally good is identical with what is simply good. What does Knauer mean by "good"? He says that he means the physical goodness of every existing thing in accordance with the scholastic axiom *ens et bonum convertuntur*. Scholastic reflection regarded the good as one of the transcendental determinations of being, which does not concern being in itself but relationship to another (*secundum ordinem ad aliud*), more precisely to the will. All that is known is also wanted, for wanting is related to perfection and every being is perfect to the extent to which it is actual (*in quantum est in actu*).[15] If I understand Knauer's specific theory correctly, he is saying: X is some perfection (value)[16] that can become an object of interest. X is **simply good**,[17] and therefore **morally good**, if it is willed by person S in such a way that physical evil possibly associated with X is not objectively part of S's intention. In such case X merely determines S's intention. Simply and therefore morally good is therefore primarily some value, if only it enters S's intention. One could probably say that human action is morally good, if the value specifying the agent's intention is morally good.[18]

The opposite of physical good is physical evil, which Knauer does not define in any way and does not try to ground it in some metaphysics. He reckons that all people know physical evil from experience: we all know that pain, disease, ignorance, a missing limb, blindness, etc. are cases of physical evil. Human action often or perhaps always causes or admits some physical evil, but "to cause or admit physical evil" is not equivalent with moral evil. A surgeon obliged to amputate a limb causes physical evil (a missing limb is an example of physical evil), but his action is morally right (good). According to Knauer it accords with the principle of double effect generally determining in what circumstances it is morally licit to admit or cause a physical evil. But it plays a much more important role, for it is a hermeneutic principle in light of which we interpret the very basic concepts of morality, such as the concept of moral evil. That consists in admitting the existence or causing a physical evil for which we do not have a commensurate reason (*ratio proportionata*).

We will return to the concept of commensurate reason later, as well as to Knauer's own formulation of the principle of double effect. First I must remark on his understanding of the traditional concepts *finis operis* and *finis operantis*.[19] In the second chapter we encountered this distinction in expounding the basic principles of Thomas Aquinas's moral theory. Aquinas understands *finis operis* as the object of the action itself, though he specifies sometimes that this object is some thing (*res aliena* in the case of theft) and, at other times, that it is the action itself (*suscipere aliena*). But whether the object of the action is a thing, a state of affairs or the action itself (the extrinsic act becomes the object of the intrinsic act), a relationship to the order of reason is always assumed, not the thing itself in its physical reality (e.g. money) or the action described merely behaviourally (transfer of money to own pocket). The object of theft is money belonging to someone else who did not consent to it being transferred, the action is a theft if it is an actualization of an intention to take over the property of another without his consent.

*Finis operantis* corresponds to the circumstance why (*cur*) and can be either a further act, or an end to which another act is subordinated as a means.

In his paper Knauer criticizes what he views as a frequent interpretation of the end of action (*finis operis*), according to which it is the extrinsic act that can be simply observed. An action is specified by the intention, which is why it cannot be determined simply based on its observable, "physical" manifestation. Thomas Aquinas advocated the doctrine that the object of intention is the object of an act of the will (intention is an act of the will), which comprises an implicit reference to the means employed to attain the end. Some thing, state of affairs or action becomes the end of an action (*finis operis*) because the agent focusses on it as on the object to which the action is directed and in which it finds completion. But Knauer advocates a very different and highly surprising and non-standard theory of intention.[20] First he distinguishes between two meanings of the concept "intention": one is encountered in psychology, the other one in ethics. Psychological intention corresponds to what the agent consciously focusses on in his action (approximately intention in Aquinas's sense). What matters, however, is moral intention, specified not by what the agent intends, what he aims at, what he plans and what means he chooses for his action, but objectively by the existence or non-existence of a commensurate reason. A commensurate reason answers the question whether admitting or causing a physical evil is justifiable: in case *S* acts in such a way that there is a commensurate reason for his action, then *S*'s action is motivated only by the positive value which is *ipso facto* intended and belongs to the end of the action (*finis operis*) of *S* himself. But if there is not a commensurate reason for *S*'s action, then according to Knauer his action is motivated by physical evil, which becomes the object of the intention and the internal object of the action (*finis operis*). Let us note how unusual Knauer's conception is: what the object of the intention is is not determined by the human being who chooses an end and the means to attain the end, but the existence or non-existence of some objective criterion of the admissibility of actualizing the action (commensurate reason). Let us take a look at the following example:

- **Chemotherapy.** Patient *X* suffers of cancer. The physician *Y* prescribes a cycle of chemotherapy, as a result of which the tumour is reduced to operable size. But chemotherapy also has harmful consequences: *X* feels weak, suffers hair loss and often feels ill.

Aquinas and his modern advocates in the field of ethics would say that Y carried out an action (administering chemotherapy) with two consequences: (i) the good consequence is the reduction of the tumour, making possible its surgical removal; (ii) the bad consequences are nausea, weakness and hair loss. Y's proximate intention (*finis operis*) is applying chemotherapy (which comprises all the necessary means, choice of appropriate medicine, prescribing it, choice of the way, modality of application, etc.), the remote intention (*finis operantis*) is, let us say, preparing the patient for an oncological operation. The bad consequence of chemotherapy is neither an end (final or intermediate), nor a means to attain the end, so it is neither part of the end-means structure nor object of intention. It is unintended, merely foreseen and accepted as a necessary and unfortunately irremovable part of chemotherapy. The fact that the weakness, nausea and hair loss are not part of the physician's intention is not determined by any objective criteria but by the intentional structure of his action.

Knauer would proceed differently. He would focus on the physical good and evil that can be brought about by the action: tumour reduction and preparing the patient for operation is a physical good, while weakness, nausea and hair loss are examples of physical evil. By his action the physician Y actualizes (whether directly – causes, or indirectly – admits) physical good and evil; whether it is a case of moral good or moral evil is determined by the existence or non-existence of a commensurate reason. If such a reason exists, then Y's action is motivated by the good, only the good itself enters the object of the action (*finis operis*), while the evil is, in Knauer's defined moral sense, unintended. But if a commensurate reason for the action does not exist, then – regardless of the psychological intention – what is morally intended is evil, which becomes part of the action's end.

From what I have said so far the contours of a radically new conception of morality can already be fairly clearly perceived. It is therefore not surprising that the formulation of the principle of double effect is also radically different from the ones we have encountered in the preceding two chapters. According to Knauer the principle of double effect says[21]:

- The bad effect of one's action can be admitted if it is not intended in itself but is indirect and justified by a commensurate reason.

This formulation states that the bad effect must be indirect. But Knauer does not mean the traditional distinction between direct and indirect consequence in the sense of physical causality, but again a certain moral distinction.[22] We have seen that what determines whether some X is intended or unintended is not determined by the mental states of the agent, but by the existence or non-existence of a commensurate reason.

As a result the condition "if it is not intended in itself but is indirect" is redundant and can be left out. In that way we obtain the final version of the principle of double effect according to Peter Knauer[23]:

- **Principle of double effect.** The bad effect of one's action can be admitted if one has a commensurate reason for it.

## Reformulation of Traditional Ethics

What has been said above unambiguously shows that in Knauer the principle of double effect and in fact the whole conception of moral action is reduced to the existence or non-existence of good reasons to act, the existence or non-existence of a commensurate reason for the action. But Knauer leaves the clarification of the concept "commensurate reason" for later chapters of his paper and first tries to show that the ethical tradition before him in fact assumed and implicitly applied the principle of double effect reduced to the existence or non-existence of a commensurate reason.[24] In traditional ethics the claim is often encountered that some actions are of their nature and regardless of the circumstances always bad: we speak of intrinsically bad actions (*intrinsice mala*). An example can be the intentional killing of an innocent human being, which according to this theory is forbidden regardless of the consequence (good or bad) that could follow from it. Intrinsically bad behaviour (killing an innocent being) is forbidden by negative moral norms (*praecepta negativa*), which are valid at all times and in all circumstances (*semper et ad semper*), while the often less specific positive moral norms (*praecepta positiva*)[25] are valid at all times, but not in all circumstances (*semper sed non ad semper*).[26]

Knauer admits that the category of intrinsically bad action exists, but he does not restrict it to several key types of action. Intrinsically bad actions are forbidden in all circumstances, while other types of action are forbidden in some circumstances and not in others (e.g. Catholics are obliged to attend the Sunday mass but if they are ill they need not fulfil their obligation). The German theologian claims that if $\varphi$ is an action for which there exists a commensurate reason $P$, then $\varphi$ does not represent a case of intrinsically bad action. But if $P$ is lacking, $\varphi$ becomes an intrinsically bad action. Since the existence or non-existence of $P$ is a criterion of the morality of $\varphi$ (if $P$ exists, $\varphi$ is moral (good), otherwise it is immoral), the categories "immoral" and "intrinsically bad" coincide in Knauer's thinking. The German Jesuit does not deny that some concepts implicitly include reference to their moral inadmissibility (e.g. "murder"), but that is because murder is a case of killing a human being for which there is no commensurate reason. Let us note that the commensurate reason in fact enters the specification of the action itself (it becomes part of *finis operis*). Let us compare the following two examples:

1   **Self-defence.** X defends himself against unjust aggression on the part of Y and, not having another option, kills the aggressor.
2   **Murder.** X attacks an innocent passer-by and kills him.

The physical description of X's action is identical in both scenarios: X lifts up a weapon with the trigger mechanism unlocked, points at Y, moves the trigger with his finger, the gun fires and the bullet kills Y. But in the first case X had a commensurate reason for his action. It means not only that his action can be justified by the principle of double effect, it is moral and is motivated only by a good intention (in the moral sense), but also that X committed a certain type of action: killing in self-defence. In the second scenario X has no commensurate reason for his deeds, which is why his action cannot be justified by the principle of double effect, it is motivated by a morally bad intention and as such immoral. The non-existence of a commensurate reason also specifies that in the second scenario X committed a different type of action: murder. From the moral point of view murder is always forbidden, but only because it is an instance of killing without commensurate reason.

In contemporary bioethics it is intensively debated whether there is a morally significant difference between killing and letting die. Killing is an example of breaking a negative norm, which is valid *semper et ad semper*, while letting die breaks a positive norm enjoining respect and protection of human life, which is valid *semper sed non ad semper*. The difference between killing and letting die can be illustrated with the following example:

1   **Killing.** Peter desires the property of his rich uncle, whose heir he is. One evening he sneaks into the bathroom when his uncle is having a bath and drowns him.
2   **Letting die.** Peter desires the property of his rich uncle, whose heir he is. One evening he sneaks into the bathroom when his uncle is having a bath. At that moment the uncle accidentally hits his head and slips under water. Peter stands and watches his uncle drown.

Some contemporary authors would say that the two scenarios differ in Peter's causal contribution to his uncle's death: in the first scenario Peter is the cause of his death, while in the second one Peter merely does not interfere with the existing fatal sequence of events culminating in the uncle's death. However, regardless of causality, Peter is morally guilty in both scenarios. Knauer would agree with these authors, though for somewhat different reasons. He would say that in the second scenario

Peter had no commensurate reason not to respect the positive moral norm obliging him to save his uncle's life. If that is so then from the moral point of view, Knauer says, Peter is the cause of his uncle's death, regardless of what the "physical" causality was. In other words, Peter broke the negative norm "you will not kill" since, without the existence of a commensurate reason, he broke the positive norm commanding him to protect human life. Knauer in fact claims that negative norms are contained in positive norms: not respecting positive norms without a commensurate reason is identical with actively breaking negative norms.[27]

Knauer illustrates his theory with a simple example[28]: an oncologist decides to administer chemotherapy to a patient. He knows very well that chemotherapy markedly improves the patients' state of health, or can even result in full recovery. But it is accompanied by unpleasant side effects: nausea, weakness and hair loss. Knauer claims that if the oncologist has a commensurate reason for his action (administering chemotherapy), then the negative effects of chemotherapy follow from it indirectly. By his action he breaks a positive moral norm but there is a commensurate reason for it. If the physician had no commensurate reason for his action, it would be an instance of breaking a negative norm.

### Commensurate Reason

The concept of commensurate reason plays a key part in Knauer's thought since, by being incorporated in the author's reformulation of the principle of double effect, it defines the basic concepts of morality and serves as a criterion of good and bad action. We can summarize the individual definitions in a semi-formal form.

1   Let $\varphi$ be an arbitrary action, $S$ an arbitrary agent, $C$ a bad effect and $P$ a commensurate reason. We define:

    a   **The morally bad.** If there is no $P$ for $\varphi$, then $\varphi$ is a morally bad action. If $\varphi$ is a morally bad action, then $\varphi$ is intrinsically morally bad.

    b   **The morally good.** If there is $P$ for $\varphi$, then $\varphi$ is a morally good action.

    c   **Moral intention.** If there is $P$ for $\varphi$, then $C$ is not the object of $S$'s moral intention. If there is no $P$ for $\varphi$, then $C$ is the object of the moral intention and enters the specification of *finis operis*.

    d   **Moral causality.** If there is $P$ for $\varphi$, then $C$ is an indirect consequence of $\varphi$. If there is no $P$ for $\varphi$, then $C$ is a direct consequence of $\varphi$.

But what is a commensurate reason? It is not any reason, since according to Knauer agents have some good reason for every action, whether good or bad (a thief stealing money does not choose evil – theft – as the reason for his activity but a certain good he wants to attain by his action).[29] The reason must be commensurate, but to what? Knauer denies that commensurate reason could refer to comparing the good and evil that are the consequence of some action, since he believes that qualitatively different values cannot be compared. But he is unable to present a precise definition of the key concept of his revolutionary moral theory and offers only some examples to illustrate its content. Let us take a look at two of them.

1   **Speed limit.** Contemporary human life is impossible without means of transport and traffic, which at the same time pose risks to it. Therefore there are restrictions to regulate speed, which limit our freedom but on the whole contribute to making traffic safer for everyone. If someone breaks the speed limit, his action contradicts the overall aim of speed regulation and as such is irrational.
2   **Studying.** A student wants to master as much study matter as possible, which is why he studies day and night without proper rest. As a result he eventually breaks down and does not attain his end. His action is irrational, since it does not follow the best path to fulfilling its finality.

These two examples (Knauer gives three altogether) serve to illustrate the concept of commensurate reason. It seems that a commensurate reason for an action exists when the relevant good in the action is pursued in a rational way, which means in the best way possible. Knauer also says that moral evil is admitted or caused without a commensurate reason if there is a long-term contradiction between a certain value and the way of realizing it. The student best realizes the value of knowledge by studying rationally: he does not forget to eat, drink, rest and also take exercise. Increased safety for all persons involved in traffic is compromised if someone drives faster: his action contradicts the value pursued for all by speed regulation.

Knauer's analysis of the key concept of his ethical system – the concept of commensurate reason – is not very clear and does not provide explicit instructions how to determine whether a commensurate reason did or did not exist for a certain action in particular situations. But we do get a basic idea and could apply it e.g. in the following way:

1   **Without commensurate reason.** A physician applies certain chemotherapy to his patient in order to improve his state of health so that the tumour will diminish, and the patient can undergo an oncological operation. The chemotherapy has a number of side effects. At the same time the physician knows that another form of treatment exists (e.g. biological treatment), which facilitates the same health improvement at least as effectively. Despite that he does not prescribe it

for the patient[30]; his action therefore lacks a commensurate reason (the action's end could have been attained in a better way).

2  **With commensurate reason.** An oncologist deliberates what treatment to prescribe for his patient. He assesses the state of his health, type of tumour, the patient's expectations and apprehensions, present state of therapeutic possibilities, etc. Based on this complex analysis he chooses chemotherapy as the best way of preparing the patient for an operation. There is a commensurate reason for his action, because he has taken all the options into account and chosen the action which best fulfils its end.

The moral good, as these examples show, consists in the best possible realization of some value. An action that realizes the chosen value in this way is one for which there is a commensurate reason, while an action that is suboptimal lacks it.

The commensurate reason expressed in the formulation of the principle of double effect has a hermeneutic function: it defines the basic concepts of morality. But a moral theory constructed in this way differs radically from the traditional ethics from which it emerged, not only at the general level of moral theory itself, but also in the final moral evaluation of particular instances. To conclude let us take a look at two examples that have already been discussed above:

1  **Hysterectomy.** A pregnant woman has been diagnosed with uterine tumour which cannot be cured in any other way than by excising the uterus together with the foetus. The foetus will die, but the woman will be saved. According to traditional ethics this is a licit action within the application field of the principle of double effect. Knauer will agree with this conclusion, but his justification will be different (though verbally – principle of double effect – identical): the physician has a commensurate reason for his action, which is why the action can be designated as morally good, regardless of the physical death (death of foetus) it gives rise to. But let us imagine that the physician can save the uterus, on the condition that he will excise the foetus which will die. According to traditional ethics the principle of double effect does not apply to this situation, since the death of the newborn as a means to the given end is part of the physician's intention. But Knauer would not agree: if the physician can save the woman and her uterus, his action is better than if he excised the uterus with the foetus. So there is a commensurate reason for excising the foetus, and with respect to the definitions above the physician is not the cause of the foetus's death from the moral point of view, and it is not part of his intention. While in the case of hysterectomy Knauer conforms to traditional ethics, he evaluates the case of foetus excision with uterus retention in exactly the opposite way.

2   **Ectopic pregnancy.** According to Knauer traditional ethics states that removing a foetus from an oviduct is not morally licit, because it is an instance of breaking the negative commandment "you will not kill." But the German theologian argues: negative norms apply only to cases of directly admitting or causing physical evil, which is equivalent to the claim that it applies to cases when there is no commensurate reason for the action. Since the physician does have a commensurate reason to excise the foetus,[31] his action is moral and cannot be classified as murder of an innocent human being.

## One or Three Principles?

In the second chapter I discussed in detail the version of the principle of double effect presented by Thomas Aquinas, the Dominican theologian and philosopher of the 13th century, in an answer to the question concerning the moral admissibility of defending own life in *Secunda secundae* of his *Summa theologiae*. The third chapter captures significant moments of the historical development of the principle of double effect up to mid-19th century, when the first edition of the *Compendium of Moral Theology* by the French moral theologian Jean Pierre Gury appeared. Finally in this chapter I focussed on a fairly modern version of the principle of double effect, presented first in the French and later in the English language by the German Jesuit theologian Peter Knauer.

Let us take one more look at all three versions of the principle of double effect.

1   **Thomas Aquinas.** An act of self-defence can have two consequences: a good one (saving own life) and a bad one (killing the aggressor), if it holds that:

a   The remote intention is good (conserving one's own life);
b   The proximate intention is good (fending off force by force);
c   The action is proportionate to its end.

2   **Jean Pierre Gury.** Person $S$ is allowed to actualize action $\varphi$, from which two consequences $C_1$ and $C_2$ follow, of which $C_1$ is good and $C_2$ is bad, if the following four conditions are satisfied:

a   $S$'s end is honest (*honestus*);
b   $\varphi$ is good or at least indifferent;
c   There is a grave reason (*ratio gravis*) to actualize $\varphi$ and there is no other reason preventing the actualization of $\varphi$ (e.g. some preceding obligation not to act).

3   **Peter Knauer.** We can admit a bad effect of our action if we have a commensurate reason for it.

Already at first sight it is evident that these are very different formulations; Aquinas's formulation is restricted to a particular case and is not formulated in general terms as the two later ones. But the differences between these formulations are due not only to how the principle of double effect is defined, but also to the general ethical context in which they are set, and also to the role they play in it.[32]

Thomas Aquinas discusses the principle of double effect as the 178th moral question of the total number of 304 questions of *Secunda secundae*, in *quaestio* 64, article 7. *Secunda secundae* assumes *Prima secundae* which deals with general moral questions, the structure of human action, its moral character, the intrinsic and extrinsic principles of human action. Aquinas's version of the principle of double effect is formulated in an answer to a particular moral problem and can be interpreted as an application of the general principles of moral evaluation of human action of *Prima secundae*. According to these principles killing the aggressor is licit if it holds that: (i) the agent's remote intention is good (IaIIae, q. 18, a. 4, ad 3); (ii) the proximate intention, object of action, is good (IaIIae, q. 18. a. 2); and (iii) the circumstances must be adequate (IaIIae, q. 18, a. 3 and a. 10). Rather than one principle, in Aquinas's treatise the principle of double effect is the sum of three general moral principles according to which human action is evaluated.

Over the course of history the position of the principle of double effect in the context of moral theology gradually changed, as it gradually came to play an ever more significant role. The process finally culminated in the *Compendium theologiae moralis* by Jean Pierre Gury. Gury discusses the principle of double effect already in the introduction to his compendium, in the exposition of human action. But we do not find Aquinas's subtle analyses of the intentional structure of human action in Gury; he ultimately reduces it to the mere actualization of the potency to act, i.e., to the physical execution of some action. But in Gury's work the principle of double effect is not the mere application of several moral principles; it becomes a general moral principle in itself with a significant role in the entire context of moral theology.

In Peter Knauer's work the principle of double effect becomes the most important moral principle on which the entire moral theory is constructed. It does not merely answer the question in what circumstances one is allowed to actualize an action causing physical evil, but in its hermeneutic function makes it possible to re-define the concepts of moral good and evil, moral intention or moral causality (direct or indirect). So, over the course of several centuries the principle of double effect was transformed from a marginal form of applying the general principles of the moral evaluation of human action to a hermeneutic principle serving as the main pillar of the entire moral theory.

The three authors also differ in their understanding of intention. Thomas Aquinas presents a sophisticated theory of intentions and their relationship to the totality of action and the means to fulfilling its ends. An intention is an act of the will with respect to some end (which is the object of the intention), which implicitly involves reference to means, which as means to the intended end are part of the intention (they are *in intentione* or fall *sub intentione*). According to Aquinas unintended bad effects are the product of intentional action (the agent knows that his action will have the respective consequences), but are not the object, whether of the action (*finis operis*) or of the agent (*finis operantis*), which is why they are not means to attaining the end. The concept of intention also implies the extent of obligation to action (and thus moral gravity): if someone makes killing a casual passer-by the object of intention, his obligation to act is markedly higher (the killing has already become the end of an action) and regulates possible further deeds (if he does not succeed in killing the passer-by with the first shot, he will shoot again). If a certain consequence is merely foreseen by the intellect and is not intended, the agent's obligation to actualize it is quite different. A physician prescribing chemotherapy foresees the negative effects; but if he could, he would prevent their actualization.

Gury, as I have already said, does not present any subtle and complex analysis of human action and his treatise *De actibus humanis* can be conceived as a clarification of the conditions of and impediments to the voluntariness of actions. In explaining the conditions of validity of his version of the principle of double effect the author assumes the distinction between intended and merely foreseen consequences, but it is unclear what the significance of this distinction is based on. The French theologian defines action simply as the actualization of some cause and it is unclear what the structure of this action is.

In his distinction between moral and psychological intention Peter Knauer quite radically breaks with the preceding tradition. While the psychological intention roughly corresponds to Aquinas's conception of intentions, the moral intention is quite different. It is not the agent who decides whether some physical good or evil becomes the object of an intention, but the existence or non-existence of a commensurate reason. We can speak of a good intention when there is a commensurate reason for the action; in the opposite case the intention is bad. Commensurate reason is also a defining element of action: if e.g. X shoots a man Y without commensurate reason, it is a case of murder. The bad consequence of the action (death of a human being) becomes the object of the moral intention and enters the definition of the action itself. While the difference between the intended and the merely foreseen consequences of an action plays an important role in Aquinas's ethics and also appears in Gury's description of the conditions of the validity of the principle of double effect, in Knauer's ethical system this difference becomes quite meaningless.

There is another significant difference between Aquinas's and Gury's version of the principle of double effect on the one hand and Knauer's formulation on the other. Both Aquinas and Gury underscore that the action itself must be morally good or at least indifferent. Let us say that a physician contemplates applying chemotherapy. That is at least morally indifferent, which is why further conditions of applying the principle of double effect can be considered: the good consequence is intended, while the bad one (nausea, weakness, hair loss…) is merely foreseen. A condition of the possibility of applying the principle of double effect is a moral deliberation determining whether the considered action is moral or immoral prior to the application itself. On the other hand, Knauer defines the concept of moral good and moral evil by means of the principle of double effect. Every action results in some physical evil or good: if there is a commensurate reason for the action, the evil is outside the agent's moral intention and his action can be characterized as morally good. In the opposite case it is morally bad. So applying the principle of double effect is not preceded by a moral deliberation which determines whether the considered action is morally good or not: that is determined by the application itself.

In his formulation of the principle of double effect Aquinas states that an action (in his case fending off force by force) must be proportionate to its end (*proportionatus fini*). That means that the defender must take into account all the consequences of his action, make some form of comparison and decide accordingly whether his action is proportionate to his finality. Let us take a look at the following three examples:

1  **One childless aggressor.** Y brutally attacks X. X defends himself and it turns out that the only effective way of fending off the attack (force by force) is using a weapon, which results in Y's death.

2  **One aggressor with offspring.** Y brutally attacks X. X knows that Y is an inhabitant of the same town, whom he occasionally sees with his three small children. X defends himself and it turns out that the only effective way of fending off the attack (force by force) is using a weapon, which results in Y's death.

3  **Three aggressors.** Three aggressors brutally attack X. X defends himself and it turns out that the only effective way of fending off the attack (force by force) is using a weapon, which results in the death of all three aggressors.

In evaluating these three scenarios consequentialists would take into account all the consequences of X's action: in the first case it is a life for a life, in the second case the father of three children dies, in the third case one life is bought with the death of three human beings. But Aquinas does not reason in this way and his requirement that the action must be proportionate to its end does not comprise such comparison of the action's consequences.[33] I understand Aquinas's requirement as follows:

- Action $\varphi$ is proportionate to its end $E$, if there are actions $\varphi_1, \ldots, \varphi_n$ such that each action $\varphi_1, \ldots, \varphi_n$ attains the end $E$ and at the same time each of them causes more **unnecessary** harm than action $\varphi$.

Let us now return to the individual scenarios. In the first scenario one aggressor attacks. The defender can run away ($\varphi_1$), defend himself with a sword and stab the aggressor's leg ($\varphi_2$), or fend him off with a lethal strike ($\varphi_3$). If the defender can run away, then $\varphi_1$ is the optimal action (it causes the aggressor no harm) and attains end $E$. If he cannot run away and manages to paralyze the aggressor by injuring his limb ($\varphi_2$), then the defender's action is again proportionate to the end, since $\varphi_2$ causes less harm than action $\varphi_3$ (if it was possible for the defender to merely injure the aggressor and he would nonetheless actualize $\varphi_3$, the harm would be unnecessary). Finally, if it is not possible to defend oneself in any other way than by killing the aggressor over the course of the fight, then the defender's action is proportionate to $E$ and the harm done is necessary for attaining $E$ (there is an action that will attain $E$ and cause unnecessary harm, e.g. killing the aggressor in an unnecessarily brutal way). Quite analogical reasoning can also be applied to the other two scenarios: so according to Aquinas the "amount" of physical evil with respect to proportionality to the end of self-defence is non-additive. Whether the defender kills one or five aggressors is relevant only with respect to whether his action is proportionate to attaining the end of self-defence, i.e., protecting his life. The proportionality of which *Doctor angelicus* speaks is therefore the proportion between the act and its end (*act/end proportion*).[34]

Aquinas's understanding of the proportion between an action and its end is not retained in the modern formulations of the principle of double effect already since Gury's *Compendium of Moral Theology*. The fourth condition of the principle of double effect Gury states is that the reason for the action must be serious (*adest ratio gravis ponendi causam*) and the agent must not bound by an obligation not to act. Gury further states that the natural equality of human beings (*aequitas naturalis*) obliges us to avoid evil (*ad vitanda mala*) and doing harm to our neighbours (*ad praecavenda proximi damna*), insofar as it is possible for us (*quando id facile possumus*). Kaczor interprets this requirement as a requirement to compare the possible harm imminent on us and the one imminent on our neighbours, i.e., as a requirement to compare to effects of the same action (*effect/effect proportion*).[35]

Although Peter Knauer's formulations are similar to those of Tomas Aquinas (he speaks of a certain disproportion between an action and its end), the examples he gives to illustrate the concept of commensurate reason show that in fact he means the relationship between the action's consequences. One of these examples is the case of the imprudent student who wants to master the subject of his study perfectly and studies hard without attending to the needs of his body (quality food, sufficient exercise and rest). Eventually the student breaks down and does not attain his end, whereas if he had studied proportionately to the possibilities of his situation, ate well and rested, he would have coped with his end much better. In fact, Knauer is comparing the consequences of one action (intensive unreasonable study) with the results of another action (reasonable study within the limits of human physical possibilities): his commensurate reason therefore applies to the consequences of an action (*effect/effect proportion*).

In the second to fourth chapter of this work I dealt with the history of the principle of double effect, first in the Dominican philosopher and theologian of the 13th century Thomas Aquinas, later in Tommaso de Vio, Francisco de Vitoria, the Salamanca school, Jean Pierre Gury, and finally in Peter Knauer. The overview and explication of their views unambiguously shows that to speak of the principle of double effect is to a great extent inadequate. Although in the history of moral thought there have been reflections associated with the admissibility of an action having good and bad consequences, these reflections are set in different ethical contexts, assume different conceptions of the nature of human action (philosophy of human action), in some cases they provide different answers to particular moral dilemmas and are formulated very differently. We should therefore not speak of the principle of double effect, but at most of principles of double effect: each of them has its place in a certain system of thought and the systems are not equivalent. To conclude let us see what form Knauer's principle of proportionality, the core of his conception of the principle of double effect, takes in the thought of the American theologian Garth L. Hallett.

## The Proportionalism of G. L. Hallett

Garth L. Hallett, an American moral theologian and like Jean Pierre Gury and Peter Knauer member of the Society of Jesus, is the author of the book *Greater Good. The Case for Proportionalism*,[36] in which he as first of the advocates of this tradition attempted to present theological and philosophical arguments for proportionalism, or for his version of it.[37] I will not lay out all of Hallett's conception of morality; I only want to focus on the form the principle of double effect takes in it.

The American moral theologian believes that the basic logical line and law of Christian moral thought must be value maximization.[38] The requirement of maximization is at the heart of proportionalism and replaces the role played by the principle of double effect in Peter Knauer's thought. But Hallett and Knauer share the conviction that human action does not acquire moral evaluation independently of the principle of double effect in Knauer and the criterion of value maximization in Hallett.[39] This criterion takes the following form[40]:

- **Value maximization.** In an objective and prospective orientation a certain action is right if and only if it promises to maximize values to the same or almost the same extent as all alternative actions. No kind of values is excluded, whether they are human or other values, moral or "physical" values, consequentialist or non-consequentialist.

Hallett underscores that value maximization takes the form of the criterion of rightness, i.e., the principle determining on what conditions some action can be evaluated as right or wrong. It is therefore not a method enabling us to establish in practice whether a certain action promises to maximize values to the same or almost the same extent as all alternative actions. With respect to method specification Hallett is a pluralist and excludes no procedure: intuition or critical thinking, customs or deliberation, imagination or the intellect, authority or private judgment. But not all methods are compatible with maximizing values: Hallett warns that consulting *Mein Kampf* will not be a good method.[41]

In his formulation Hallett speaks of prospective orientation, orientation to the future, evaluation of possible actions, not actions that have already taken place. Since the future and factors that can appear in the future are hard to grasp, he does not require certainty as to whether our action will be the one that will maximize values. It is fully sufficient that there is a promise: the considered action could satisfy the criterion of rightness. This promise can also be expressed as probability of maximizing values by the action.

It may be surprising for many that the criterion of value maximization focuses only on prospective action, action that can take place in the future. But Hallett believes that the purpose of ethics is practical, it ought to guide us in our actions. In his view this coincides with the fact that ethical deliberation appears when the possibilities of value maximization in a possible action are evaluated, not when past action is considered.

The criterion of value maximization also speaks of objectivity, to which Hallett assigns a very strong meaning: his proposal is that no heed should be paid to what reasons the agents had for their actions and how well or poorly grounded these reasons were. The rightness or wrongness of an action is determined only by objective facts, not by fallible human cognition.[42] It seems to me that here the American theologian draws the consequences of Knauer's theory, according to which the *finis operis* of an action is not determined by the agent's intention (in Aquinas's classical sense), but by the existence or non-existence of a commensurate reason and based on that by the corresponding physical good or evil. I don't find Hallett's requirement sensible; after all, we humans act based on our convictions which can be better or worse, grounded or ungrounded. If we evaluate moral action with reference to purely objective facts, our theory will fast diverge from basic moral intuitions. Let us imagine the following example:

- **Hunter.** In hunting season a hunter is out hunting and sees a wild boar run into a shrub. The hunter has good reasons to believe that there is a wild boar in the shrub: it is hunting season, there are signs everywhere telling people not to enter the forest. He saw a wild boar running into the shrub and did not see it run out. He believes that if there was someone else in the shrub, he or the boar would have run away. He sees a movement, aims his rifle and shoots. But when he walks up to the shrub he finds that he has shot a man.

The hunter has good reasons to believe that there is a wild boar in the shrub and his intention is to kill a wild animal. He has good and grounded reasons for his action, but nonetheless, according to Hallett's criterion, his action was wrong. Of course that does not mean that the hunter is a bad man; but his deed was objectively wrong. But such a solution to the problem of rightness and wrongness of human action is deeply non-intuitive, since in ethics we are not interested only in the consequences of actions measured by objective facts, but also in the extent of the agent's involvement in his deed and its consequences. For the case is different when the hunter knows that there is a man in the shrub (let us say his rival in love) and makes use of the fact that a boar had run into the shrub and when the hunter fires at his target based on a grounded conviction. Besides, if the criterion of maximization is really to serve as practical guide for action, it will constantly generate uncertainty as to whether an unexpected factor (objective fact) appears that will make our action wrong.

Hallett's objective focus on action also excludes motives and intentions, whereby it inadmissibly instrumentalizes human action. Let us again take a look at a particular example[43]:

- **Visiting Granny.** Jack and Jill's granny is in hospital. They both decide to visit her, though for a different reason (motive, traditionally *finis operantis*). Jack loves his Granny and wants to comfort her in her solitude. He brings her flowers, and they spend a pleasant afternoon together. Of course Granny is overjoyed by his visit. Jill's intention is quite different: she would like to inherit Granny's property. That is why she visits her in hospital, but like Jack she brings her flowers, makes a pleasant and friendly appearance, and Granny is overjoyed by her visit.

James Rachels, from whose book this example comes, claims that Jack and Jill have done the same, and we must therefore evaluate their actions as the same: if Jack's action was right (with respect to its consequences), Jill's action must also be evaluated as right (it had the same consequence). Hallett would probably disagree, as he would say that in evaluating Jack's and Jill's action we must take into account all values, including the value of the action itself. Jack's visit was a token of love, Jill's a token of calculation. That is why it is not the case that Jill's action was right because Jack's action was right. However, let us note well: why was Jill's action a token of calculation (and therefore did not realize the value that was realized by Jack's action)? Because she did it with a certain intention, which enters its evaluation. If we altogether disregard the agents' intention or motive for the action, we reduce their deeds to mere "doing" rather than action. Hallett allowed himself to be too consumed by the prospective outlook of his criterion of rightness. On his view we ought not to ask, "With what intention should I visit Granny?" but "Why should I visit Granny?". The answer is obvious: because my visit promises to maximize some values (or almost maximize). But if the value of the action itself is to be included among these values, we cannot disregard the intention: only intention determines that Jack's visit was a manifestation of respect and love, while Jill's strove to manipulate the ill Granny.

Hallett's criterion of value maximization is the culmination of the gradual process of transformation, in which the principle of double effect gradually changed from one of many moral rules to the only criterion of rightness. While Knauer defined key moral concepts, including the concept of moral good and evil, by means of the existence or non-existence of a commensurate reason (i.e., by means of the principle of double effect) Hallett allows not only ontic or physical, premoral values to enter the promise of value maximization, but also moral values, such as love or justice. That also implies that moral values cannot be defined by means of premoral values: the criterion of value maximization does not define moral values; it merely determines in what relationship our action must be to the whole spectrum of values – physical, moral, human, and others. An action is right if it promises to maximize values to the same or almost the same extent as all alternative actions.

## Conclusion

This chapter presents the culmination of the history of the principle of double effect since its beginning in the work of the Dominican Thomas Aquinas up to the modern advocates of a radically modified version of this moral principle, the German theologian Peter Knauer and his American confrére from the Society of Jesus Garth L. Hallett. The description of the historical development of the principle of double effect and its analysis have shown that it is altogether inadequate to speak of the principle of double effect and *ipso facto* of its history. Over the course of time different formulations of a moral principle applicable to actions having good and bad consequences crystalized. In Aquinas it is especially the case of self-defence; later authors broadened the application field of the principle, while at the same time adopting assumptions markedly different from the ones endorsed by Aquinas. Each formulation of the principle of double effect is set in a certain ethical context, in which it plays a fundamentally different part. Aquinas formulates his principle as an explication of already existing principles of moral evaluation of human action, while Knauer defines all important moral concepts, including the concept of moral intention, causality, or good and evil, by means of commensurate reason, which is at the heart of his version of the principle of double effect. Hallett does not speak of principle of double effect anymore; instead he postulates the criterion of value maximization and includes not only physical or ontic values but also moral ones, not only the value of the consequences of an action but also of the action itself. Hallett's criterion does not have the same hermeneutic function that the principle of double effect takes in Knauer, but it defines the rightness or wrongness of our actions.

These historical chapters aimed to set the principle of double effect in a historical and ideological context. In the literature we often encounter the claim that a modern formulation of the principle of double effect first appears in the work of the Salamanca school theologians,[44] some even claim that it appears in Thomas Aquinas. These claims quite ahistorically tear the principle of double effect out of the context in which it played the appropriate part and from which it derived validity. Thomas Aquinas, Jean Pierre Gury and Peter Knauer presented very different versions – not of the same principle, but of the way how they coped with actions having good and bad consequences. To speak of the principle of double effect thus becomes meaningless. If we do want to retain the name, we ought rather to use the plural: principles of double effect. That holds not only for the characters we have met so far, but generally. Even today, as we will see in the following chapters, there are different principles of double effect in the literature, not one principle in different formulations.

## Notes

1 Peter Knauer, "La détermination du bien et du mal moral par le principe du double effet." *Nouvelle Revue Théologique* 87, no. 4 (1965): 356–376.
2 Cf. Peter Knauer, "The Hermeneutic Function of the Principle of Double Effect." *The American Journal of Jurisprudence* 12, no. 1 (January 1967): 132–62.
3 In this overview I draw on the so far only elaboration of the history of proportionalism penned by Bernard Hoose, cf. Bernard Hoose, *Proportionalism.*

*The American Debate and Its European Roots* (Washington, DC: Georgetown University Press, 1987).

4 Today it is claimed that if the contralateral tube is intact, the risk posed to fertility is very low. The discussion took place in the 1970s.

5 Cf. Bernard Häring, *Medical Ethics* (Slough: St. Paul Publications, 1972), 108.

6 Cf. Bernard Hoose, "*Proportionalism*," 6 (including the presentation of Cornelius Van der Poel's view).

7 Ibid., 9–10.

8 We encountered a similar view in Thomas Aquinas, who believed that e.g. sexual intercourse can in one case be an instance of morally right action (manifestation of love between spouses) and in another case an instance of immoral adultery.

9 Bernard Hoose, "*Proportionalism*," 10–11.

10 Garth L. Hallett, *Greater Good. The Case for Proportionalism* (Washington, DC: Georgetown University Press, 1995).

11 Bernard Hoose, "*Proportionalism*," 13–20.

12 Cf. Marciano Vidal, *Manuale di etica teologica. Parte seconda. Morale dell'amore e della sessualità* (Cittadella: Assisi, 1996), 648–649.

13 Peter Knauer, "The Hermeneutic Function," 132.

14 Ibid.

15 Cf. Leo J. Elders, *La metafisica dell'essere di san Tommaso d'Aquino in una prospettiva storica*. Vol. 1. *L'essere comune* (Città del Vaticano: Libreria editrice vaticana, 1995), 140.

16 Although Knauer presents no theory of values in his paper, he seems to identify the physical good with values.

17 Note that $X$ is not merely good, but *simply good*.

18 Peter Knauer, "The Hermeneutic Function," 133.

19 Ibid., 135–136.

20 Christopher Kaczor, *Proportionalism and the Natural Law Tradition* (Washington, DC: The Catholic University of America Press, 2002), 38.

21 Peter Knauer, "The Hermeneutic Function," 136.

22 Bernard Hoose, "*Proportionalism*," 31.

23 Peter Knauer, "The Hermeneutic Function," 137.

24 Ibid., 137–140.

25 Cf. Alfonso Gómez-Lobo, *Morality and the Human Goods. An Introduction to Natural Law Ethics* (Washington, DC: Georgetown University Press, 2002), 58. Positive moral norms tend to be less specific, as they do not determine how they are to be fulfilled. Let us imagine two norms: a negative one (you may not kill an innocent human being) and a positive one (respect human life). While the negative norm clearly determines what we may not do (kill), the positive norm can be fulfilled by a number of deeds (including not killing innocent human beings).

26 Cf. John M. Finnis, *Moral Absolutes. Tradition, Revision, and Truth* (Washington, DC: The Catholic University of America Press, 1991), 27–28.

27 Peter Knauer, "The Hermeneutic Function," 139.

28 Ibid., 140. I have modified the example.

29 Here Knauer implicitly endorses Thomas Aquinas's idea, according to which humans cannot choose evil as evil: their choice is always motivated by some real or apparent good. Drug addicts do not inject heroin because (motive for action) it causes physical evil (they do not choose evil), but because it causes pleasure.

30 In order not to complicate the example let us assume that the physician did not have good reasons (e.g. lack of financial means) for not prescribing biological treatment.

31 This means that it is the best way to save the mother's life. If a better option existed, making it possible e.g. to implant the foetus in the uterus when it has been extracted from the oviduct, there would not be a commensurate reason for merely excising the foetus.

32 Christopher Kaczor, "*Proportionalism*," 34–44.

33 Ibid., 40–41.

34 Cf. Brian V. Johnstone, "The Meaning of Proportionate Reason in Contemporary Moral Theology." *The Thomist: A Speculative Quarterly Review* 49, no. 2 (1985): 223–247.

35 Christopher Kaczor, "*Proportionalism*," 41.

36 Garth L. Hallett, "*Greater Good.*"

37 Proportionalism as a trend in moral theology is not easily characterized as a whole. The individual proportionalists often differed in their assumptions and conclusions, though they agreed in the conviction that contraception is not illicit in all circumstances.

38 Garth L. Hallett, "*Greater Good,*" 1.

39 Knauer speaks of human action being good or bad, while Hallett claims that it is right or wrong.

40 Garth L. Hallett, "*Greater Good,*" 2.

41 Ibid., 4.

42 Ibid., 7.

43 I borrowed it from James Rachels, *The End of Life. Euthanasia and Morality* (Oxford: Oxford University Press, 1990), 93.

44 For example James Rachels, "*The End of Life,*" 16.

# 5 The Principle of Double Effect and Trolleyology

## Introduction

The beginnings of trolleyology were quite modest. In 1967 the British moral philosopher Philippa Foot published a paper dealing with the problem of abortions and the principle of double effect. One of the many thought experiments appearing in the paper was a runaway tram inevitably rushing towards a switch. The unhappy tram driver notices that beyond the switch there are five persons working on one rail, while on the other rail there is only one person working. If he does nothing, the tram will keep on and kill five workers. But if the driver changes the trolley's direction, he will kill only one colleague of theirs. What is he to do?

As I have said, the tram makes only a brief appearance in the paper. It is merely one of the scenarios: made-up situations helping the author test our moral intuitions and solutions to difficult, morally deeply dilemmatic cases. Foot attempted to show that although the principle of double effect is a strong instrument making it possible to explain why very similar scenarios are morally asymmetric (what is forbidden in one is morally licit in another), she has a stronger instrument at her disposal. Her brief mention gave rise to trolleyology, a part of moral philosophy trying to find ever further, ever more complicated scenarios with the runaway tram and its possible victims.

In this chapter my aim is not merely to present the ideas of other thinkers (specifically the British theorist and philosopher of law H. L. A. Hart, the British philosopher Philippa Foot and her American colleague and opponent J. J. Thomson) and the basics of trolleyology. My aim is rather more ambitious: over the course of analysing and critically discussing these authors' ideas and arguments I want to attempt a step-by-step defence of the principle of double effect, clarify the relationship between proximate and remote intention, the relationship between end and means, and show its explanatory power.

In the historical part of this work I concluded that it is historically and theoretically inadequate to speak of the principle of double effect: there are different versions of this moral principle, set in different ethical systems, in which they play a lesser, greater, or even fundamental, hermeneutic function. In this chapter I will speak of the principle of double effect as it is most commonly understood today:

1   **Principle of double effect.** From the moral point of view it is possible to actualize action $\varphi$ having a good effect $E_1$ and a bad effect $E_2$, if the following four conditions are satisfied:

   a   $\varphi$ must be at least morally indifferent (good or indifferent);
   b   $E_2$ must not be a means to $E_1$;
   c   $E_2$ must not be an object of intention (intended). $E_2$ is merely foreseen.
   d   There must be a commensurate and sufficiently grave reason to actualize $\varphi$.

Since the fourth condition is not discussed in this entire chapter, I will mostly omit it (I will discuss it more in the following chapter).

## H. L. A. Hart

The famous British theorist and philosopher of law H. L. A. Hart, author of the influential treatise in philosophy of law entitled *The Concept of Law*, deals with the problem of intention and principle of double effect in his paper *Intention and Punishment*.[1] Hart points out how the role of intention and the distinction between the intended effect of an action and a merely foreseen one is differently understood in criminal law and elsewhere (e.g. in the common understanding of words such as "intention" and "intentionally"). Let us take a look at a specific example:

•   **R. v. Desmond, Barrett and Others.** In 1868 a group of Fenians[2] decided to liberate two of their co-fighters. One of them, Desmond, laid dynamite to the prison wall and blew it up. The liberation failed and several persons living in the vicinity of the explosion died.[3]

Of course one can ask – and the question is without doubt ethically relevant – whether Desmond killed the innocent victims of his attempt to liberate his co-fighters intentionally. Since his action was not aimed to the production of that effect, whether as an end of the action or as an end of the agent (it was not an object of his intention, whether proximate or remote), it can be designated as not falling into the intention (Thomas Aquinas would say that it was *praeter intentionem*). But for the purposes of criminal law the production of a foreseen (or foreseeable) negative effect (death of innocent human beings) is sufficient, regardless of the fact that perhaps Desmond did not wish for it, did not aim his action at it, it was not part of his intention. The jury was similarly instructed e.g. in the case R. v. Woollin, House of Lords. Woollin was charged with murder of his child and convicted upon admitting that he had injured the child's head and the child subsequently died of the injury. In the appeals process the jury was instructed that it can determine the intention based on whether a given effect was an almost certain consequence of the defendant's action and he was aware of the consequence. In this way it is also possible to resolve the following case, often discussed by experts in criminal law[4]:

- **Bomb on board.** *A* decided to obtain insurance money for goods that will be transported by plane. He places a bomb on board of the plane, which will explode shortly after take-off. Of course *A* is aware that the pilot will die, but it is not the end of his action: *A* merely wishes that the goods for which the insurance company will pay him compensation are destroyed.

*A* can claim that it was not his intention to kill the pilot. Thomas Aquinas would agree, though he would claim that his action was morally illicit, since it was a case of damaging the property of another and fraud, moreover resulting in the death of an innocent human being. Peter Knauer, on the other hand, would judge this case in light of the principle of double effect and ask whether *A* had a commensurate reason for his action. He would conclude that he did not: the evil he caused (the pilot's death) would thus become part of the moral intention and the form of killing the pilot would be characterized as direct killing (though *A* would claim that he had killed the pilot indirectly by blowing up his goods). Since the pilot's death is a virtually certain consequence of the bomb's detonation, the jury could legitimately conclude that *A* had killed him intentionally.

Hart comments on Desmond's case:

> The law therefore does not require in such cases that the outcome should have been something intended in the sense that the accused set out to achieve it, either as a means or an end, and here the law diverges from what is ordinarily meant by expressions like 'he intentionally killed those men'.[5]

The expression "*S* did *X* intentionally" is commonly understood to mean that *S* aimed to produce *X*, *X* became the end of his action or a means to some other end. But if *S* does not focus on *X* in his action, whether as the end of his action or as a means to attain that end, one cannot say that *S* did *X* intentionally (*X* was part of his intention). An exception to this understanding of "*S* did *X* intentionally" are situations when some consequence of an action is so firmly linked to the action that it immediately and invariably accompanies it. Here Hart touches on a problem known thanks to Philippa Foot as *the closeness problem*. Let us take a look at the following example of Hart's:

- **Breaking a glass.** Peter decides to make noise by breaking a glass with a hammer. Later he claims that he merely wanted to attract attention by the noise made by the hammer striking the glass. But it was not his intention to break the glass.

The connection between the action (striking the glass with a hammer), whose end (*finis operantis*) is to attract attention (Peter struck the glass with a hammer so that the noise would attract attention), and another consequence of that action (breaking the glass) is not contingent: striking a glass forcefully with a hammer always breaks it. In Hart's view it is therefore impossible to claim that Peter did not intend to break the glass: there is a non-contingent (Hart says that probably conceptual) relationship between the action and its effect. In connection with the closeness problem the question is also discussed in ethics and bioethics whether an agent can legitimately claim that he did not intend a certain consequence of an action (e.g. the death of a foetus), although he did intend something that is necessarily associated with it (e.g. crushing the foetus' head in craniotomy). In later chapters I will deal with this problem in more detail.

Theorists of law frequently distinguish between *direct intention* and *oblique intention*. In Hart's view this distinction between that which is directly intended and that which is merely foreseen as a concomitant consequence of an action is inadequately employed in the traditional doctrine of the principle of double effect, which the British theorist of law associates with Catholic moral theology. Hart is critical of applying the principle of double effect while discussing two cases we are already familiar with:

2  **Hysterectomy.** A pregnant woman's uterus is affected with cancer and must be removed or the woman will die. The surgeon removes the uterus (action) in order to save her life (*finis operantis*). But together with the uterus an immature foetus comes out and dies. But the foetus' death is not part of the surgeon's intention: his proximate intention is to remove the uterus; the remote one is to save the patient's life.

3  **Craniotomy.** Hart associates craniotomy with difficult childbirth, when in order to save the mother's life it is necessary to crush the foetus' head and remove it from the mother's body.

In the first case the foetus' death is an unintended, though foreseen and admitted consequence of the action (extracting the uterus), while in the second case death is the end of the surgeon's action (the surgeon must crush the head = kill the foetus in order to save the mother). Catholic moralists therefore admit hysterectomy as licit and reject craniotomy as an instance of breaking the moral norm forbidding intentional killing of innocent human beings. Hart disagrees: he believes that in the case of craniotomy the foetus' death is also unintended. The surgeon in fact intends to remove the foetus, its death is not the object of his intention whether as a means or as the final end of the action. On Hart's view the main difference between hysterectomy and craniotomy consists in different causal structure, which is also differently expressed in language. In the case of hysterectomy it is a matter of intentionally killing an innocent human being, while in the case of craniotomy it is possible to speak of consciously causing the foetus' death. According to Hart this different causal structure and its verbal expression in the two cases does not correspond to any morally relevant dichotomy.

The problematic part of Hart's analysis of the principle of double effect and its application to cases of hysterectomy and craniotomy is his claim that over the course of craniotomy the foetus' death is merely a secondary and foreseen consequence, which is neither an end nor a means to attaining an end (extracting the foetus). The British theorist of law evaluates the surgeon's action only in its physical manifestation and in connection with its objective ends: the physician must extract the foetus in order for the woman to survive. His end is extracting the foetus, which is why his action must be teleologically evaluated with respect to this finality. But I find Hart's analysis untenable. Let us say that the end of the surgeon's action is only extracting the foetus (*finis operis*) in order to save the mother's life (*finis operantis*). Crushing the foetus' head therefore cannot be characterized as the end of the action, but it is evidently a means: the surgeon can extract the foetus because he first crushes its head. If he could choose a different means, if he did not have to crush the foetus' head, he would probably choose it. But in this particular case he chose craniotomy as a means to fulfilling his proximate and remote intention. It is inconceivable how Hart can claim that the child's death is not a means to attaining the physician's end.

Let us grant that the physician's intention is not to kill the foetus, but to remove it from the mother's body by means of crushing its head. We can compare the following two scenarios:

1  **Killing the foetus.** A physician must extract a foetus from the mother's body and has no other option than to crush its head. The physician's intention is to kill the foetus **by** crushing its head **in order to** save the mother's life.

2  **Crushing the head.** A physician must extract a foetus from the mother's body and has no other option than to crush its head. The physician's intention is to crush the foetus' head in order to save the mother's life. But his intention is not to kill the foetus.

The two scenarios differ in that in the first one the foetus' death is part of the physician's intention, while in the second case the physician claims that he did not intend the foetus' death: he merely foresaw is as a negative consequence of his action. Does the principle of double effect make it possible to distinguish between the two scenarios and entitle the physician to perform the operation in the second case? The answer is negative: even though proponents of the principle of double effect will mostly agree that the physician's intention is different in the first and second scenario, which is why their action can be described differently (in the first case it is a matter of intentionally killing the foetus, in the second one of mutilating the foetus resulting in death), their deed is illicit.

Hart claims that the difference between hysterectomy and craniotomy is based merely on the verbal expression of a morally insubstantial difference between consciously killing a foetus (hysterectomy) and intentionally killing a foetus (craniotomy). But this difference is not morally irrelevant, as the following two scenarios show:

1   **Dentist.** A dentist must drill a patient's bad tooth. He is well aware that he will cause the patient pain, but he does not intend this negative effect of his intervention: he intends to drill the tooth (*finis operis*) so that his patient's teeth are healthy (*finis operantis*).
2   **Sadistic dentist.** A dentist must drill a patient's bad tooth. He is well aware that he will cause the patient pain and is overjoyed by that. The pain caused becomes one of the ends of his action: he does not merely want to repair the patient's teeth, but also to cause him pain.

Both dentists cause their patients pain: in the first case causing pain can be characterized as conscious (consciously causing pain), while in the second case it is not only conscious but also intentional. This difference between consciously and intentionally causing pain is not merely verbal and does not reflect a merely different and ethically irrelevant causal structure, as Hart claims in the case of conscious and intentional killing. After all, the second dentist will be correctly characterized as a sadist and the patient's pain as a manifestation of his sadism. The difference between intentionally and merely consciously causing pain is not only ethically relevant: the intention is a guiding moment of the action, which can be characterized as actualization of the corresponding intentions. The dentist of the first scenario will probably try to eliminate the negative effect of drilling the tooth to the highest possible extent and will proceed with consideration and sensitivity. He is aware that his action will cause some pain (in this respect causing pain is a conscious consequence), but it is not his end. The sadistic dentist, on the other hand, wants to cause pain and acts accordingly; the pain caused is not a merely conscious consequence of his action, but an intended one.

Hart's criticism of the principle of double effect is incorrect: there is a morally relevant difference between intentionally killing an innocent human being (the death is the action's end) and consciously killing an innocent human being.

## Philippa Foot, Double Effect, Positive and Negative Duties

In 1967 the British philosopher Philippa Foot published a paper entitled *The Problem of Abortion and the Doctrine of Double Effect*, containing a brief mention of a tram rushing along a rail line.[6] Foot could not have guessed what an enormous response her thought experiment will raise and that it will become the object of discussions and polemics still alive today. A large number of philosophers later focussed attention on imaginary scenarios, in which a runaway tram or train is inevitably approaching a switch, bridge, loop, or turnstile and will kill five unlucky persons, unless someone interferes. The driver can change the trolley's direction, a casual passer-by can change the switch, another casual passer-by can push a very fat man off a bridge so that his body would stop the trolley, and so on. To Foot's paper we owe the birth of trolleyology, the investigation, mental and at present often even empirical, of imaginary scenarios ingeniously constructed to help test our moral intuitions and moral principles.[7] That is why David Edmonds has called Foot the George Stephenson of trolleyology.[8]

In her paper Foot focusses on the problem of abortion and the principle of double effect. She finds the core of the principle of double effect (she speaks of the doctrine of double effect) in the distinction between intended and merely foreseen consequences. The expression "double effect" in the doctrine's specification refers to two effects a certain action can have: (i) one effect is intended, whether as an end or as a means, and (ii) the other effect is merely foreseen. Employing the terminology introduced above it is possible to speak of direct and oblique intention: a direct intention relates to an intended effect, while an oblique intention relates to a merely foreseen effect. Foot formulates the doctrine of double effect as follows:

- **Doctrine of double effect.** Sometimes it is possible to cause an obliquely intended effect that cannot be intended directly.

The sense of this formulation is quite simple: there are consequences of action that morally cannot be intended directly (the sadistic dentist intends the pain he causes), but it is possible to intend them obliquely (merely foresee them). The doctrine of double effect states that there is important **moral asymmetry** between the first type of action (the negative effect is directly intended) and the second type of action (the negative effect is intended merely indirectly): the first type of action is illicit, the second type of action is licit when certain conditions are met (a dentist can cause pain, if it accompanies a necessary medical intervention).

When she has presented her formulation of the principle of double effect, Foot focussed on the critical reservations raised by H. L. A. Hart. As we have seen, Hart had claimed that the foetus' death is not the result of an intention: the physician, strictly speaking, does not need to kill the foetus, his intention is to remove it from the mother's body. He must crush its head, but he does not intend its death: that is merely an unwanted, though foreseen consequence of his action. In her answer to this interpretation Foot introduced a problem into philosophical discourse which the principle of double effect and its proponents are still tackling today: the closeness problem.

Let us take a look at the following possible interpretation of the physician's action in foetal craniotomy. The physician carries out a certain action (crushing the foetus's head), which has two consequences: (i) one of them is removing the foetus from the mother's body and thereby fulfilling the end of the physician's action (saving the mother's life), and (ii) the other, the negative one, is killing the foetus. The physician's proximate intention is crushing the head and extracting the foetus, the remote intention is saving the mother's life. The negative effect is not intended by the physician, but merely foreseen and accepted. But Foot correctly notes that the two events – crushing the foetus's head and killing it – are so *close* to each other that the principle of double effect cannot be applied to them. I understand it to mean that killing the foetus is intrinsically linked to the operation of crushing the head: by crushing the foetus's head the foetus is put to death. In the present circumstances it is difficult to imagine that a human being could live with a crushed skull and damaged brain. To illustrate the concept of closeness Foot gives the following, now already famous example:

- **Speleologists.** A group of speleologists unwisely let an obese member of the expedition lead them out of a cave. But the mouth is narrow, he gets stuck and cannot move. By unhappy coincidence the water level in the cave starts rising and the speleologists face the danger of drowning. But they have dynamite and two options: either they blow the cave's mouth up (and kill the expedition member stuck there), or they will all drown.

With this thought experiment Foot wants to illustrate the absurdity of Hart's proposal. Let us imagine that an advocate of the principle of double effect argued as follows. The speleologists want to blow up the blocked cave mouth in order to save their life. Their proximate intention is to blow up the mouth, their remote intention is to save their lives. Their action has two consequences: (i) the cave's mouth will open up, and they will be saved, and (ii) the bad consequence, unintended but foreseen, is the obese colleague's death. Foot correctly notes that it would be absurd if the speleologists claimed "we didn't want to kill our colleague, merely to blast him to pieces and so open up the cave's mouth." As crushing the foetus's head is intrinsically linked to killing it, so blasting up the speleologist's body is intrinsically linked to killing him.

While Hart deemed the principle of double effect invalid and relying on morally irrelevant distinctions, Foot takes it very seriously. In the remaining part of the paper she argues as follows: there are scenarios which are intuitively morally asymmetric and their asymmetry can be explained by the principle of double effect. If we give it up and do not offer an alternative explanation of this asymmetry, strongly rooted intuitions will remain without a rational explanation. But if an alternative explanation exists, which will also be more expedient (simpler, with fewer contradictory assumptions, etc.), then the principle of double effect can be given up and the alternative explanation accepted.

Let us now take a look at two examples of morally asymmetric scenarios (I have adapted some of them).[9]

1   **Innocent victim.** A little girl has been murdered in town and the whole town is up to riots and violence. The judge knows that unless he very quickly finds a culprit and has him executed, the violence will escalate and more innocent human lives will fall victim to it. He therefore decides to accuse a petty criminal and alcoholic, whom he knows to be innocent. A trial takes place, the death sentence is pronounced and soon carried out. The people in the town calm down and return to their normal lives.

2   **Runaway tram.** A tram with damaged brakes is rushing towards a switch, beyond which it will go on to a rail on which five persons are working. On the other rail only one person is working. The tram driver has two options: either he will do nothing (and five persons will die), or he will change the trolley's direction and only one person will die. The driver decides to change the direction and the tram kills only one person.

The two scenarios have something in common and they also differ in some aspects. They also differ in the intuitive reaction of most people: (i) the first scenario describes an evident act of injustice in which the accused person is innocent, and his life becomes a means to attaining some, though laudable, ends; (ii) in the second scenario we intuitively regard what the driver does as morally licit and correct. The reaction of a pilot trying to stir an airplane plummeting to the earth to an area as little populated as possible is regarded as similarly laudable.

But the two scenarios also have something in common, some sort of possible "moral arithmetic": in both it is possible to add up and compare the numbers of victims of the different variants of action. Let us say that we know that the number of victims of the violent riots in the first scenario will be five. We thus face the alternative of one (innocent) human life or five (innocent) human lives. In the second scenario the options are the same: either five human lives will fall victim to the runaway trolley, or only one. There is an influential school of moral philosophers – the **consequentialists** – who evaluate human action, its correctness or incorrectness, only based on its consequences.[10] But these consequences must be evaluated according to some key: What consequences are good and what consequences are bad? Linking consequentialism to a theory of values, welfare or well-being results in some version of **utilitarianism**. An act-utilitarian evaluates the consequences of individual deeds. Without having to specify the theory of values precisely, it is easy to agree that, for consequentialists, five lives outweigh one life. An act-utilitarian could therefore reason as follows:

- **An act-utilitarian.** According to my moral theory I evaluate only the consequences of human action. The judge has two options: (i) to accuse an innocent person (moral arithmetic: one life against five) or (ii) not to accuse an innocent person (moral arithmetic: five lives against one). The tram driver also has two options: (i) to change the tram's direction (moral arithmetic: one life against five) or (ii) not to change the tram's direction (moral arithmetic: five lives against one). In both cases the agent ought to choose to sacrifice one life. So the two scenarios are not morally asymmetric after all.

But the solution a utilitarian could offer contradicts our moral intuitions. Some utilitarians believe that moral intuitions are not a good starting point and criterion of moral deliberations, but at present authors adhering to this tradition mostly believe that moral intuitions are important and try to harmonize their theories with them.[11] And these moral intuitions say that there is in fact a moral difference between the two scenarios, explained precisely by the principle of double effect. It is not applicable to the first scenario, as the judge must intend the death of the innocent person as a means to attaining his end. But the tram driver's situation is different. One action (change of the tram's direction) has two consequences: (i) saving the lives of five workers on one rail or (ii) killing one worker on the other rail. The driver's proximate intention is changing the tram's direction, his remote intention is saving the five workers. The death of the sixth one is not intended, it is not a means to attaining the driver's end and is merely foreseen and accepted. If the worker could see the tram in time and step aside, the driver would be much relieved: his death was not his end, or a means, so that his action was not guided by the intention to kill him. Let us compare that with a different example:

- **Murderer.** A tram driver has for a long time been cultivating murderous intentions towards X. One day his tram's brakes stop working and the tram is rushing down a slope towards a switch beyond control. The driver notices that there are five persons working on one rail, only one on the other. He suddenly realizes that the sixth worker is X. Without hesitation he redirects the tram to the rail where X is working and the tram kills him.

In this case X's death is not merely foreseen: it is part of the driver's intention guiding his action. If X noticed the tram in time and stepped aside to safety, the driver would not be relieved: his plan would have failed and this failure would guide his further steps. He would not give up his murderous intention, would plan further steps and one day he would kill X e.g. with poison.

Let us take a look at another pair of intuitively morally asymmetric scenarios:

1  **Precious medicine.** A physician has only one dose of a precious medicine, which can save the life of one patient. Just before the medicine is applied five patients appear in the hospital, each of whom only needs one fifth of the medicine to save his life. The physician changes his plans and administers the medicine to these five new patients. The result of his action is death of one patient and saving the life of another five.

2  **Transplantation.** In hospital five patients are awaiting the transplantation of five different organs. Donors cannot be found and the time is running short. A young homeless man comes to have a minor wound treated. His health is good and all his organs are suitable for transplantation. The physician kills him and uses his organs for transplantations. He kills one person, but saves five.

Again we will judge that the physician in the first scenario acted correctly, while the physician in the second scenario acted incorrectly; the moral arithmetic is sound (one life redeemed by five lives), but only in the first scenario the physician did not kill the patient and the principle of double effect can be applied to his action. Let us again note the role of intention as the mental state guiding the action (*intention in action*) and other possible deeds. If it happens that in the last moment another dose of that precious medicine arrives, the physician will without doubt be relieved and rather than five lives will save six. But the physician in the second scenario must kill the patient: if he e.g. found out that the amount of the deadly potion administered had been insufficient, he would have to act again and inject another dose.[12]

To support the validity of the principle of double effect Foot introduces one other highly interesting argument: if this principle did not hold, we would be at the mercy of the whims of a sadistic tyrant, who could present us with the following alternative[13]: (i) either we will torture one person, or (ii) he will torture five persons. The principle of double effect justifies us in rejecting to torture one person, though we foresee that the consequence of our rejection will be the suffering of five persons.[14]

As I have already said, Foot quite reasonably thought that it is implausible to reject the validity of the principle of double effect, unless an alternative and better explanation of the moral asymmetry captured by the preceding two pairs of thought scenarios is available. For otherwise, fundamental moral intuitions would be left without a rational explanation. Foot believed that she had found an alternative explanation. It consisted in the distinction between positive and negative duties and assigning higher value in practical moral deliberation to the negative ones. Foot does not present a more detailed description and explanation of the difference between positive and negative duties, she relies entirely on the basic definition, which I will attempt to formulate as precisely as possible[15]:

1   **Negative duty.** Person $S$ has a negative duty $P_n$ if there is an action $\varphi$ such that $P_n$ forbids $\varphi$.
2   **Positive duty.** Person $S$ has a positive duty $P_p$ if there is an action $\varphi$ such that $P_p$ prescribes $\varphi$.

An example of negative duty can be the duty not to kill innocent human beings or not to steal, an example of positive duty can be e.g. the duty to take care of own children. Foot says that it is useful to extend the set of positive duties to include actions that are strictly speaking not obligatory (e.g. helping strangers in need, which is not a strict duty and is rather a manifestation of human virtues).

Let us now take a look at how the distinction between positive and negative duties explains the moral intuitions associated with our two pairs of thought scenarios.

1   **Innocent victim.** The judge faces a dilemma in which the negative duty not to kill (or not to arrange the death of) an innocent human victim clashes with the positive duty to prevent the death of five human beings. When negative and positive duties clash, moral arithmetic does not hold: negative duties always have priority over positive ones. Therefore the judge must not have the innocent human victim killed.
2   **Runaway tram.** The tram driver's situation is different. He must choose between breaking the negative duty not to kill one person and breaking the negative duty not to kill five persons. Since the conflict concerns duty of the same type (negative), moral arithmetic comes into play and determines that the driver ought to change the tram's direction and kill only one person.
3   **Precious medicine.** The physician faces a choice comprising the breaking of duties of the same type, positive ones (to help his

patients). Since it is again a case of clash of the same type of duties, with respect to moral arithmetic he will choose to save five lives over saving only one.

4   **Transplantation.** The situation is different for the physician in the last scenario. He must choose between the negative duty not to kill his patient and the positive duty to help five patients. It is a clash of different types of duty, which is why moral arithmetic is irrelevant: the physician must not kill the patient and if he did he would act incorrectly.[16]

The moral intuitions associated with these four scenarios are very well explained both by the principle of double effect and by the distinction between positive and negative obligations. That is why Foot introduces a scenario in which her solution departs from the solution based on the validity of the principle of double effect[17]:

• **Poisonous gas.** The lives of five patients can be saved only by means of preparing a poisonous gas. The physician knows that over the course of the preparation the gas will enter the room next door, where it will kill one patient who for some reason cannot be moved. Nonetheless the physician prepares the gas; the end of his action is to prepare the gas and save five patients, the death of the patient next door is merely an unintended, though foreseen consequence.

This scenario is similar to the one with the precious medicine, but according to Foot it is different: if the relatives of the poisoned patient sued the hospital, their suit would probably be successful. Foot wants to illustrate the advantage of her solution as to the moral asymmetry between different situations, but when she wants to persuade us that the scenario introduced above is better solved by her distinction between positive and negative duties, she switches from moral discourse to legal one. Let us leave aside the fact that without rigorous legal analysis it can hardly be claimed that the poisoned patient's relatives could hope to succeed with their suit, while the relatives of the patient who did not receive the dose of the necessary medicine could not. The essential point is that the legal level of the problem does not reflect the moral level, and if law does provide some answers to our questions, it does not mean that these answers need to be applied in the sphere of morality.

In connection with this scenario Foot notes that we will probably be loath to imagine that some human being is made use of, e.g. over the course of biomedical research. It is hard to say why she made that comment: the case of the patient poisoned with the gas is certainly not a case of patient exploitation. The need of the situation demanded producing a medicine which will save five human lives. Unfortunately, one patient will die because for some reason it is not possible to move him away from the room into which the gas leaks. But this patient's death is neither an end nor a means, the patient is not made use of in any way: his death is an unintended consequence of producing the medicine.

According to Foot her solution forbids physicians to prepare the gas and thereby save the lives of five patients at the expense of one patient's life. It is a case where the positive duty to help (save a life) and the negative duty not to kill collide; negative duties outweigh positive duties. Advocates of the principle of double effect could disagree and claim that (i) the action itself (preparing the gas) is morally neutral; (ii) the agent's end is good (save five human lives); (iii) only the good effect (saving lives) is intended, while the bad one is merely foreseen and necessitated by the circumstances; or (iv) the bad effect is neither an end nor a means to attain an end. The scenario *The poisonous gas* will probably not determine which of the solutions is correct, because our intuitions concerning it will differ. But let us take a look at the following situation:

- **Mountain climbers.** A group of five mountain climbers and their equipment are hanging on a rope held by a last climbing cam. The equipment is hanging at the end of the rope and straight down below it there is another climber sleeping in a sleeping bag. The climbers know that the cam will not hold them much longer and must quickly decide: either they cut off the equipment, which will drop on the sleeping climber and kill him, or they will all fall down and die. Let us also assume that if the cam came loose and all of them fell down, the direction of their fall would change and they would not hit the sleeping climber. The climbers quickly decide and cut off the equipment. As it falls it kills the sleeping climber.

I think that in this scenario we will intuitively incline to the opinion that it was permissible to cut off the equipment. But this scenario is analogical to the preceding one: there are five lives at stake as opposed to one, it is necessary to do something that will lead to the death of one climber, there is a conflict between the positive duty to help oneself and others and the negative duty not to kill the sleeping climber.[18] Foot would have to say that the climbers may not cut off the equipment because they would thereby break a negative duty, while, on the other hand, proponents of the principle of double effect would advocate the view that it is licit to cut the rope since: (i) the action itself (cutting the rope) is morally indifferent; (ii) the (remote) intention is good (saving own life); (iii) the sleeping climber's death is not intended, whether as an end or as a means; and (iv) the climber's death is therefore not a means to saving their lives.

Foot illustrates the superiority of her solution with an example in which she states only legal reasons (the possible success of a suit), not moral ones. Furthermore I have constructed an analogical imaginary situation, that of the climbers, which is ever more realistic than Foot's example of the poisonous gas, which operates in favour of the principle of double effect. And this situation is not the only one, as the American philosopher and theorist of law Judith Jarvis Thomson shows.

## J. J. Thomson and the Loop Version

Another important figure in the history of trolleyology is the American philosopher and theorist of law Judith Jarvis Thomson. While Philippa Foot was the first to set off a tram with damaged brakes to speed through the thought scenarios of moral and experimental philosophers, Thomson gave trolleyology its final form in her two papers *Killing, Letting Die, and the Tram Problem* of 1976[19] and *The Trolley Problem* of 1985.[20] Especially in her 1985 paper she critically analyzes Foot's solution to the problem of morally asymmetric scenarios, from among which she selects especially the following two[21]: (i) A surgeon needs to obtain five organs in order to save five patients. He suddenly finds out that a young man has come to the hospital for a regular yearly check-up, whose organs happen to be suitable for transplantation. Is it morally licit to kill the young man and transplant his organs? (ii) A trolley driver finds out that the trolley's brakes are out of order and it is rushing to a switch, after which it will proceed on a rail on which five persons are working. There is only one person working on the other rail. May the driver change the tram's direction and kill one worker?

Let us recall that Foot's answer to the first question is negative: what is involved is the positive duty to help patients waiting for transplantation and the negative duty not to kill a possible organ donor; negative duties outweigh positive ones. But her answer to the second question is positive: here two negative duties clash and moral arithmetic comes into play. According to Foot we ought to prefer killing one person to the lives of five persons.

In her polemic Thomson formulates Foot's position with the following pair of propositions[22]:

1 Killing one is worse than letting five die.
2 Killing five is worse than killing one.

The first proposition explains why it is illicit for the surgeon to obtain the necessary organs by killing the young man, while the second one explains why it is possible for the trolley driver to change its direction. But this apparently simple and attractive solution will not work if the thought scenario is changed; rather than of a trolley driver we will speak of a casual passer-by (Thomson calls this scenario *Bystander at the Switch*)[23]:

- **Casual passer-by**. A man is strolling along a rail and is approaching a switch. There are five persons working on one rail, there is only one worker on the other. The man suddenly notices a trolley rushing at a great speed towards a switch, to go on to the line where five persons are working. There is a lever at the switch making it possible to change it. If the passer-by does nothing, the trolley will kill five persons; if he changes the switch, only one person will die.

Let us notice the differences between this scenario and the situation described by Foot. The tram driver is responsible for the safety of passengers and other traffic participants, including workers on the rail. If he does nothing, he will kill five persons; if he changes the direction, he will kill only one person. The situation in which the casual passer-by finds himself is different: he has no moral obligation to workers on the rail comparable to the tram driver's moral obligation. But what is most important, if the passer-by does nothing, the trolley will kill five persons, but he will not participate in their death in any way. But if he decides to intervene and changes the switch, one person will die as a result of his action. Thomson, who like Foot relies on moral intuition, believes that despite these differences it is licit to change the switch.

But this conclusion is problematic for Foot's conclusion, as it contradicts her conviction that killing one person is worse than letting five persons die. If the passer-by did nothing, he would let five workers die; but if he changes the trolley's direction, he will kill one person. But the principle of double effect need not tackle this problem: (i) the action itself (changing the switch) is morally indifferent, (ii) the agent's end is good (saving five human lives), (iii) killing the worker on the other rail is neither an end, nor a means to saving a life, (iv) the negative effect is not intended, and (v) there is a commensurate reason for the action (one life versus five). The principle of double effect thus acquires a dialectical advantage as compared to the solution to the problem of morally asymmetric scenarios presented by Philippa Foot.

The principle of double effect also answers the question whether action is possible in the following scenario[24]:

- **Fat man on the bridge**. A tourist is standing on a bridge over a trolley rail and beyond the bridge there are five persons working on the rail. Next to him a very fat man is leaning against the railing and out over the rail line. The tourist suddenly notices that there is a trolley rushing along the line, whose brakes are apparently out of order. If it goes on in its course, it will kill all five workers on the rail. The tourist is an expert in trolley traffic and realizes that if he throws the fat man off the bridge and he will drop down in front of the trolley, it will stop and not crush into those five men.

Now we already have the pair of morally asymmetric scenarios constituting the core of modern trolleyology. Foot, like Thomson, would reply that it is morally unacceptable to throw the fat man off the bridge. A proponent of the principle of double effect would take the same stance. Foot would regard the scenario as an instance of breaking the rule that killing one is worse than letting five die (breaking a negative duty is worse than breaking a positive one), while Thomson would regard throwing the fat man off the bridge as an instance of infringing on his rights (e.g. the right not to be thrown off a bridge). But while for Thomson and proponents of the principle of double effect the two scenarios are really morally asymmetric (in the first case the passer-by may change the switch, in the second one the tourist may not throw the fat man off the bridge), for Foot they are ultimately not asymmetric: the casual passer-by may not change the switch.

Thomson introduces another interesting scenario to illustrate how difficult it is to determine when, as Kant would say, we approach persons not as ends, but as means. Let us recall the situation in which the transplantation surgeon finds himself: he needs the organs of a healthy person who has come to the hospital for a routine check-up. If this man suddenly disappeared, the surgeon could not carry out his plan. Is he therefore a means to attaining the surgeon's plan? Let us compare that with changing the switch: the casual passer-by changes the switch and the trolley is rushing to the rail on which only one person is working. If he noticed the trolley in time and jumped to safety, would it frustrate the plan of saving the other five? Most certainly it would not. Based on this difference, can we claim that the young man in the hospital is a means, while the worker on the rail is not a means to attain the action's end? Thomson believes that we cannot and introduces the following thought experiment (known in the literature as *Loop*)[25]:

- **Loop.** A casual passer-by is approaching a rail of an interesting disposition. Beyond the switch the rail does not go straight but turns around and eventually connects to another rail beyond a switch, so that they form a closed loop. On one rail, immediately beyond the switch, there are five persons working, there is one person on the other. The passer-by suddenly notices that a trolley is rushing towards the switch whose brakes are apparently out of order. By his side there is a lever with which he can change the switch, so that the trolley will not continue along the original rail and kill five workers; but it will kill the one. The passer-by is an expert in traffic and notices an interesting fact: the five workers on the one rail are slim, so that if the trolley crushed into them, it would kill all five, in turn, and then stop. But the worker on the other rail is very obese and if the trolley crushes into him, it will stop. But if he was slim or was not on the rail, the trolley would return along the connected rail to the switch and kill those five workers.

In the original scenario the rails beyond the switch are not connected, so if the worker jumped aside, the passer-by's end (*finis operantis*) would nonetheless be fulfilled: he would save all five workers, and his action would moreover not have the foreseen negative effect. But in this case it does not hold: if the obese worker avoided the trolley, it would return along the loop and frustrate the effort to save his colleagues. It appears that his death must be a means to saving those five, unlike the original scenario of changing the switch and similarly to the case of the transplantation surgeon. But Thomson's conclusion is different: she believes that we are morally justified to change the switch in this scenario as well, while the surgeon may not kill the young man. If that is so, then the necessity of some person's death (the young man in case of the transplantation, the obese man in case of this adapted scenario of switch-changing) does not mean that the person automatically becomes a means.

But Ezio di Nucci interprets the *Loop* version of the switch-changing scenario to speak against the principle of double effect, as he believes it to show that the difference between means and mere unintended consequences is not morally relevant.[26] In case of the *Loop* version the obese man's death seems to be a means to attaining an end (saving the lives of his five colleagues), since if he managed to jump aside in time, the effort to save them would fail. Since – at least according to Thomson – the switch may be changed in this scenario as well, the distinction between the means (which are intended) and the unintended negative consequences of an action is morally irrelevant.[27]

I agree that the *Loop* version of the switch scenario could present a problem for advocates of the principle of double effect. But not because of what moral intuitions say about it. In fact, Thomson appeals not so much to intuitions as to something else: she says that merely changing the rail's shape cannot change the moral qualities of the scenario. It is contested whether the fact that the obese worker's death is a necessary condition of saving the lives of his colleagues implies that this death is a means to attaining the action's end. I believe that it does not.

Let us return to the original version of the scenario. A casual passer-by is standing by the switch and can change it. His action (*finis operis*) consists in changing the switch, which is the result of all physical sequences of actions he carries out (he approaches the switch, grasps the mechanism's lever, moves it in the required direction, changes the switch). The proximate intention is therefore changing the switch and this action is morally indifferent. The remote intention (*finis operantis*) is to save the lives of five persons. The action has two consequences: (i) one is good and fulfils the remote intention (saving five lives), and (ii) the other one is bad (death of one worker). The bad consequence is not the object of an intention, whether proximate or remote, and is not a means to attaining the end. The means to attaining the action's end (*finis operis*) or fulfilling the proximate intention is all that makes it possible to move the mechanism and change the switch, the means to attaining the agent's end (*finis operantis*) or fulfilling the remote intention is changing the switch and all that serves to make it possible to change it.

Let us now take a look at the *Loop* version. The casual passer-by's proximate intention is to change the switch (*finis operis*), his remote intention (*finis operantis*) is to save five innocent human lives. The means to fulfilling this agent's end is changing the switch and all that is necessary to change it, i.e., the means necessary to fulfil the proximate intention (the means necessary to fulfil the action's end are in this act simultaneously the means to fulfil the agent's end, whereby the means to fulfil the *finis operantis* is also the action itself). If the proximate end is successfully fulfilled, the trolley will change its course and kill the obese worker, as a result of which it will stop and not kill his colleagues. But if this worker was not there, or if he was slim and his body did not stop the trolley, the agent's end (saving five human lives) would not be attained. It is evident that the passer-by would not change the switch in such conditions. The question is whether the fact that the obese person's death is necessary implies that he becomes a means to fulfilling the end. My answer is negative. The means to fulfil the agent's end is not the obese worker's death but changing the switch; the means to fulfil the action's end is the physical sequence of actions leading to changing the switch. The passer-by changes the switch **in order to** save five human lives, it cannot be claimed that he kills the obese man **in order to** save his colleagues.

An important role that intentions play in actions is that they relate them to further action: these intentions restrict or determine how we will act.[28] If the death of the obese worker was an end or a means, then the passer-by would have to react to the fact that he noticed the trolley in time and jumped off the rail. He would have to e.g. try to push him into the trolley's path. But if this worker's death is a mere unintended, though necessary consequence, he will act differently. Let us say that he changes the switch, the worker notices the trolley in time and jumps aside to safety. The passer-by will not attempt to push him into the trolley's path, he will merely acknowledge that although the proximate intention of his action was fulfilled, the remote intention failed to be fulfilled (all five workers will eventually die). This role of intentions is actions is of utmost importance and ethically relevant, as the following two scenarios show:

- **Murderer.** A physician learns that his grateful patient in the terminal stage of disease has made him his heir. But he is afraid that his relatives' visit could change his mind and decides to murder him. He injects him with a deadly cocktail of chemicals and quickly leaves the room. When he returns after some time he finds the patient still breathing. He takes a syringe and injects a higher dose of the same substance in his circulation. The patient's breathing stops.

- **Paliativist**. A physician decides to alleviate the great pains of his oncological patient and injects a large dose of a pain relief substance in his circulation. He consulted the decision with the patient in advance and warned him that such high dose can radically shorten his life. But neither of them can see another way out and the patient agrees with the solution. After some time the physician returns to the patient's room and finds him sleeping calmly; the pain has gone and the patient did not die. The physician does nothing.

In the first scenario death is the end of the action and a means to fulfilling the agent's end (getting the inheritance). Since the first murder attempt failed, the physician changed his plans and carried out a second murder attempt, successfully this time. In the second scenario death is a possible, unintended but foreseen consequence of the physician's action. When the physician found out that the patient had not died, he did not need to look for other means of killing him: his death was neither his end, nor a means.

If my analysis has been correct, then the *Loop* version of the switch-changing scenario does not present a problem for advocates of the principle of double effect. The obese worker's death, though it is necessary for the agent's end to be fulfilled, is in fact neither an end nor a means of the action. However, I willingly acknowledge that my solution is controversial and may be thought of as not entirely convincing. There are other solutions to the Loop case mystery though. Some philosophers for instance believe that it is in fact impermissible to switch the trolley. We have seen that Thomson argues that an extra track in the Loop scenario cannot change its moral character. But Whitley R. P. Kaufman convincingly argues that Thomson is committing a category error.[29] Consider the following three scenarios:

1   A person P aims at a target on a removable wall, pulls the trigger, the bullet leaves the barrel and after travelling a distance $t$ it hits the target.
2   A person P aims at a target on a removable wall, closes her eyes without knowing that in the meantime somebody has removed the wall, pulls the trigger, the bullet leaves the barrel and after travelling a distance $t^*$ it hits a person working behind the wall.
3   A person P aims at a target on a removable wall when at once she realizes that the wall has been removed and behind the wall there is P's personal enemy. P pulls the trigger, the bullet leaves the barrel and after travelling a distance $t^*$ it hits the person and kills her.

These scenarios have something in common: physically speaking, from the perspective of their physical movements, all three persons moved in the same way: aimed, pulled the trigger, hit a target. However, they also differ somehow. In the first scenario the bullet travelled a distance $t$, in the second and third it travelled a distance $t^*$. In the second and third scenario the wall was removed uncovering a person working behind it. Last but not least, contrary to the first, in the second and third scenario that person was hit by the bullet and killed. Do these facts change the moral character of the three scenarios?

It seems that the difference in distance travelled by the bullets (extra tract in the Loop case) has no bearing on the moral evaluation of $P$'s action, but the fact that in the second and third situation the worker is hit and killed makes a moral difference. As Kaufman puts it:

> In any significant moral action, there will always be material factors that, while by themselves not intrinsically morally salient, will become so because of their impact on morally significant factors such as physical harm to people. If the man is present to ensure that the five people on the track will not die, then the moral nature of the action has changed.[30]

I agree with Kaufman, but still I believe that we must make a more nuanced distinction as I tried to suggest by introducing the second and third scenario. What is morally salient in these cases and what clearly distinguishes them is the fact that the death of the worker is intended by $P$ in the third scenario and as such it constitutes an obvious instance of a murder. Whereas the second person might defend herself by saying, "I didn't intend to kill the worker, I was just playing with my gun and trying 'blind-shooting' at the target without knowing that the wall had been removed," the same excuse is not available to the third shooter. From the facts as we know them, she intended to kill her enemy and it is rational to attribute this intention to her which is determining the nature of her action.

If I'm correct in insisting that, beside the material factor mentioned by Kaufman, we must also pay close attention to the intentions with which the act itself was actualized, then it follows that my analysis of the Loop case might be correct. In no way it demonstrates that it is indeed correct, but corroborates it by showing that material factors become morally salient only when related to our intentions and plans.

Kaufman in his paper defends another possible response to the Loop case which some advocates of the principle of double effect may find convincing. He states it as follows:

> "[...] what makes Thomson's Loop variant so ingenious is that it creates an ambiguous borderline case, a case midway between the Standard case (clearly foreseen harm) and Fat Man case (clearly intended harm). [...] But if the case can be understood as presenting an ambiguity between intended and foreseen harm, then the proper interpretation of the Loop case under the DDE is that DDE gives no clear, determinate result. Reasonable people could reasonably disagree."[31]

I must admit that Kaufman solution has something attractive. He's right that the Loop variant is situated at (maybe behind) the border separating morally clear cases from those that are not. And I believe that morality is a land hemmed in insecurity which grows stronger as we get closer to what Saul Smilansky calls black holes in the moral universe,[32] the parts of our lives where moral intuitions go crazy and sound moral principles lead to sometimes contradictory conclusions. If my analysis turned incorrect, I could happily go with Kaufman solution, as I don't think uncertainty in the morality is a defect that can always be fixed. As Aristotle notes in his *Nicomachean Ethics*,[33] in every area of inquiry we can attain as much precision as the object of inquiry itself allows. In my opinion, therefore, the sphere of applicability of the principle of double effect will always contain grey areas where our intuitions will be insecure and divided and where rational people will disagree about whether the principle is applicable or not. This insecurity and vagueness is inherent in the very nature of moral inquiry, which is not *more geometrico demonstrata*. The best we can do is try as hard as we can to make sense of our moral living in human society by postulating abstract moral principles or rules and norms and by finding a reflexive equilibrium (which is *semper reformandum*) between them and our moral practices.

## Conclusion

This fifth chapter was not merely an historical exposition of the principle of double effect. I discussed the theory of intention and criticism of the principle of double effect presented by the well-known British theorist and philosopher of law H. L. A. Hart, then I focussed on the theory of positive and negative duties proposed by the British moral philosopher Philippa Foot, and I concluded the exposition by extending the traditional trolleyology scenarios as presented by Thomson up to the *Loop* version. But in presenting and analysing the views of these three thinkers I was not merely interested in what they wrote, what arguments they presented, or what conclusions they reached. I primarily tried to illustrate the principle of double effect in practice, the way its advocates can – or, in my view, ought to – argue and how they should solve moral dilemmas. Over the course of the chapter the role of proximate and remote intention, the relationship of means to end (means of the action and action as means to the final end) and also the great explanatory power of the principle of double effect was clarified. I do not claim that the thought experiments and moral intuitions associated with them prove the validity of this moral rule. But they constitute a firm starting point for further reasoning.

## Notes

1 Cf. Herbert L. A. Hart, "Intention and Punishment," in *Punishment and Responsibility. Essays in the Philosophy of Law*, ed. Herbert L. A. Hart (Oxford: Oxford University Press, 1975), 113–135.

2 The Fenians, an Irish republican brotherhood, were originally founded in 1858 in the USA. They wanted to overthrow the British government in Ireland.

3 Herbert L. A. Hart, "Intention and Punishment," 119.

4 Jonathan Herring, *Criminal Law. The Basics* (London: Routledge, 2010), 19.

5 Herbert L. A. Hart, "Intention and Punishment," 120.

6 Cf. Philippa Foot, "The Problem of Abortion and the Doctrine of Double Effect." *Oxford Review*, no. 5 (1967): 5–15. Reprinted in Paul Woodward, *The Doctrine of Double Effect: Philosophers Debate a Controversial Moral Principle* (Notre Dame, IN: University of Notre Dame Press, 2001), 143–155. In the following I will refer to Woodward's collection.

7 Trolleyology is presented in very accessible form by Thomas Cathcart, *The Tram Problem or Would You Throw the Fat Guy Off the Bridge?* (New York: Workman Publishing, 2013). Cf. also Francis Kamm, *The Trolley Problem Mysteries* (New York: Oxford University Press, 2019).

8 Cf. David Edmonds, *Would You Kill the Fat Man? The Tram Problem and What Your Answers Tell Us about Right and Wrong* (Princeton, NJ: Princeton University Press, 2014), 13.

9 Philippa Foot, "The Problem of Abortion," 147.

10 Cf. Julia Driver, *Consequentialism* (New York: Routledge, 2012).

11 Cf. Tim Mulgan, *Understanding Utilitarianism* (Stocksfield: Acumen, 2007), 55–59; Tim Mulgan, *The Demands of Consequentialism* (New York: Oxford University Press, 2001).

12 By that I am not implying that the physician in the second scenario is overjoyed by his action and would not be relieved if another solution was found. But there is no other solution and if he wants to perform the organ transplantations and save five lives, he must terminate one.

13 Philippa Foot, "The Problem of Abortion," 149.

14 The scenario with the tyrant is similar to an objection raised by Bernard Williams against utilitarianism. Imagine that Jim comes to the square of a small South American town. There are 20 terrified Indians standing at a wall and a group of armed men in uniforms around them. The uniformed men first question Jim, and eventually their captain makes the following proposal to him: if he, as an honorary guest, shoots one Indian, all the others will be set free. But if he does not shoot one of the Indians, all will be executed. Williams claims that according to utilitarianism, as he understands it, Jim ought to kill the Indian because that is the correct action for the given situation. Cf. John J. C. Smart and Bernard Williams, *Utilitarianism: For and Against* (Cambridge: Cambridge University Press, 1973), 98–99.

15 Philippa Foot, "The Problem of Abortion," 150–151.

16 In her paper *Morality, Action, and Outcome* Foot again endorses her conviction that negative duties prevail over positive duties. But furthermore she distinguishes between a situation when some person sets off a sequence of events with some results (a physician performs a sequence of actions at the end of which there is a patient's death, so that the patient's death can be imputed to him) and a situation when some sequence of events has already begun and the person merely does not interfere (allows a non-swimmer to drown) or changes its direction (the driver changes the tram's direction to the rail where only one person is working). Cf. Philippa Foot, "Morality, Action, and Outcome," in *Morality and Objectivity: A Tribute to J. L. Mackie*, ed. Ted Honderich (London: Routledge, 1985), 23–38.

17 Philippa Foot, "The Problem of Abortion," 152.

18 If someone wanted to intensify the analogy between the two scenarios, they can imagine that there is a seventh climber whose life is not endangered (he

has his own rope), is by the rope close to the equipment and the five colleagues are begging him to cut the equipment off.

19  Cf. Judith J. Thomson, "Killing, Letting Die, and the Trolley Problem." *Monist* 59, no. 2 (1976): 204–217. Reprinted in *Ethical Theory: An Anthology.* 2nd ed., ed. Russ Shafer-Landau (Malden, MA: Wiley-Blackwell, 2013), 543–551. All quotations are from this edition.

20  Cf. Judith J. Thomson, "The Trolley Problem." *The Yale Law Journal* 94, no. 6 (1985): 1395–1415. While Foot, whose native language was British English, used the term "tram" in her thought scenarios, American English uses the word "trolley." That is why at present this field is called trolleyology.

21  I described them in detail in the part of this chapter devoted to Philippa Foot and will mention them again here only briefly.

22  Judith J. Thomson, "The Tram Problem," 1396–1397.

23  Ibid., 1397. Cf. also a mildly different version in Judith J. Thomson, "Killing, Letting Die," 545. I adapted the scenarios somewhat.

24  Cf. Judith J. Thomson, "The Tram Problem," 1409. Cf. also Judith J. Thomson, "Killing, Letting Die," 545.

25  Judith J. Thomson, "The Tram Problem," 1402–1403.

26  Ezio di Nucci, *Ethics without Intention* (London: Bloomsbury, 2014), 76. In fact, many philosophers consider the Loop case as decisively refuting the validity of the principle of double effect, for example Peter Singer, "Ethics and Intuitions." *Journal of Ethics* 9, no. 314 (2005): 31–352. However, Singer seems to ignore the fact that people's intuitions are split 50/50 on the question whether it is morally permissible to switch the trolley in the Loop case.

27  But Di Nucci eventually reaches a different conclusion: he does not deny that if this scenario was acceptable (the switch may be changed), the distinction stated above would be morally irrelevant; he rejects the very possibility that changing the switch agrees with moral intuitions. However, it is doubtful whether he means the same by moral intuition as Thomson does: his conception of moral intuitions is an empirical one, relying on empirical results of experimental philosophy. These show that while in the case of the original scenario (*The casual passer-by*) 76.85% people would change the switch, in case of the *Loop* version the number for and against is roughly 50 to 50 (depending on the order in which the scenarios are presented). Cf. Ezio di Nucci, "*Ethics without Intention*," 71–76.

28  Christopher Kaczor, *Proportionalism and the Natural Law Tradition* (Washington, DC: The Catholic University of America Press, 2002), 107–108.

29  Whitley R. P. Kaufman, "The Doctrine of Double Effect and the Trolley Problem." *Journal of Value Inquiry* 50, no. 1 (2016): 21–31.

30  Ibid., 27.

31  Ibid., 30.

32  Saul Smilansky, *10 Moral Paradoxes* (Malden, MA: Blackwell, 2007).

33  Aristotle, Nicomachean Ethics. 1194b, 12–14.

# 6  Defence of the Principle of Double Effect

## Introduction

Though the preceding chapters where prevalently historical in character, they nonetheless also served to illustrate and explain the following concepts and principles, on which the principle of double effect and its application to difficult moral situations comprising the production of good and bad effects rely. In this last chapter I will attempt to systematically summarize and expound the conclusions I reached in the preceding chapters and so offer a certain defence of the principle of double effect.

## *Reductio ad unum principium?*

In contemporary bioethical and practical ethical treatises the principle of double most frequently takes the following form[1]:

- **Principle of double effect (Beauchamp-Childress):**

  - **Nature of act.** The act must be good or at least morally indifferent (independently of its consequences).
  - **Intention of agent.** The agent intends only the good effect. The bad effect can be foreseen, tolerated and admitted, but it must not be intended.
  - **Distinction between means and consequences.** The bad effect must not be a means to attaining the good effect. If the good effect was a direct causal effect of the bad effect, it would be intended by the agent in his effort to attain the good effect.
  - **Proportion between good and bad effect.** The good effect must outweigh the bad effect.

As we can see, the principle of double effect comprises altogether four conditions: the first one speaks of the nature of the action itself (it must be at least morally indifferent), the second one focusses on moral psychology and requires the agent to intend only the good effect of his action, the third condition requests that the good effect not be attained by means of the bad one, and finally the last condition states that a commensurate reason for the action must exist, expressed by the requirement that the good effect is to outweigh the bad one. In the preceding chapters we have seen that a large number of formulations of the principle of double effect have appeared in the history of moral thinking, among which there are sometimes even essential differences, including the context – ethical theories – in which they are situated. But Ezio di Nucci, whom we have met in the preceding chapter, approaches these formulations quite ahistorically and tries to prove that they (i) are equivalent and (ii) can be reduced to one single principle. He demonstrates the equivalence of these versions of the principle of double effect by reducing them to a single principle. Let us now examine the versions of the principle of double effect analysed by Di Nucci and his reductionist effort. He cites six different formulations of the principle of double effect in all, but three will suffice for our purposes (we are already familiar with two of them; I somewhat adapt)[2]:

- **The principle of double effect (McIntyre):** Sometimes it is licit to cause a harmful event as a merely foreseen effect, which it would not be licit to cause intentionally.
- **The principle of double effect (Mangan).** Person $S$ can actualize an action having a good effect and a bad effect, if the following four conditions are satisfied:
  - The action itself is of its object good or at least indifferent;
  - Only the good effect is intended, not the bad one;
  - The good effect must not be reached by means of the bad effect;
  - There is a proportionately grave reason to permit the production of the bad effect.
- **The principle of double effect (Gury).** It is licit to actualize a morally good or indifferent cause from which two consequences follow – one good and one bad – if there is a proportionately grave reason for it, the agent's final end is good and the bad effect is not a means to the good effect.

Two formulations of the principle of double effect (Beauchamp-Childress, Mangan and Gury) contain the explicit requirement that there should be a commensurate (or proportionately grave) reason to carry out the action having not only a good effect but also a bad one, while one of them (McIntyre) does not. But Di Nucci believes that it is contained in the single word "sometimes": **sometimes** it is licit to cause some harmful event as a merely foreseen effect, which it would not be licit to cause intentionally. According to him "sometimes" implies that it is not licit to actualize the action based only on the distinction between intended and merely foreseen effect. Other conditions must be satisfied, expressing the proportion between the good and the bad effect, such as e.g. five lives against one in the classical runaway tram scenario. I agree that the word "sometimes" can play a similar role as the one played by the fourth condition in the other two formulations of the principle of double effect, but it does not seem appropriate to me to replace an explicitly formulated condition of the possibility to actualize some action with merely vaguely admitting the possibility that sometimes such action is morally licit. The equivalence of "sometimes" and "there is a proportionately grave reason to permit the production of the bad effect" is evident only if we interpret "sometimes" to mean "if there is a proportionately grave reason." I therefore do not regard giving up this condition up as reasonable.

The second condition of the principle of double effect states that the bad effect must not be intended; only the good effect may be intended (and of course the action itself). The third condition expresses the requirement that the bad effect must not be a means to attain the good effect. The concept "means" can be interpreted in two ways: intensionally and extensionally[3]. Let us take a look at the following two examples:

1    **Intensional means.** Peter is standing on a bridge over a tram rail in the company of a very obese gentleman who is leaning over the railing. Beyond the bridge along the rail five persons are working. Peter suddenly notices that a tram is rushing on the rail, whose brakes are apparently out of order, and realizes that if he pushes the obese gentleman into the tram's path, he will stop it and save the five workers' lives. He decides instantly and pushes the obese gentleman onto the rail.
2    **Extensional means.** Peter is standing on a bridge over a tram rail in the company of a very obese gentleman who is leaning over the railing. Beyond the bridge along the rail five persons are working. Peter has been toying with the idea of murder for a long time already and now a perfect opportunity has arisen. Without hesitating he pushes the obese gentleman off the bridge. Without realizing it he thereby stops a runaway tram and saves the lives of the five workers on it.

In the first scenario the obese gentleman is an intensional means to Peter's end: Peter wants to stop the tram and save the lives of five workers on the line, which is why in his plan of action he chooses to push the obese gentleman off the bridge as a means: the pushing is a means to fulfilling the end of the action (*finis operis*), and thereby also the agent's end (*finis operantis*). In the second scenario Peter does not intend to stop the tram and save someone's life. His has murderous intentions, which he realizes by pushing the obese gentleman off the bridge. Peter's victim falls onto the rail and stops the runaway tram which does not kill the five persons working on the rail; but Peter did not want to stop the tram (*finis operis*) and was not trying to prevent losses of innocent human lives (*finis operantis*).

In the first scenario pushing the obese gentleman off the bridge was a means in an intensional sense (Peter intends this action as a means to stop the tram), in the second scenario it is a means merely in an extensional sense (Peter did not intend this action as a means to stop the tram). The exposition in the preceding chapters has shown that advocates of the principle of double effect interpret the concept of means intensionally: $X$ is a means to fulfilling the end of the action and of agent $S$, if and only if $X$ is intended as a means. This intensional interpretation can be formulated as follows:

- **Intensional means.** If person $S$ intends to carry out action $\varphi$ in order to fulfil its end $E$, then $X$ is an intensional means to fulfilling $E$, if and only if $S$ intends $X$ as a means to actualizing the end $\varphi$ (*finis operis*) or as a means to actualizing $E$ (*finis operantis*).

This definition shows that the means to actualizing $E$ can be the action $\varphi$ itself and *ipso facto* also all means serving to fulfil the end $\varphi$.[4] It is evident that there is a necessary connection between the concept "to be an intensional means" and the concept "to be intended": if $X$ is a means, then it is intended, if $X$ is not a means, then it is not intended. So it holds that "for every $X$ which is a means it holds that $X$ is intended," but it does not hold that "for every $X$, if $X$ is intended, then $X$ is a means." More formally, if "$I$" is the predicate "to be intended" and "$M$" is the predicate "to be a means," it holds that:

- $\forall X(M(X) \rightarrow I(X))$
- $\sim \forall X(I(X) \rightarrow M(X))$, i.e., it holds that $\exists X(I(X) \wedge \sim M(X))$

The ends of actions are intended, but they need not be means, the final end of an action is not a means. From $\forall X(M(X) \rightarrow I(X))$ it immediately follows that the last conditions in the three formulations of the principle of double effect (Beauchamp-Childress, Mangan and Gury) is redundant and can be omitted.[5] In his monograph Di Nucci offers two possible explanations of the existence of this redundant condition: (i) either the authors were not aware of this redundancy, or (ii) they admitted the possibility of means that are not intended, i.e., they denied the validity of $\forall X(M(X) \rightarrow I(X))$. I believe that there is a much simpler explanation: both Mangan and Gury were moral theologians concerned about the education of priests and moral guidance of the faithful. The third condition can be of merely didactic significance: it makes practical deliberation easier, without requiring priests, confessioners and moral advisors to speculate about the relationship between "to be intended" and "to be a means."

Finally, the first condition in the formulation of the principle of double effect remains: the action itself must be good, or at least indifferent. Di Nucci believes that even this essential condition is redundant.[6] The author asks: how can some action $\varphi$ be morally evaluated without respect to its consequences? The moral evaluation of $\varphi$ is presented by the principle of double effect, so it is not possible to judge $\varphi$ alone. But advocates of the principle of double effect often (though not all) endorse the view that there are negative moral precepts (*praecepta negativa*) valid always and everywhere (*semper et ad semper*). An example of such a precept is the prohibition of killing an innocent human person: it is a type of action that is morally evil of its nature (*ex obiecto*), independently of its consequences. Di Nucci is aware that this is a possible answer when he admits that the principle of double effect need not be the moral criterion of the correctness or incorrectness of $\varphi$, but the **criterion of justification**: on some conditions it is possible to actualize an action that is at least indifferent, having not only a good effect but also a bad one. But even if that were the case, the first condition would be redundant, because if $\varphi$ is a bad (incorrect) action, then if person $S$ actualized $\varphi$, it would have to intend something bad (the actualization of $\varphi$), which is forbidden by the second condition of the principle of double effect. I believe that this conclusion is correct (although $\varphi$ actualizes some end of its own, with respect to the agent's end $\varphi$ is a means), but it does not follow from it that the first condition is redundant. Di Nucci overlooks the **role** this condition plays: it functions as a criterion of selecting possible actions. Conditions 2–4 process actions (i.e., determine whether they are admissible), but only actions first "selected" by the first condition. In some types of action there is no point deliberating whether it is or is not intended; they are simply excluded from the very beginning.

Although the third condition is really redundant, it has an important didactic function; I therefore decided not to omit it. The principle of double effect is not merely an abstract moral principle, but also a guide for practical choices. Its use is not reserved for those who have theoretically mastered all the relationships between the concepts occurring in its formulation: it is intended for all those who share a certain minimum of moral theory (see below) and want to decide accordingly when solving morally unclear situations. In the following pages I will therefore attempt to defend the principle of double effect in the following formulation:

- **Principle of double effect:**

  - **Nature of act.** The act must be good or at least morally indifferent (independently of its consequences).
  - **Intention of agent.** The agent intends only the good effect. The bad effect can be foreseen, tolerated and admitted, but it must not be intended.
  - **Distinction between means and consequences.** The bad effect must not be a means to attaining the good effect.
  - **Proportion between good and bad effect.** The good effect must outweigh the bad effect.

# Are Hysterectomy and Craniotomy Morally Equivalent?

In the second section (*Reductio ad unum principium?*) of this chapter I distinguished between extensional and intensional means (more precisely: between the extensional and intensional interpretation of the concept "means") and defined intensional means as follows: If person $S$ intends to actualize action $\varphi$ in order to fulfil some end $E$, then $X$ is an intensional means to fulfilling $E$, if and only if $S$ intends $X$ as a means to actualizing the end $\varphi$ (*finis operis*) or as a means to actualizing $E$ (*finis operantis*). But some authors see a tension in applying the distinction between extensional and intensional means within the principle of double effect, which they think leads to inadequate conclusions. Nancy Davis speaks not of intensional and extensional means, but of *agent-interpretation* and *event-interpretation* (interpretation from the point of view of the agent and from the point of view of the event).[7] Let us recall two scenarios from the medical milieu:

1   **Hysterectomy.** A pregnant woman's uterus is affected with cancer and must be removed or the woman will die. The surgeon removes the uterus (action) in order to save her life (*finis operantis*). But with the uterus he also extracts the immature foetus, which dies. But the foetus's death does not fall under the surgeon's intention: his proximate intention is removing the uterus, the remote intention is saving the patient's life.
2   **Craniotomy.** A woman is undergoing a difficult childbirth and eventually it turns out that the only way to save her life is to crush the foetus's head. The assistant performs craniotomy and saves the woman's life.[8]

Advocates of the principle of double effect interpret the two scenarios as morally asymmetric: hysterectomy is morally licit, since the foetus's death is only an unintended consequence of the action (extracting the uterus), while craniotomy is a case of directly killing an innocent human being and as such is morally illicit. Davis explicates the structure of the argument against the moral admissibility of performing craniotomy in the following way[9]:

1   Performing craniotomy is necessary to save the woman's life.
2   Craniotomy is therefore a means to save the woman's life.
3   Craniotomy will kill the foetus.
4   Therefore the foetus's death is a means to save the woman's life (from 2. and 3.).
5   The principle of double effect forbids the use of evil means.
6   The killing of an innocent person as a means is evil.
7   The principle of double effect forbids killing the foetus (5. and 6.) and *ipso facto* carrying out craniotomy (3.).

What interpretation of the concept "means" is employed in the argument, or better, to what interpretation are advocates of the principle of double effect obliged by the requirement of maintaining the argument's validity? The argument's second step says that craniotomy is a means to saving the woman's life, the third step then states that craniotomy will cause the foetus's death. From that the fourth step of the argument derives: the foetus's death is a means to saving the woman's life. The transition from 2 and 3 to 4 is backed by the following notion of the relationship between means and causality: if *X* and *Y* are events and *X* is the cause of *Y*, then *X* is a means to *Y*. To reach the conclusion that the foetus's death is a means to saving the woman's life, the concept of means must be interpreted extensionally (*event-interpretation*), since an intensional interpretation requires the foetus's death to be part of the physician's plan, that the physician intends it as a means to actualizing his end. But, as H. L. A. Hart suggested, the physician's intention can be only to crush the foetus's head, not to kill it. In other words, for the above argument to remain valid the foetus's death must be conceived as a causal consequence of crushing its head and this causal relationship between the events (crushing the head – foetus's death) as the basis of the specification that the foetus's death is a means to save the woman's life. On the intensional interpretation of the concept of means the argument would not be universally valid: sometimes it would be valid, at other times it would not. But advocates of the principle of double effect regard craniotomy as morally illicit, they do not claim that sometimes it is licit and sometimes it is not.

The extensional interpretation of the concept "means" guarantees the validity of the argument forbidding craniotomy. The problem is that it also forbids carrying out hysterectomy, regarded by advocates of the principle of double effect as a paradigmatic example of an action with two effects whose actualization is morally licit, since the death of the foetus is unintended and merely foreseen. Let us take a look at the structure of the argument against the admissibility of carrying out hysterectomy:

1 Carrying out hysterectomy is necessary to save the woman's life.
2 Hysterectomy is therefore a means to save the woman's life.
3 Hysterectomy will kill the foetus.
4 The foetus's death is therefore a means to save the woman's life (from 2. and 3.).
5 The principle of double effect forbids the use of evil means.
6 The death of an innocent human being is an evil means.
7 The principle of double effect forbids killing the foetus (5. and 6.) and *ipso facto* carrying out hysterectomy (3).

The structure of this argument is identical to the structure of the argument forbidding craniotomy, and as in that case the transition from second and third step to the fourth one is crucial: the foetus's death is a means to save the woman's life. This conclusion is valid only assuming the extensional interpretation of means (one event – hysterectomy – causes another event – death of foetus). This interpretation is required by consistence: it is not possible to interpret means intensionally in one case and extensionally in another. We could interpret it intensionally: then the argument against the admissibility of craniotomy will not be universally valid, hysterectomy will be morally licit and the two scenarios will sometimes be morally equivalent and sometimes not. Means can also be interpreted extensionally: then the two scenarios will always be morally equivalent and hysterectomy will be illicit, as is craniotomy.

But, as we have seen, means must be interpreted intensionally. Does that mean that we need to resign on moral asymmetry between craniotomy and hysterectomy? I believe not. In the case of craniotomy we must discern in what sense the foetus's death is a means and draw the corresponding conclusions. The physician wants to save the mother's life, it is the architectonic plan of his action (*finis operantis*), the final end of his effort (*finis ultimus*), the object of his remote intention. To be able to actualize that plan he must crush the foetus's head (including the brain) and extract the foetus from the mother's body. So crushing the head is a means only relatively to the final end, but at the level of action it is not a means but the result of the action or the object of the proximate intention (*finis operis*). The core of the principle of double effect has not as yet come into play, we are merely considering at a general level whether the action in question (crushing the head) is a type of action to which a deliberation based on the principle of double effect can be applied.

Recall that in Thomas Aquinas the object of intention, which specifies the kind of action, is always some state of affairs or an action related to the order of reason. Let us take a look at the following two scenarios:

1   **Thief**. Thief *X* itches for his neighbour's watch. *X* tracks the neighbour's habits and notices when he leaves the watch unobserved. On one such occasion *X* takes the watch and hides it away in his home.
2   **Absentminded professor**. An absentminded professor works in a lab with his colleague who wears a similar watch. One day he sees a watch on the table and without much thinking puts it on and goes home. There his wife finds that it is not his watch.

The end of the thief's action is to appropriate the property of another, which is the defining specification of theft. Again the distinction between the "physical" (observable) sequence of actions (*X* enters the room, grasps the watch, puts it in his pocket, goes home and hides it away there), i.e., action *in genere naturae*, and its evaluation as a human action (*in genere moris*) is important. The end of the action (*finis operis*) is taking the property of another without authorization (theft). Let us imagine that the thief would defend himself: I did not want to steal the watch, the word "theft" did not appear in my mind at all! I just liked it, so I took it. *X* need not be lying, it is quite possible that he did not think of his action as of a theft, i.e., he did not explicitly apply the description "theft" to his action. But that is not essential: the intention of his action was to take his neighbour's property without authorization, which is objectively theft; *ex obiecto* his action must be characterized as theft.

The absentminded professor's situation is different: his plans also did not comprise the concept "theft." But the end of his remote intention was not to take another person's property without authorization. The professor believed he was taking his own watch, and when his wife realized his error he returned the watch with an apology (his action would become a theft if he still kept the watch after that).

Elizabeth Anscombe is critical of some opponents of the principle of double effect and claims that they inadequately understand intentions as internal mental acts that can be produced at will.[10] If the thief forms the alibistic mental intention "to borrow the neighbour's watch," then this conception does not make it possible to speak of theft (even though the thief does not intend to return the watch). Intentions are mental states with some content: the content of these states is actualizing some action (the action can be characterized as actualization of the content of the corresponding intention) and the character of this action is not determined merely based on a verbal description. Theft is unauthorized taking the property of another, and if the action's end is the unauthorized taking of such property, then it is a theft whether the agent is willing to admit it or not.

Let us now return to craniotomy. The end of the physician's action is crushing the foetus's head; the physician can say: my action is true under the description "crushing the foetus's head," but it is not true under the description "killing the foetus" because I do not intend to kill the foetus. But crushing the foetus's head is a way of killing it: in the moment when the physician crushes the head, he kills the foetus. We would hardly accept the defence of a murderer who would claim: I did not want to kill my victim; I only wanted to stab him in the heart. Similarly inadequate would be the reaction of a physician carrying out abortions: I don't want to kill foetuses, I only want to terminate undesirable pregnancies. Crushing the head is killing the foetus, stabbing a knife in the heart is killing the victim and vacuum aspirating the foetus out of the uterus is killing the foetus.

This reflection implies that craniotomy and hysterectomy are morally asymmetric scenarios, since the end of the physician's action in hysterectomy is removing the uterus, not killing the foetus. Removing the uterus cannot be characterized as direct killing of the foetus, since its death is a consequence of extracting the uterus, whereas in the case of craniotomy the foetus's death is not a consequence of crushing the head: crushing the head is killing the foetus. When a physician extracts a uterus affected with cancer that is precisely what he is doing: extracting the uterus (*finis operis* is extracting the uterus and all the surgeon's actions are aimed at fulfilling this proximate end). A consequence of extracting the uterus is the foetus's death. But when the physician is crushing the foetus's head, he is killing it. Its death is not a consequence of fulfilling some proximate end that could be characterized as "not killing the foetus." The moral asymmetry between hysterectomy and craniotomy is not based on applying the principle of double effect to both situations, determining that in the former the foetus's death is not a means to save the woman's life, while in the latter it is. It is based on the fact that crushing the foetus's head is an *ex obiecto* morally illicit action, since it breaks the negative moral norm forbidding direct killing of an innocent human life. As such it is an illicit means to fulfilling the agent's end (*finis operantis*), but it is not excluded from applying the principle of double effect primarily as a means, but as the action itself.

Davis grants that Anscombe's criticism of the "Cartesian" conception of intentions is correct, though not unproblematic. Let us take a look at the following two scenarios (I adapt)[11]:

1    **Alleviating pain.** A physician is trying to alleviate the pain of his oncological patient with medicine $M$. But the pain is unmanageable and the physician must choose a dose which he knows will kill the patient. He applies the medicine in his circulation and the patient dies.
2    **Euthanasia.** A physician knows that his patient is suffering unrelievable pain and has repeatedly asked him for a merciful death. The physician consults the situation with other experts, the patient is competent and persists in his request, and the decision to carry out euthanasia is made. The physician approaches the patient's bedside and injects a high dose of $M$ in his circulation; shortly afterwards the patient dies.

Why is this pair of scenarios problematic? We have reached the conclusion that the thief cannot claim that theft was not his intention; his intention is partially determined by extramental reality in its relationship to the order of reason. The murderer cannot claim that he did not want to commit murder, but merely to immerse a knife in the heart of his rival in love: conscious and intentional immersion of a knife in a heart is an act of murder. The physician cannot claim that his intention does not comprise killing the foetus: intended crushing the head is an act of killing the foetus. Let us name the physician from the first scenario $P_1$ and his colleague from the second scenario $P_2$: is it possible to claim that $P_1$ did not kill his patient while $P_2$ did? And is it also possible to claim that the patient's death in the first scenario was not a means to attaining the end (relieving the patient's pain)?

$P_1$ wants to relieve the patient's pain, that is his architectonic end (*finis operantis*), whose structure is impressed on the action as a whole. He fulfils this end by means of a certain action (injecting opioids in the patient's circulation). Can this action be viewed as alleviating pain, although it is an extensional means to the patient's death? The proximate intention is to alleviate pain. The physician proceeds *lege artis*, gradually increasing the dose when the previous one was not effective. Eventually he must increase the dose in such a way that he foresees that it will result in the patient's death. But this action resulted from continual and explicit effort to alleviate pain. Let us say that $P_1$ has the dose $D$ in a syringe, which he foresees will result in the patient's death. But he is not applying the dose in order to kill the patient, but in order to effectively alleviate his unmanageable pain. Therefore the physician is not trying to kill the patient, but to relieve his pain; if the patient survives the dose $D$, the physician will not inject another dose to kill him. There is also the relationship between the intention to alleviate pain and other intentions: some are forbidden, others on the other hand required. If the physician can administer a medicine reducing the negative effects of opioids and decreasing the risk of undesired death, he will most certainly do so. But the character of the action's end forbids him to administer a medicine reinforcing the deadly effect of opioids.[12]

$P_2$'s situation is quite different. The patient's death is the object of his proximate intention, the end of his action (*finis operis*); he is therefore bound to fulfil this end. Let us imagine that he administers the dose $D$ to his patient, which he expects to be lethal; but the patient does not die. Unlike $P_1$, $P_2$ will have to increase the dose: the end of his action has not been attained, so he must try to kill the patient again. The intention to kill the patient also places some requirements on other possible intentions: if there is a medicine reducing the lethal effect of the medicine, $P_2$ will not administer it to his patient. It would contradict the end of his action.

This analysis implies that in the first case the patient's death is a mere unintended effect of the physician's action, while in the second scenario it is a means to attaining the architectonic end of the action (relieving pain).[13] But the analysis does not imply that euthanasia is immoral: some advocates of the principle of double effect can regard euthanasia as morally licit. It implies only that in the first scenario the patient's death is not a means to fulfilling the end of the action and the agent's end, while in the second scenario it is a means to fulfilling the agent's end.

## Are Intentions Irrelevant?

The role of the preceding chapters was not merely historical. Over the course of laying out the history of the principle of double effect and the discussion in modern trolleyology I gradually specified the conception of this important moral principle, its possibilities and manners of application, and also the role played by intentions. I distinguished between proximate intentions, relating to the classical concept of *finis operis* (end of action), and remote intentions, relating to the classical concept of *finis operantis* (agent's end). This terminological distinction can be illustrated with the following example:

- **Quenching thirst.** Peter is very thirsty, which is why he decides to drink water. The end of his subsequent action (*finis operantis*) is the object of his remote intention. The object of his proximate intention is the end of his action (drinking a glass of water, *finis operis*). The proximate intention sets the plan of carrying out the action and determining the ordered means-end structure. Peter must carry out a sequence of physical actions: get up from the chair, go to the kitchen, take a glass out of a cupboard, turn the water on, pour it into the glass, lift the glass up to his mouth and drink. The selected means are contingent (Peter could have drunk in the bathroom, from a cup), but some means are necessary to fulfil the end of his action, and once they are chosen, they become part of the plan and are employed one by one over the course of the action (actualization of the proximate intention).

Let us notice the relationship between the end of the action and the agent's end, the object of the proximate intention and the object of the remote one. The action's end (drinking a glass of water) is the real end at the level of action (action in its physical manifestation), to which the corresponding means relate. But with respect to the agent's end the end of his action is a means to fulfilling this final end: Peter drinks water in order to quench thirst. The concept of means therefore comprises both the individual acts of which the action is composed (taking out the glass, turning the water on, filling the glass, lifting the glass up to the mouth and drinking) and the action as a whole (Peter drinks water). Furthermore, the relation "to be a means" is transitive. At the general level a binary relation $R$ on a set $X$ is called transitive if for each member $\alpha, \beta, \gamma$ of $X$ it holds that is $\alpha$ is in relation $R$ to $\beta$ and $\beta$ is in relation $R$ to $\gamma$, then $\alpha$ and $\gamma$ are also in relation $R$. Formally:

- **Transitive relations.** Relation $R$ on set $X$ is transitive, if it holds: $\forall \alpha, \beta, \gamma \in X : \alpha R \beta \wedge \beta R \gamma \rightarrow \alpha R \gamma$.

So if $X$ is a means to action's end $\varphi$ and $\varphi$ is a means to the agent's end, then $X$ is a means to the agent's end (putting a glass of water to the mouth is a means to the action's end, the action is a means to quenching thirst, so putting a glass of water to the mouth is a means to quenching thirst). If some means to the action's end (to fulfilling the proximate intention) fails, then *ipso facto* a means to fulfilling the agent's end (to fulfilling the remote intention) fails. But it can happen that the action fulfils its end, but the remote intention will remain unfulfilled. Let us take a look at the following example:

- **Loan for studying.** Peter decides to lend his friend some money to pay for his studies. His action consists in withdrawing money from the bank, transporting the money to his friend and handing it over. The proximate intention specifies this action as a loan (the money is Peter's and Peter hands it over with the intention of lending it). *Finis operis* is fulfilled at the moment when Peter hands the money over to his friend. However, the friend uses the money to buy a car. So even though Peter's proximate intention is fulfilled, the remote intention (*finis operantis*) is not fulfilled.

Proximate and remote intentions, as these examples illustrate, specify human action *in genere moris* and also determine the conditions of fulfilment, i.e., conditions on which the action's end and the agent's end are fulfilled. But is it possible to claim that intentions are also important from the moral point of view? And if so, in what sense?

The American philosopher James Rachels is one of many authors denying that intentions play an essential role in ethical evaluation of human action. He supports his conviction with the following thought experiment we are already familiar with[14]:

- **Visiting Granny.** Jack and Jill's granny is ill in hospital. Both want to visit her, but for quite different reasons: Jack sincerely loves Granny and wants to make her happy, Jill would like to come into her property. Both visit Granny, in turn, bring her flowers and chocolates, whereby they make her very happy.

According to Rachels Jack and Jill *did the very same thing* and consistence obliges us to evaluate similar (in this case identical) actions similarly (in this case identically). We would probably tend to think that Jack did a good thing, behaved well and morally, while Jill's action was simply immoral. But Rachels forces us to admit under the pressure of consistence that their actions are morally equivalent: if Jack's action is correct, then Jill's action must also be correct; and if Jack's action is not correct, then Jill's action is also not correct (or conversely: if Jill's action is good, then Jack's action is also good). What did Jack and Jill do? They made Granny happy, so their action was correct regardless of the intention (in this case the remote intention or motive). Rachels distinguishes between the action's correctness or incorrectness, which is evaluated based on what persons do, not based on their intentions, and the good or bad character of the agents, to which intentions are related: Jack's character is good,

Jill's character is bad. Rachels concludes his thought experiment with the following words:

The traditional view says that the intention with which an act is done is relevant to determining whether the act is right. The example of Jack and Jill suggests that, on the contrary, the intention is not relevant to deciding whether the act is right or wrong, but instead is relevant to assessing the character of the person who does it, which is another thing entirely.[15]

Rachels uses the noun *"intention"* in the context it is evident that he means the intention, or better, the motive of the action. From the point of view of moral evaluation of human action the intention (motive) is irrelevant, the important matter is what the agent did, is doing, or will do. Let us imagine the following scenario:

- **Hostile relatives.** Jack's Granny, whom he loves very much, is ill, and he decides to visit her. He has no idea that at Granny's bedside he will meet her sisters, who sincerely resent Jack. He makes Granny happy, but in her three sisters he stirs strong negative emotions.

How would Rachels evaluate this scenario? Since he may not take the motive of Jack's visit into account, he would focus on what Jack did: he made Granny happy, but at the same time he put her sisters out of humour. Rachels could not say: Jack made Granny happy with his action, but he did not aggravate her sisters; he was making Granny happy. The problem is that it is not what Jack wanted to do that determines whether he made Granny happy or her sisters upset, but the consequences of what he did. Let us say that Jack is very nice to Granny, gives her flowers, chocolates, talks to her kindly: and the nicer he is to Granny, the more upset and disgusted her sisters are. On Rachels's conception Jack made Granny happy with his action, but at the same time he made her sisters upset. So if Rachels were to evaluate whether Jack's action was correct or not, he would have to consider not only Granny and the joy Jack's visit has given her, but also the negative emotions of her three sisters, and he would probably reach the conclusion that Jack's action was not correct. This is equivalent to the claim that Jack's action is morally evaluated based only on its consequences: in accordance with act-utilitarianism. And here the problematic vicious circle appears: act-utilitarianism is an ethical theory, which regards the intentions of agents as irrelevant in evaluating their deeds. So it cannot be employed to prove that intentions are irrelevant in morally evaluating human action.

Notice how Rachels takes the possibility to act morally correctly away from us and makes us subordinate to unexpected circumstances. Jack's motive is good: he wants to make the granny he loves very much happy. He goes to see her in hospital, but besides Granny he meets her three sisters, who have no liking for him. Our deeply rooted intuitions say that Jack behaved correctly, that his action, not only his character, was correct and praiseworthy. But if we accepted Rachels's theory, we would have to conclude that Jack's action was not correct: the intention is irrelevant, it is only important what he caused with his action (moral arithmetic: he made one person happy, three persons upset). That is why the British philosopher Anne Maclen calls Rachels's conception of human action instrumental[16]:

- **Instrumental conception of human action**: For person $S$ to act means to bring about some change in the world.

According to this instrumental conception Jack's and Jill's actions were really identical: both brought about the same change in the world (made Granny happy). The problem with the instrumental conception of human action does not consist only in that it eliminates the role of intentions in its ethical evaluation; it entirely removes intentions, so that the only thing that is left are the physical manifestations of the action and the changes it brings about. The inadequacy of this conception can be illustrated with the example we are already familiar with from the second chapter, where we illustrated the difference between human action *in genere naturae* and *in genere moris*:

1   **Poisoning**. Jack takes a glass containing a liquid in his hand, raises his hand, puts the glass to his lips and swallows. After a while symptoms of poisoning appear and shortly afterwards Jack dies.
2   **Suicide**. Jill takes a glass containing a liquid in her hand, raises her hand, puts the glass to her lips and swallows. After a while symptoms of poisoning appear and shortly afterwards Jill dies.

On Rachels's conception Jack and Jill did the same: they carried out the same sequence of actions and their action brought about the same change. But let us now take a look at the two agents' intentions: Jack was thirsty, wanted to drink (*finis operantis*), which is why he put the glass to his mouth and drank (*finis operis*). He was not aware that the glass contains not water, but strong poison which will shortly end his life. If we take *finis operis* and *finis operantis* (or the proximate and remote intention) of Jack's action into account, we find that it is a case of tragic error, not suicide. The situation is different in Jill's case: Jill wanted to commit suicide, which is why she drank a glass of poison. Let us note that *finis operis* and *finis operantis* coincide: Jill drank poison in order to commit suicide, but drinking poison is an act of suicide (*ex obiecto*, i.e., *finis operis*). If we leave intentions aside, as Rachels suggests, we are unable to distinguish between Jack's and Jill's action: but the fact that the former is a case of tragic error, while the latter is an act of suicide, is of utmost importance for ethical evaluation of their action.

Let us now return to the visiting Granny scenario. Is it really possible to say that Jack and Jill did the same thing? We must distinguish among (i) their actions, (ii) the consequences of their actions, (iii) the proximate intentions and (iv) the remote intentions. Both visited Granny in hospital (i), and their action was guided by the same proximate intention (iii). The consequence of visiting Granny was the same (ii): so how do Jack's and Jill's actions differ? They differ in the remote intention (iv): Jack's visit was disinterested, he visited Granny **to** make her happy, **to** express his love for her, while Jill visited Granny **to** inherit her property. This can be summarized in the following table:

Here we can again illustrate the role of the relevant intentions. The proximate intention immediately determines the type of action Jack and Jill performed (they visited Granny in hospital). The remote intention expresses the motive, the reason why Jack and Jill visited Granny. From the second chapter we know that Thomas Aquinas regarded remote intentions as in a sense more formal than proximate intentions, since they imprint further character on acts already specified by a proximate intention. That is how it is also in this case: Jack visits Granny, but that is not all. Jack visits her to express his love for her. This fact speaks not only of Jack's character, but also of the action itself. Jack is a good man, but also his action is an expression of love; Jack visited Granny (action specified by the proximate intention), but the visit itself was a manifestation of love and respect (the further formal specification of Jack's action). Jill also visited Granny, but the motive of her visit was quite different and this motive allows us to characterize her visit not as an expression of love, but as deceit, an attempt at manipulation. So the remote intention speaks not only of Jill's character, but also of the character of the action itself.

Rachels claims that Jack and Jill did the same thing. In fact he is saying: let $T$ be some type of action (visiting Granny in hospital). Jack visited Granny in hospital and made her happy ($\varphi_1$), Jill visited Granny in hospital and made her happy ($\varphi_2$). The instrumental conception of human action holds, so that we are only interested in what Jack and Jill did, what changes in the world their actions brought about. That implies that $\varphi_1$ and $\varphi_2$ are instances of the same type of action $T$, or in other words that $\varphi_1$ and $\varphi_2$ are type-identical actions ($\varphi_1 =_T \varphi_2$). But if $\varphi_1 =_T \varphi_2$ holds, then no description $D_i$ may exist such that $D_i$ is true of $\varphi_1$ and at the same time is not true of $\varphi_2$ (and vice versa). But if we

*Table 6.1* Proximate and remote intentions

|  | Action | Consequence | Prox. intention | Rem. intention |
|---|---|---|---|---|
| Jack | Visiting Granny | Pleased Granny | To visit Granny | To express love |
| Jill | Visiting Granny | Pleased Granny | To visit Granny | To get inheritance |

do not accept Rachels's inadequate and argumentatively insufficiently grounded conception of human action, we will easily find at least two descriptions $D_1$ and $D_2$ where the former is a true description of Jack's action but is not a true description of Jill's action and the latter is a true description of Jill's action but is not a true description of Jack's action. $D_1$ can be "is a manifestation of love and respect," $D_2$ can be "is an effort to manipulate." The first description is true of Jack's action but it is not a true description of Jill's action, while the second description does not hold of Jack's action but is a correct description of Jill's action. That immediately implies that although Jack's and Jill's actions may be type-identical in their physical realization and consequences (*in genere naturae*), they are not type-identical as human actions (*in genere moris*).

In what follows I propose to speak of the proximate intention as of **characterizing intention** (or **c-intention**) and of the remote intention as of **final intention** (or **f-intention**). The example with Jack, Jill and their visit at Granny's bedside in the hospital also shows why intentions are important in the moral evaluation of human action and what role they play in it. Let us take a look at the following table:

We will evaluate Jack's action as good or correct, because the object of the action (object of c-intention) is morally indifferent and the f-intention is good (Jack's visit at Granny's bedside was an expression of love and respect), while Jill's action will be evaluated as bad or incorrect, since while the object of the action (object of c-intention) is morally indifferent, the f-intention is bad (Jill's visit at Granny's bedside was an attempt to manipulate her). Utilitarians, especially act-utilitarians, will not agree with this analysis, but the goal of my work is not to refute utilitarianism, but to clarify the conditions and context in which the principle of double effect can be applied.

In the conclusion of the historical chapters devoted to the development of the principle of double effect (or more precisely principles of double effect) I stated that the individual versions of this moral rule play a role in a certain context, in a certain type of ethical deliberation. The example with Jack and Jill shows what the minimum condition of the applicability of the principle of double effect is: it must be what J. L. A. Garcia calls "*intention-sensitive ethics*," i.e., ethics that is aware of how important the role of c- and f-intentions is in characterizing the action itself.[17]

*Table 6.2* Evaluation of c- and f-intentions

|  | Action | Consequence | c-intention | f-intention |
|---|---|---|---|---|
| Jack | Visiting Granny | Pleased Granny | Indifferent | Good |
| Jill | Visiting Granny | Pleased Granny | Indifferent | Bad |

## T. M. Scanlon and the Illusory Appeal of Double Effect

In his book *Permissibility, Meaning, Blame*[18] Thomas Scanlon also devotes attention to the ethical relevance of intentions. He acknowledges that intentions do play some part, which he calls the predictive meaning of intentions, but on their own, without regard to the action's consequences of which they are predicated, they are not determinative of whether an action is morally admissible or not. Let us take a look at the two following, already familiar scenarios:

1   **Dentist.** A dentist must drill a patient's bad tooth. He is well aware that he will cause the patient pain, but he does not intend this negative effect of his intervention: he intends to drill the tooth (*finis operis*) so that his patient's teeth are healthy (*finis operantis*).
2   **Sadistic dentist.** A dentist must drill a patient's bad tooth. He is well aware that he will cause the patient pain and is overjoyed by that. The pain caused becomes one of the ends of his action: he does not merely want to repair the patient's teeth, but also to cause him pain.

Scanlon raises the following question:

> But the question I am interested in is whether an agent's intention is itself directly relevant to the permissibility of an action—whether, holding effects (or expected effects) constant, the permissibility of an action can depend on the agent's intention in performing it or, more generally, on what he or she saw as a reason for the action.[19]

Let us construe the two scenarios above so that the two dentists cause the same pain and both attain the same effect: the patient's healthy teeth. We may seem to have found an answer to Scanlon's question; the action's consequences are constant (absolutely identical in the two scenarios), the scenarios differ only in the intentions (the sadistic dentist intends to cause pain) and we will probably all agree that the sadistic dentist's action is morally inadmissible, while his colleague's action was right. But apparently it will not be that simple. Scanlon could insist that while the sadistic dentist causes the same amount of pain as his colleague does, he nonetheless causes more of it than would be necessary to perform the action.

Thus Scanlon could say that the two scenarios ultimately differ in something else than the intention: precisely in that the sadistic dentist causes more pain than is necessary, so that the patient's pain is not proportionate to the intervention (the same intervention could be carried out with lesser pain). But why is the pain proportionate in one scenario and not in the other? It cannot be merely due to the amount of the pain caused, as that is identical in the two scenarios. The answer is that the sadistic dentist causes pain intentionally and therefore causes more of it than if its role in his plan was merely that of an unintended consequence of his action. Let us imagine two possible worlds $w_1$ and $w_2$; the two worlds are fully identical and they differ only in that in world $w_1$ the sadistic dentist has not yet satisfied his desire and intentionally causes pain, while in world $w_2$ causing pain is no part of his intentions. Let us say that in $w_1$ the amount of pain caused (intensity × duration) equals $P$, while in $w_2$ it equals $Q$; $P > Q$. Let us further assume that the non-sadistic dentist also causes pain, whose value equals $R$; $R = P$. Obviously, the amount of pain itself cannot explain why the pain caused in $w_1$ in disproportionate, since $P = R$. The difference consists in something else, namely in that the scenarios $w_1$ and $w_2$ differ, and they differ precisely in that in one the dentist causes pain intentionally, while in the other he does so unintentionally.

An advocate of the principle of double effect could thus say that in the case of the scenarios dentist – sadistic dentist intentions play a double role. On the one hand, as we have seen earlier, they determine the nature of the action itself, that is, they subordinate some physical execution of a series of actions under morally relevant categories (the sadistic dentist essentially tortures his patients, so that his action can *in genere moris* be correctly characterized as torture). On the other hand it makes it possible to determine whether a certain pain is proportionate to the action's ends or not.

Of course, Scanlon would object that in fact my exposition fails to answer two of his important objections:

1  Regarding the (in)admissibility of actions, intentions alone are irrelevant.
2  There is no way to explain why the difference between intended and merely foreseen consequences should be morally relevant.

However, I believe that Scanlon starts from a certain incorrect conception of the role of intentions in ethics and in the application of the principle of double effect. In my discussion of the role of intentions in ethics I have tried to show that intentions are in fact not morally relevant on their own. Their relevance is derivative, yet essential: they make it possible to classify the physical manifestations of human action (*in genere naturae*) into the corresponding moral categories (*in genere moris*). Endorsing this ethical rule does not oblige advocates of the principle of double effect to acknowledge some deeper, independent role of intentions in the ethical evaluation of human action. This function of intentions as moral classifiers of action types is reflected in the very conditions of the applicability of the principle of double effect which state that the action as such, independently of its consequences, must be at least morally indifferent. Intentions play an important role here, but not the kind of role ascribed to them by Scanlon.

But another question still remains open, namely why the distinction between an evil effect that is intended and one that is not intended (it is not an object of a c- or f-intention and thus plays no part in the plan of the action finally determined by the f-intention) and is merely foreseen should be morally relevant. One of the possible and often quoted answers is to be found in Thomas Nagel who writes:

> [...] to aim at evil, even as a means, is to have one's action guided by evil. ... But the essence of evil is that it should *repel* us. If something is evil, our action should be guided, if they are guided by it at all, toward its elimination rather than toward its maintenance. That is what evil *means*. So when we aim at evil we are swimming head-on against the normative current. Our action is guided by the goal at every point in the direction diametrically opposite to that in which the value of that goal points.[20]

Nagel's reasoning seems clear here: evil is intrinsically something that ought not to be whether an end or a means of our action (it ought to repel us). But when we act in such a way that the evil effects do not become objects of our intentions (c- and f-intentions), then, if the evil effects cannot be eliminated, there are situations in which such actions are morally admissible. But some authors hold that Nagel is wrong and that an evil can be an end or a means of action. Let us take a look at the following scenario[21]:

- **Painful therapy.** A patient suffers from a disease that for a long time proceeds without painful symptoms. But if it was left untreated it would eventually reach a very painful phase. There is a treatment that must be applied in the painless phase. Although it is painful, it causes lesser pain than the disease would cause later on.

Shelly Kagan, the author of this scenario, believes that it shows that there are situations in which it is possible to intentionally cause pain. He characterizes pain here as a necessary means of treating the disease (the pain stimulates the production of hormones and antibodies that are necessary for the cure), not merely as a side effect of the therapy. But I do not believe that he has succeeded to show that an evil can become an end or a means of our action.

Let us imagine a physician applying this painful procedure. If we asked him whether he was intentionally causing his patient pain, he would probably answer that he was not. The pain is not the reason for his action and his action cannot be characterized as causing pain. In fact the physician is applying a *painful therapy*. It seems to me that there is a world of difference between causing pain for the pain itself and applying a treatment that is necessarily painful. The physician wants to cure his patient and the only treatment available causes pain, but the pain itself, separated from the therapy, is no part of the physician's intention. The physician applies a "painful therapy," which is a correct description of his action; the reason (f-intention) for his action is curing his patient, the means is a painful therapy, not pain as such (an evil). In other words, the pain taken on its own is not an object of a c-intention; it is not what the physician does. The object of the c-intention is a painful therapy, viz. a therapy that unfortunately is necessarily painful.

Let us recall the example with limb amputation and mutilation. If a physician amputates a gangrenous limb, he causes some evil, if we construe the non-existence of the limb as a physical evil. It would be difficult to deny that the amputation is what the physician is doing (c-intention) in order to (f-intention) cure the patient, but the bare fact that a physical evil becomes the object of a c-intention does not mean that the physician is acting immorally. An amputation is in full accord with the principles of medical ethics and *lege artis* and the focus on a physical evil does not imply the inadmissibility of the action at the moral level (*in genere moris*). A physical evil (pain, amputated limb) is not automatically projected onto the level of moral evil and morally inadmissible action. A different situation arises in the case of a mutilation, when someone amputates a limb only and precisely because he is thereby causing a grave damage. In such situation it is no longer a case of amputation, but a case of mutilating a human being, which is without doubt morally inadmissible. We can thus specify Nagel's claim in order to make it accord with the way advocates of the principle of double effect frequently construe ethics: no moral evil, viz. types of action that are determined and inadmissible at the moral level, such as murder, torture or mutilation, may become the object of an intention.

L. W. Sumner in his book *Assisted Death* also raises an objection against Nagel's reasoning for the inadmissibility of intentionally causing pain.[22] It is very simple in core: it is possible that someone intentionally causes evil even though the evil repels him (for example, he or she causes pain to a child in order to save someone else's life). But Sumner focusses too closely on one word in the sentence "But the essence of evil is that it should *repel* us"; it is then easy to construct a counterexample in which we cause an evil for some grave reason while it still holds that it repels us. But Nagel's text seems to me to provide a clear clue as to how his idea can be grasped more precisely.

In distinguishing between intended and merely foreseen evil consequences intentions are important for at least two reasons:

1   They determine the way agents relate to the evil consequences.
2   They can determine the extent of the evil consequences.

Let us first take a look at the first reason, which is clearly outlined in Nagel's text. Let us consider two agents, $A_1$ and $A_2$. $A_1$ does not intend the evil consequence $P$ of his action and merely foresees it, while $A_2$ intends the evil consequence $Q$. How do the two agents differ? $A_1$ acts in a way that necessarily includes $P$, which he cannot eliminate. Although he does not intend $P$, it provides him with reasons for action that are morally good: $A_1$ tries to limit $P$ to the least possible extent. A dentist knows that drilling teeth causes pain and mental stress that can sometimes be pronounced. He is aware that if he wants to restore health to his patient's teeth (f-intention), he must drill the bad tooth (c-intention). The negative consequences of drilling teeth give him reasons to act in a certain way, for example, trying to set the patient at ease by gentle behaviour, applying a sufficiently efficient anaesthetic, etc. The dentist relates to the negative consequences in a certain way and construes them as providing reasons for a certain kind of action and also reasons for not acting in a certain way (being too rough, refusing to apply an anaesthetic, etc.)

$A_2$ intends the evil consequence $Q$ and relates to it in a way that is different from the way $A_1$ relates to $P$; he tries to reinforce $Q$, eliminates forms of action that could decrease $Q$; in brief, he construes $Q$ as providing reasons for action that are very different from $A_1$. A sadistic dentist intends the pain which he causes by his action. His f-intention may be restoring health to his patient's teeth, but since pain is part of his c-intention, his action cannot be construed merely as drilling teeth; it is a case of tormenting the patient, maybe even of torture. This dentist acts in such a way in order to torment the patient, behaves roughly, does not apply anaesthetics or applies them in insufficient amounts. Note that when the evil effect becomes part of the dentist's plan of action, it co-determines the very nature of his action at the moral level; it is no longer merely a case of drilling a tooth, but of tormenting the patient.

Thus the distinction between an intended and a merely foreseen effect determines an important and morally relevant difference in how agents relate to the evil consequence and what reasons for action this effect provides in their perspective. But it can also determine the very extent of the evil effect. We have seen that the difference between a dentist and a sadistic dentist need not consist in the overall amount of pain caused; that can be identical. But the sadistic dentist causes more pain than he would if he were not a sadist, precisely because the pain is intended. And again, the extent of the harm caused is a morally relevant factor, if it exceeds the limits of harm occurring in case the harm was not intended.

A brief summary. I agree with Scanlon that intentions taken on their own do not determine whether a certain action is morally licit or not. But this need not agitate advocates of the principle of double effect, since applying this principle does not require any such independent relevance of intentions. But I disagree with Scanlon in that we do not have good reasons to construe the distinction between intended and merely foreseen consequences as morally relevant, since this distinction determines the agents' attitudes to the evil effects, the reasons for action provided by the evil consequences, and it can also determine the extent of these evil consequences. Intended evil consequences as the objects of intentions also co-determine the nature of the act itself and can thus change its evaluation (licit-illicit). All these factors are morally relevant.

## F. Kamm and the Principle of Triple Effect

Let us now return for a moment to the scenario described on p. 124:

- **Dentist.** A dentist must drill a patient's bad tooth. He is well aware that he will cause the patient pain, but he does not intend this negative effect of his intervention: he intends to drill the tooth (c-intention) so that his patient's teeth are healthy (f-intention).

The dentist's final intention (f-intention) is to restore health to his patient's teeth, his action (c-intention) is drilling a tooth; this is at the same time a means to fulfilling the f-intention, and, through the transitivity of "being a means," all that is a means to fulfilling the action determined by the c-intention is also a means to fulfilling the f-intention. The dentist foresees that drilling the tooth will cause some discomfort or even pain in the patient, he does not intend that and it is no part of his structured end-means plan to fulfilling the final end of his action: restoring health to the patient's teeth. This scenario represents a paradigmatic situation of applying the principle of double effect – an action $\varphi$ (drilling a tooth), which is at least morally neutral, has two effects: (i) one good $D_1$ (restoring health to the patient's teeth), (ii) one evil $D_2$ (discomfort and pain), (iii) $D_2$ is not intended, merely foreseen, (iv) $D_2$ is not a means to attaining $D_1$, (v) there is a proportional reason to actualize action $\varphi$.

Note that both consequences give the dentist a reason to act: $D_1$ provides a reason for the dentist to drill the bad tooth; $D_2$, although it is unintended, nonetheless provides reasons for the dentist to act in certain ways: for example, to try to set the patient at ease by gentle behaviour; to apply a sufficient amount of local anaesthetic; or, in particularly grave cases, to anesthetize the patient fully. But the American philosopher Francis Kamm holds that this does not exhaust all the possible ways a rational agent can relate to the consequences of her actions. Let us take a look at an example Kamm uses to illustrate her idea[23]:

- **Party.** Adam has decided to hold a party in order to have fun with his friends. But at the same time he knows that mess will occur over the course of the party, and also that his friends will feel indebted to him and will help him to clear up the next day. Since Adam does not want to clear the mess up alone, he understands the indebtedness and the associated help with clearing up as a condition of holding the party at all. But he does not hold the party in order for his friends to feel indebted to him, or in order for his friends to help him clear up; he holds it because he knows that his friends will feel indebted to him and will help him clear up.

The final end of Adam's action (f-intention) is that he and his friends have good fun; the means-action (c-intention) is holding a party. This action has two consequences: (i) fulfilling the f-intention (people had fun) and (ii) a feeling of indebtedness and help with clearing up. Let us say together with Kamm that feeling indebted is something negative, thus the second consequence of the action can be considered evil. It now seems feasible to apply the principle of double effect and, since all of its conditions are met, proclaim that Adam's action is morally admissible. But Kamm believes that there is another factor at work. Adam intends to hold a party (c-intention) in order to fulfil his final intention (having fun with friends), which is a good consequence of actualizing the c-intention in action. The evil intention is not intended, but it is also not merely foreseen: Kamm underlines that Adam holds the party because the evil effect will occur; otherwise he would not hold it. Advocates of the traditional principle of double effect do not account for such a relationship of the rational agent to the evil consequence (I act in a certain way because I know that the evil effect will occur; if I knew that it would not occur, I would not act). This is why Kamm formulates her doctrine of triple effect, giving it the following shape:

- **Doctrine of Triple Effect (DTE).** A greater good than we cause and whose expected existence is a condition of our action, but which we do not necessarily intend, may justify a lesser evil that we must not intend but may have as a condition for action.

The choice of the term "triple effect" may seem misleading. While it is true that the consequences of Adam's party include not only a feeling of indebtedness on the part of Adam's friends, but also mess, this does not justify speaking of a triple effect. Returning to the dentist example, it is possible to distinguish between various kinds of evil consequences: the patient may feel panic, stress, acute pain, but it is not necessary to speak of a principle of quadruple effect (healthy teeth, panic, stress, pain), since all three evil consequences are understood as belonging to one category (evil effect) and relate to the agent in the same way (as unintended, albeit foreseen). But Ezio Di Nucci in his book *Ethics Without Intention* claims that Kamm introduces a new type of means; it is necessary to distinguish between "in order to" means and "because" means, yielding the following quadruple[24]:

1   Ends: to have fun
2   IOT-Means (In Order To-Means): to organize the party

3   BO-Means (Because Of-Means): my friend's feeling of indebtedness
4   Side Effects: the mess that my friends will help me clear up

However, this interpretation is misleading. In the overall plan structured by f- and c-intentions (why and what) means are only what serves to actualize the action (c-intention) and its final end (f-intention). But creating a feeling of indebtedness and making friends help Adam clear up after the party have no part in the plan structured like this (I do not need to create a feeling of indebtedness to organize a party and it is also not necessary for Adam and his friends to have fun). I therefore do not hold that distinguishing between IOT-means a BO-means based on Kamm's example is correct and justifies choosing the term "triple effect."

Kamm seems to have something else in mind. She wants to say that advocates of the principle of double effect do not distinguish between two possible ways of relating to the evil consequences of actions: one is the relationship of not intending but foreseeing; the other is the same as the first, but we also relate to it as to a condition of actualizing the given action. But even so it is not particularly clear why we should speak of a triple effect; there are two effects (a good one and an evil one), we can just have a more complex relationship to the evil one than to something we do not intend and merely foresee.

With her party example Kamm wants to show that the evil effect can sometimes be a reason for action (we act because something will occur), but still the action will be morally licit since it is not what we intend. The feeling of indebtedness, which Adam assumes his friends will experience, is not intended, but on the other hand it provides Adam with reasons for action; if he knew that it would not occur, he would not hold the party.

It does not seem to me that the fact that the evil action provides reasons for action distinguishes the principle of double effect from DTE. Let us recall the dentist example: the evil effect of drilling a tooth is psychological discomfort and pain, which gives the dentist reasons to act as considerately and gently as possible. But the dentist does not construe his relationship to these negative effects as strongly as Kamm construes the feeling of indebtedness that forms in Adam's friends, i.e., as a condition of actualizing the action. Quite on the contrary: he construes it as something that he must try to eliminate, or at least minimize. And despite the merely partial or zero success he is nonetheless morally justified in drilling the tooth.

I believe that Kamm had not sufficiently taken into account a fact she herself mentions: the evil effect that prompted her to introduce DTE is *a condition of actualizing the action*; if Adam knew that his friends would not feel indebted to him and would not help him clear up, he would not organize the party. It seems to me that as a condition of actualizing the action it must be intended by the rational agent precisely as such, or more exactly, its being fulfilled must be intended. When Adam holds a party because he knows that his friends will feel indebted to him and will help him clear up the mess, he incorporates the negative effect (the feeling of indebtedness) into a new plan of action whose fulfilment is intended. For example he will make an effort that his friends really have fun, he will unobtrusively indicate that mess is being generated and someone will have to clear it up the next day, perhaps he will mention at some point how much he hates clearing up, he will perhaps even narrate how he was left alone to clear up after the last party and how it spoiled the pleasure for him. In such ways he will be taking small steps towards fulfilling the condition of the party being held. Thus it seems to me that Kamm's party example allows for the following interpretation. Adam has one main plan (having fun with friends by organizing a party), of which he assumes that it will give rise to a feeling of indebtedness. Within this plan the feeling of indebtedness is an unintended consequence, but once Adam makes it a condition of actualizing the main plan he develops a new auxiliary plan. Its main end is that his friends help him clear up and the means to this end is arousing a feeling of indebtedness in them, where all that can contribute to his friends really feeling indebted are further possible means.

Kamm claims that Adam relates to the feeling of indebtedness as to a condition of actualizing his action; if that is the case, then Adam must intend this condition to be actualized. He cannot perceive it as a merely unintended consequence that nonetheless is a reason for (a condition of) the action. Let us imagine the following scenario:

- **Partially rational sadistic dentist.** The dentist understands that the end of his action (drilling a tooth) is restoring health to his patient's teeth and he is so rational that he always attempts to do that. But at the same time he wishes to cause some pain and without it he would not undertake the treatment. Thus a condition of his action always is that he causes some, even if minimal, pain (or at least psychological discomfort).

Now let us imagine that the dentist would defend himself as follows:

> I wanted to restore health to teeth. I knew that I will cause pain, it even was a condition of my action, but it was an unintended condition. Thus from the ethical point of view I acted acceptably, since the pain was never too big and the good consequence (healthy teeth) always outweighed this negative effect.

It seems to me that such defence would not stand the test. For if the dentist sets causing pain as a condition of his action motivated by a good f-intention (restoring health to teeth), he relates to it as to something structuring a parallel plan of action. He will probably apply a lesser amount of local anaesthetic, or he will apply it in a painful way, or he will find some other way to reach his parallel end. If that is so, then his action is inadmissible from the ethical point of view, since the unintended evil effect of one plan of action is transferred to another plan of action, where its actualization is a condition of carrying out the first plan. At the same time it also holds that this actualization is intended.

Let us take a look at another example introduced by Kamm[25]:

- **The Munition Grief Case.** A strategic bomber plans bombing a strategic military target. He does not intend civilian deaths, but he is aware that if he carries out the raid, it will result in the death of innocent people. But at the same time he knows that if no civilians died, the bombing would be useless as the target would very soon be rebuilt. Thus he will not do the bombing in order for civilians to die, but because he knows that some civilians will die and the resulting grief and panic will prevent the bombed target being rebuilt.

Note that even in this case it is not possible to speak of three effects. The negative consequences are civilian deaths, grief and panic, but as I have already observed this does not mean that these negative consequences should be judged in isolation and the principle of double effect should be broadened to a principle of triple or quadruple effect. Kamm believes that although the bomber knows quite well that some civilians will die, and this even provides him with reasons for action (otherwise the final end, which is weakening and demoralizing the enemy army, would not be fulfilled), their death is not intended. Therefore she regards such bombing as morally admissible, although she does not regard the terror bomber's action as admissible.

Again it seems to me that civilian deaths as a condition of actualizing the action becomes an object of intending (in order for the condition to be fulfilled) and structures a whole series of means to fulfilling this intention. Let us assume, for example, that the bombing has been planned for Monday but the bomber learns that on that day a celebration will be taking place in the target area and there will be no civilians in the vicinity of his strategic target. He therefore decides to re-schedule the raid for Tuesday, in other words, he intentionally and consciously restructures his means to fulfilling the final aim in order for it to be really fulfilled. And it need not be merely a matter of changing the timing of the raid. If he is really planning to do the bombing with the intention of killing civilians, and otherwise would not actualize his plan, he will probably adjust his action to this condition in other ways as well. For example, he will choose ammunition that will with probability hit and kill some civilians, and perhaps he will even aim the bombing in such a way that some bombs will hit the peripheral parts of his target where they are likely to kill civilians. Put simply, the fact that he will do the bombing only under the condition that he will kill someone cannot be explained in any other way than that civilian deaths as a condition of the action become an object of his intention and also makes it possible to determine the means to securing that the condition of action will truly be fulfilled.

Perhaps Kamm could object that the classical strategic bomber and her strategic bomber do not differ in that they both know that some civilians will die; there is only a difference in that the classical bomber does not link this fact to a condition of his action in any way, while the other one does. But what is really the difference, since civilians will die either way? But this objection will not stand the test, since civilian deaths provide the two bombers with different reasons for action, precisely because in the first case it is unintended, while in the other it becomes a condition of the bombing. For example, the classical strategic bomber would fly to the raid with great joy on Monday, because he would know he was going to kill no civilians; but the other would stay on the ground and fly the next day. The classical bomber would choose such ammunition that would sufficiently destroy the target while minimizing civilian casualties, while the other one would apparently choose so that it would not be possible that by a lucky accident the target would be destroyed and no civilians would die.

Unlike Kamm I believe that while the classical strategic bomber is morally permitted to bomb his target, if the conditions determined by the principle of double effect are met, Kamm's strategic bomber lacks moral justification. There is a moral asymmetry between the two cases due to the different ways in which the two bombers relate to the negative effect of the bombing.

Kamm presents her doctrine of triple effect as a broadening of the application sphere and the area of moral admissibility beyond the limits of the traditional principle of double effect. But already the very name is misleading: in fact there are the traditional two effects (or, if you wish, two categories of effects) and the only difference consists in how the rational agent relates to the evil effect. Kamm claims that he can relate to it as to a necessary condition of actualizing the action, which nonetheless remains beyond the contours traced by the structure of f-intentions and ch-intentions and is merely foreseen, not intended. But if my reasoning is correct, then the rational agent intends the necessary condition of realizing some action and he can even make it the end of a parallel plan, to which other means of fulfilment and thus the fulfilment of the condition of action itself are subordinated. Thus an advocate of the principle of double effect can regard Kamm's effort as unsuccessful: while it is true that she introduces a new way of agents' relating to the negative consequences of their actions, and it is also true that this fact is morally relevant, it is not possible to say that the situations to which the author applies her reasoning are morally admissible due to DTE. The negative effect as an intended condition of realizing the action becomes a reason due to which in these situations the action becomes morally inadmissible

## Bratman and the Three Roles of Intentions

Thomas Aquinas conceived intentions and their role in the context of his treatise on the structural moments of human action (*actus humanus*), or more precisely the intrinsic act. The human intellect (*intellectus*) is prospectively aware of the possibility of some action or fulfilling an end (buying ice cream). The ice cream is presented as something having some appeal: the notion of ice cream attracts us (we consider it *sub ratione boni*, as a possible reason for action; the result is simple wanting – *velleitas*). At this point the whole matter can come to an end; but if the intellect and the will continue to be in harmony, the ice cream becomes the object of a proximate intention (*finis operis*) and through *consilium* and *consensus* means are sought, which are eventually chosen (*electio*). The final result of this intrinsic act is an extrinsic act (*imperium* issues into *usus*) and enjoying the ice cream. Intention is therefore an act of the will, by which an object presented by the intellect as desirable (*sub ratione boni*) becomes an end. *Electio* and *intentio* are not two different acts of the will; they are one act of the will in which two important structural moments can be analytically distinguished based on different objects. *Intentio* relates to the end and implicitly includes reference to means, *electio* relates to means and implicitly includes reference to the end. In fact the proximate and remote intention frame a certain plan of the action, within which the final end is attained by different means, where the concept of means is relative: certain means can be means to the end of the action, the action can be a means to the final end, and thus by transitivity the means of the action are means to the final end, the agent's end (*finis operantis*). Let us say that Peter wants to satisfy his craving for sweets (*finis operantis*). He could have an ice cream, some chocolate, or a cream cake. He decides for ice cream, which becomes the means of satisfying his craving and the end of the action (*finis operis*). If Peter is to be able to fulfil the end of his action, he must decide whether he will go out to buy ice cream, make it at home, or have it delivered by a delivery service. He decides to go out and buy ice cream. He must get dressed, take money, walk out of his apartment, go to the nearest confectioner's, order ice cream, pay for it and eat it. All these means are part of the plan (satisfied craving for sweets), which Peter fulfils by means of various acts; in the structure of this plan the individual intentions (to take keys, leave the house, pay for the ice cream...) are subordinate to the end of the action and ultimately to the agent's end.

In the modern period the American philosopher Michael R. Bratman advocates a similar role of intentions.[26] Bratman calls his influential theory of intentions **planning theory of intention**, because it assumes that humans are planning beings and in their plans and their fulfilment intentions play a central role. Intentions are not identical with plans, they are – as in Aquinas – mental states *sui generis* representing possible actions and directing their actualization.[27] Bratman rejects reducing intentions to the pair *desire* and *belief* and the methodological priority of intentions in action, which is typical e.g. for Elisabeth Anscombe in her seminal monograph *Intention*. Humans are planning creatures and their plans involve future actions, to which intentions are related; but this relationship is as yet not a relationship of an intention to an action already in progress, but to an action which the agent intends and to which he commits himself in some way. Intention is a certain kind of pro-attitude, like a desire. But there is an important difference which can be illustrated with a simple example:

- **Chocolate cake.** Peter has been tormented by a craving for chocolate cake all day long. At the same time he would like to be on a diet and shed a kilo or two. Although the craving for chocolate cake does not leave him all day long, he does not have any.

Peter has a pro-attitude to have chocolate cake. This attitude, desire, craving or wish does not leave him all day long, but he nonetheless does not have it. The desire itself does not comprise a commitment to action. It is merely a possible motive affecting action (*potential influencer of action*).[28] On the other hand, intention does comprise commitment to action: if Peter decided (made a plan) that instead of having cake he will take some exercise and this decision became the object of his intention, it already comprises a clear commitment to action. Intentions, unlike desires and wishes, control our action (Bratman says that they are *conduct-controlling*).

In a commitment to action two components can be identified: one is volitional, the other has to do with further deliberation on possible action and is therefore the domain of practical rationality. The volitional aspect of intentions (expressed in their commitment to action) is expressed precisely by being a certain pro-attitude controlling our action. The other aspect of intentions is manifested in relationship to practical reason and deliberations associated with action; it takes two forms. One aspect of intentions is certain stability. If I decide today that I will go to the library tomorrow, this intention (prior intention)[29] is stable and it is not necessary to continually deliberate whether I will or will not go to the library. Of course, it can well happen that a friend calls me, asks me to the theatre and I decide to change my plans for tomorrow. Stability of intentions does not mean that they cannot be changed, but that as a result of their commitment to action they don't lead to further deliberations whether to actualize that action or not. After all, intention is not a mere desire; it is a conscious decision to actualize some future action, whether in near or distant future.

A prior intention to some action can lead to further intentions, which are intentions of actions that become means to fulfilling this prior intention. Today I form the prior intention to go to the library tomorrow (*finis operis*) to read some new treatise on philosophy of action (*finis operantis*). Within practical deliberation I form further intentions out of this prior intention: e.g. the intention to leave home at nine a.m., the intention to go by bus no. 7, get the book and sit down in my favourite study hall. One future intention leads to further intentions, which are situate as means to attaining some end. Thomas Aquinas's reasoning was similar: he was well aware that means are part of fulfilling some end and these means can be individual human acts, each of which is finalized by some intention.

But practical rationality is not restricted to making judgments concerning further intentions in the optics of ends and means of fulfilling plans, of which intentions are key components. An important requirement on practical rationality is consistence, which can be expressed so that intentions restrict other intentions. A trivial example is the requirement forbidding that on the way to the library I go or not go by bus no. 7. A less trivial requirement is that I do not go there by bus no. 10 (which does not go to the library) or that I do not stop at a restaurant and spend the day drinking wine. According to Bratman the two dimensions of commitment explain the characteristic role of intentions in plans, which have not only an individual dimension, but also an intrapersonal and social one.

I will now attempt to capture the concepts I have introduced in the following definitions:

1   **Intentions**. Intentions are action-controlling propositional pro-attitudes, characterized by certain stability, which in the horizon of practical rationality constitute a point of departure for deliberations giving rise to further intentions.[30]

2   **Kinds of intentions**:

   a   **Prior intentions.** Prior intentions are intentions which precede action.

   b   **Intentions in action.** Intentions in action are intentions actualized in actions.

   c   **Further intentions.** Further intentions are intentions reached by practical deliberation based on prior intentions.

3   **Action.** Action can be characterized as actualization of intentions in action. The intentions in action determine the action and the conditions of its fulfilment.

4   **Three roles of intentions**:

   a   **Volitional**: intentions are pro-attitudes regulating our action. The volitional aspect expresses the relationship between intentions and action.

b   **In the horizon of practical rationality:** (i) relationship between intentions oriented to the future and further intentions, and (ii) restriction of further intention with respect to adopted intentions.

So intentions play three important roles: (i) they express commitment to action and to its fulfilment (to fulfilling its end), (ii) they place requirements on the formulation of further intentions (e.g. over the course of searching for means to the end) and (iii) they restrict further possible intentions and thereby possible actions.

Bratman believes – and with him some advocates of the principle of double effect – that these three roles of intentions can effectively distinguish between intended ends and consequences of actions on the one hand and the conscious but unintended consequences of the same action on the other. Let us take a look at two scenarios with which the American philosopher demonstrates his conviction[31]:

1   **Strategic bomber.** A strategic bomber wants to disable the enemy. He decides to bomb an ammunition warehouse. He knows well that in the vicinity of the ammunition warehouse there is a school with children. The strategic bomber's plan is not to kill children, nor is it a means to attaining his end. He carefully selects the means (kind of ammo), chooses a suitable moment for the raid and bombs the ammunition warehouse. The unintended, but nonetheless expected consequence of his action is the death of several children.

2   **Terror bomber.** The terror bomber's end is similar to the strategic bomber's end: he wants to disable the enemy. But he chose a different strategy: he wants to terrify the enemy. He therefore decides to bomb a school with children. He chooses suitable ammo, waits for a suitable moment and drops bombs on the target. The intended result of his action is the death of several children.

The two bombers' end is the same: they want to disable the enemy. But each chooses a different strategy (another plan of carrying out/fulfilling their end): the strategic bomber decided to bomb the ammunition warehouse, while his colleague wants to drop bombs on a school with children and terrify the enemy. Bratman believes that his three roles of intentions can explain why in the case of the strategic bomber the children's death was an unintended, though foreseen consequence, while in the case of the terror bomber the children's death is a means to fulfilling his end.

Let us begin with the first role of intentions: intentions to action are the starting point of a practical deliberation looking e.g. for the means to attaining an end. The strategic bomber will choose such bombs as will most effectively destroy the ammunition warehouse and will choose such time for the raid as will minimize the casualties among innocent civilians. His colleague, on the other hand, will choose such bombs as will cause the greatest calamity among the children, kill the greatest number of them, and will embark on his mission at a time when there are most children in the school.

Let us now take a look at the second role of intentions: restricting further intentions and thereby possible action. Let us imagine together with Bratman that the terror bomber is at the same time a commander over other units. Before departing on his mission he deliberates whether to send one of his units to the school. He is well aware that his soldiers will terrify the children and force them to flee; his mission would thus come to naught. For that reason he does no issue an order to move: in other words, his prior intention to action (killing children at school), together with his knowledge and convictions, determines the possible space of permitted and forbidden intentions and their actualizations in action.

Finally there is the last role of intentions: if a person S forms an intention to action, he commits himself to actualize this action and fulfil his end. The strategic bomber drops bombs on the ammo warehouse and when he flies over to check later on he finds that the ammunition warehouse has been destroyed and by a lucky coincidence the school is intact. He returns to the base; his mission is fulfilled and no child has been injured. His colleague also drops bombs on the school, but when he flies over to check later he finds that he missed his target. He returns and drops bombs again; if the children start running away from the school after the first bombing, he will target not only the school building but also the fleeing schoolchildren. When he has killed them all, or at least a sufficiently high number of them, he returns to the base; his mission is fulfilled.

Bratman's analysis of these two scenarios is similar to my analysis employing traditional scholastic concepts. The strategic and terror bombers' remote intentions (*finis operantis*) are the same: disabling the enemy (in the first case disabling physically – destroying an ammunition warehouse, in the second case disabling morally – killing young children). The remote intention structures the overall plan, in which further intentions and their fulfilment in action play the part of means. The strategic bomber decided to bomb a warehouse (*finis operis*), his proximate intention is therefore to carry out an action which will result in dropping bombs on the ammo warehouse. To fulfil the end of the action (proximate intention) and ultimately the agent's end (remote intention) he chooses different means: he chooses a plane, selects the corresponding type of bomb, a suitable moment to set off, a suitable flight and approach coarse, and eventually drops bombs on the target. The death of children (if it occurs) is not part of the plan, or a means to fulfilling an intention, whether proximate or remote. If by chance the children are unharmed he will be happy, but if some die he will accept it as a necessary evil: a necessary, unintended, but foreseen consequence of his action.

The strategic bomber's situation is quite different. As a means to fulfilling the architectonic end of his action (fulfilling the remote intention) he chooses the death of young schoolchildren (*finis operis*). Fulfilling his proximate intention therefore requires him to choose means in such a way that his action (dropping bombs on the school) will result in as many children casualties as possible. Their death is not a means to fulfilling the end of the action (*finis operis*), but to fulfilling the agent's end (*finis operantis*), since his action cannot be evaluated otherwise than as killing innocent schoolchildren. If he did not succeed in killing the children with the first bomb-dropping, the action itself would not be fulfilled and *ipso facto* neither would the overall plan; he would have to return and drop bombs again.

## The Closeness Problem

We first encountered the closeness problem in connection with the critical reaction of Phillipa Foot to H. L. A. Hart's proposal of the possibility to redescribe craniotomy. Hart claimed that the intention of a physician carrying out craniotomy need not be to kill the foetus, but merely to crush its head.[32] Foot reacted to this proposal with the following thought scenario[33]:

- **Speleologists.** A group of speleologists have unwisely allowed an obese member of the expedition to lead them out of a cave. But the mouth is very narrow, he gets stuck in it and cannot move. By an unlucky coincidence the water level starts rising in the cave and the speleologists are in danger of drowning. But they have dynamite and two options: either they will blow the cave mouth up (and kill the member who got stuck in it), or they will all drown.

The closeness problem appears when we describe the stuck speleologists' two possible intentions: (i) to open up the cave's mouth by blowing up and killing the obese colleague, or (ii) to open up the cave's mouth by blowing up the obese colleague and tearing his body to pieces. These two intentions are similar to the possible intentions of the physician from the craniotomy scenario: (i) to save the woman's life by crushing the foetus's head and killing it or (ii) to save the woman's life by merely crushing the foetus's head. Foot argues that the two events (blasting the obese speleologist and killing him and crushing the foetus's head and killing it) are too close to each other for us to separate them. In this way the closeness problem was born, which is still regarded as the most serious objection to the applicability of the principle of double effect. We have already had the opportunity to encounter it in this chapter several times, now the time has come to deal with it systematically.

In fact, the closeness problem expresses the concern that there is no principal way of distinguishing between the means and the unintended consequences of human action. Is the obese speleologist's death a means to fulfilling his colleagues' end? It appears to be if their intention is characterized as "blow up and move away the stuck colleague," it probably is not if it is described as "blast the stuck colleague to pieces." Blasting the colleague to pieces, if it is regarded as the action's end, has an undesirable consequence: his death. But this death, say advocates of the closeness problem, is not intended, whether as the end of the action or as the agents' end. But it is highly unintuitive that the principle of double effect could not be applied to an action characterized by the intention "blow up and kill the colleague," while it could be applied to an action falling under the intention "blast the colleague to pieces."

In the following text I will first describe several attempts to solve the closeness problem; then I will attempt to present my own solution, which has already been indicated over the course of the exposition in the preceding part of this chapter and in the previous chapter.

Can the closeness problem be solved with the help of **Bratman's theory of three roles of intentions**? Ezio di Nucci claims that it cannot.[34] According to Bratman intentions have three roles:

1  They commit the agent to fulfil the action's end.
2  They lead to further intentions.
3  They determine the scope of licit intentions.

Let us say that the end of the speleologists' action is blasting their colleague to pieces by dynamite and thereby clearing up the cave's mouth and saving their lives. The final end of the action is saving own lives (*finis operantis*), the chosen means (of the action) is blasting the colleague to pieces (not killing him). Di Nucci claims that Bratman's three roles of intentions will not prove that the end of the action (object of the remote intention) is in fact killing the obese speleologist, as advocates of the principle of double effect would request. Quite the contrary: it will distinguish blasting the stuck speleologist to pieces as a permitted means from killing him, which is merely an unintended consequence. The speleologists decided to blast the colleague to pieces, they must therefore try to fulfil their end (first role of intentions). If the load they place is too weak and the explosion does not open up the cave's mouth to a sufficient extent, they will have to place another load and strive to blast the stuck body more thoroughly. The action's end leads to further intentions (second role of intentions): the speleologists must figure out where to place the load so that it will blast the body to pieces, when and how to set it off, they must hide in time before the explosion, etc. By the goal of their enterprise the speleologists' action will restrict other possible acts (and *ipso facto* intentions, the third role of intentions) that could hinder blasting the body of the unlucky expedition member to pieces. In this description the obese speleologist's death does not appear even once: it speaks of blasting his body to pieces, which is the end of the speleologists' action. According to Di Nucci Bratman's three roles of intentions can, paradoxically, be turned against advocates of the principle of double effect, because they make it possible to distinguish between blasting the body to pieces as a means to the final end and killing the speleologist, which appears here as a mere unintended negative consequence.

Let us now focus on Bratman's example of the terror bomber:

- **Terror bomber.** The terror bomber's end is similar to the strategic bomber's end: he wants to disable the enemy. But he has chosen a different strategy: he wants to terrify the enemy. He therefore decides to drop bombs on a school with children. He chooses suitable ammo, waits for a suitable moment and drops bombs on the target. The intended result of his action is the death of children.

Again Di Nucci claims that it is sufficient to redefine the bomber's intention: this time he does not want to kill children to fulfil his action's end. He will be quite content if the children look dead; so his end is not their death, but a state that will terrify the enemy. The death of children does not function here as the action's end, but as an unintended consequence. It seems as a fairly arbitrary move, an unrealizable thought scenario, in which we are toying with the possibilities of our imagination (we want the children to look dead but we don't want to kill them, although we know that if we make them look dead, they will really die). Di Nucci quotes the following historical command to British RAF pilots of 1941:

> The ultimate aim of the attack on a town area is to break the morale of the population which occupies it. To ensure this we must achieve two things: first, we must make the town physically uninhabitable and, secondly, we must make the people conscious of constant personal danger. The immediate aim, is therefore, twofold, namely to produce (i) destruction, and (ii) the fear of death.[35]

Not a word of civilian deaths. But there is no doubt that the destruction of a whole city neighbourhood will result in many casualties: can the principle of double effect be applied to this scenario? According to Di Nucci the terror bomber could speak in a similar manner: the end of his action is not to kill children, but to terrify the population by making the children look dead; their death is not his end, even though he is aware that by dropping the bombs and fulfilling his end he will kill them. But their death will be an unintended and foreseen consequence. On Di Nucci's view Bratman's three roles of intentions will again paradoxically support the conclusion that the bomber did not intend the children's death: he will strive to make the children look dead. If he does not succeed in the first raid he will come back; but not to kill the children – to make them look dead. He will choose the bomb in accordance with this end, and if he decides not to send another unit to the school, he will do so not because the terrified children would run away and he could not kill them, but because they would run away and his plan (to make them look dead) could not be realized. So Bratman's theory of intentions does not solve the closeness problem: it cannot principally distinguish between means and merely unintended consequences.

But Bratman's theory of intentions is also engaged by T. A. Cavanaugh in his monograph *Double Effect Reasoning*, where he applies it to the case of craniotomy.[36] He regards crushing the head as the end of the physician's action: the physician chooses instruments that will enable him to crush the head effectively and crushing it is a means to saving the mother's life. According to Di Nucci the problem is that in his description of craniotomy Cavanaugh does not use the description "kills": the physician chooses some means and a sequence of operations, whose final effect is crushing the foetus's head. But he does not solve the closeness problem, because he does not prove that it is not possible to intend to "crush the foetus's head" and "save the mother's life" without intending to "kill the foetus."

In his work *The Act Itself*[37] Jonathan Bennett presents another effort to solve the closeness problem. Let us imagine that the physician is crushing a foetus's head. It is apparently possible to consider a possible world in which crushing the head is not identical with killing the foetus (such a scenario is logically thinkable, it does not involve a logical contradiction). But in our actual world something like that is unthinkable: an ordinary person (Bennett uses the phrase *plain man*) will find it inconceivable that a physician could crush a foetus's head and not kill it at the same time.[38] So Bennett tentatively solves the closeness problem by means of the concept of inconceivability associated with an ordinary person: crushing the head is killing the foetus; bombing children is killing them; immersing a knife in the heart is killing a man.

This solution's problem lies at its very core: it is difficult to say who is an ordinary person and it is no less possible to determine what an ordinary person regards as conceivable or inconceivable. Must an ordinary person regard as inconceivable that blasting a man to pieces is not killing him? Must an ordinary person regard as inconceivable that to make a city neighbourhood uninhabitable by bombing it is not killing civilians? The concepts of ordinary person and inconceivability are too vague to solve the closeness problem.

Another interesting solution of the closeness problem was penned by Ralph Wedgwood.[39] Wedgwood engages Bratman's theory of intentions and distinguishes between (i) the motive governing the action and explaining the corresponding intentions (I change the switch to save five workers on the rail), and (ii) the intention itself. Intentions are mental states that cannot be conceived in a Cartesian fashion as some labels with which we designate our actions by verbal descriptions. Intentions are essential parts of action, since action is an actualization of the corresponding intentions governing the individual steps (when I want to scramble eggs, I must take them out of the fridge, break them, scramble them, prepare the pan, stir the eggs in the pan, watch their consistence and state and take them off the stove in time). According to Wedgwood this implies that an intention's content comprises events that are within the agent's control: if someone decides to blow up a plane to destroy compromising materials, his intention comprises not only destroying the documents, because the character of the action implies that blowing up the plane means that not only the documents will be destroyed, but the whole plane as well. An intention is not a mental label: if someone blows up a plane in order to destroy documents, he cannot claim that he is describing his action merely as "destroying documents" ("I did not intend to blow up the plane, I only wanted to destroy the documents"). An action is an actualization of an intention, which can be inferred precisely from what action was actualized. Through this conception of intentions Wedgwood defines the principle of double effect as follows[40]:

- **The principle of double effect (Wedgwood).** There are usually stronger reasons against the actualization of an action whose bad consequences are intended than against an action whose consequences are not intended.

Note that this version of the principle of double effect is not situated in an absolutist ethics, i.e., in an ethics that regards some types of action *ex obiecto* as intrinsically evil and altogether excluded. Wedgwood merely says that we usually have stronger reasons not to actualize an action whose bad consequences are intended, as compared to an action in which bad consequences are not intended. If I understand him correctly, we have stronger reasons not to actualize craniotomy as compared to hysterectomy, which does not mean, however, that craniotomy may not be actualized in any circumstances.

How does this author's theory of intentions in the context of his version of the principle of double effect solve the closeness problem? Let us recall the scenario with the obese man on the bridge above the tram rail. Beyond the bridge in the direction of the tram's course five persons are working, X is by the side of the obese man on the bridge and notices that an uncontrollable tram is rushing towards them. X deliberates on possible action and realizes that if he pushes the fat man off the bridge in the tram's path, the collision will stop it and save five lives. Many advocates of the principle of double effect would claim that X's intention must be "to kill the fat man" since pushing him off the bridge is nothing other than killing him. But Wedgwood disagrees: intentions cannot be verbally described at will, we must account for what X in fact did: X pushed the fat man off the bridge in order to save five lives. X's plan did not include searching for means of effectively killing him, if he miraculously survived X would not try to kill him (further intention). Does it mean that the principle of double effect cannot be applied to this scenario?

Let us imagine that someone is knocked down by a tram. Every reasonable human being with some basic awareness of morality and the ability to make *ceteris paribus* moral generalizations (e.g. generalizations of the type "when a human being is knocked down by a tram, it usually results in grave injury or death") will regard it as bad news. Wedgwood makes use of this observation to define a bad state of affairs[41]:

1  **Bad state of affairs.** A certain state of affairs S is a bad state of affairs if the following two conditions are satisfied:

   a  Virtuous agent[42] A, guided by knowing the relevant *ceteris paribus* moral generalizations, forms expectations of S due to which he will evaluate S as bad news;
   b  The state of affairs S is actualized more or less in the way A expected.

Let us return to the scenario with the obese man on the bridge. X's intention need not be, Wedgwood claims, to kill him: X needs to push him off the bridge to save the five workers on the rails by means of collision with the tram, his death is not part of X's plan. But every virtuous agent can form a *ceteris paribus* moral generalization of the type "pushing a man in the path of a tram will result in collision with the tram and cause grave injury or even death"; and that is without doubt bad news. If X pushes the obese man and the tram runs into him, then this state of affairs (man knocked down by a tram) is a bad state of affairs, and that is why the intention actualized by the action is also bad.

Wedgwood solves Foot's scenario with the obese speleologist stuck in the cave's mouth analogically. The speleologists can really intend merely to blast his body to pieces, but "to be blasted to pieces" is a bad state of affairs (more traditionally one could speak of physical evil), and *ipso facto* the corresponding intention in action is also bad.

So the principle of double effect saying that there usually are stronger reasons against actualizing an action whose bad consequences are intended can be applied to both scenarios. We have stronger reasons not to push the obese man off the bridge than to change the switch, and we have stronger reasons not to blast the body of the stuck speleologist than to carry out another action that will result in a less bad state of affairs.

I personally believe that proponents of the principle of double effect can approach solving the closeness problem in two independent ways. One is inspired by Wedgwood's solution, developed independently also by Christopher Kaczor in his monograph *Proportionalism and the Natural Law Tradition*.[43] Let us now return to **craniotomy**: the physician must crush the foetus's head to save the labouring mother's life. The physician can claim: my intention was not to kill the foetus, merely to crush its head. I am willing to grant that my action is true under the description "crushing the foetus's head," but with respect to my intention it is not true under the description "killing the foetus." The sophisticated physician can also point out that it is necessary to distinguish between the physical description of an action (action *in genere naturae*) and the action as a human act (*in genere moris*); his intention was merely to crush the head, which is why his deed ought to be evaluated as crushing the head, not as killing the foetus.

Let us say that we grant the physician's reasoning and agree that his c-intention is to crush the foetus's head, while his f-intention is to save the mother's life. Does this imply some unfavourable conclusion for the validity of the principle of double effect? Many of its opponents automatically claim that it does: if the physician's c-intention is not to kill the foetus, then he does not use the foetus's death as a means to fulfilling his f-intention. That is without doubt true (if we grant the validity of the physician's reasoning), but it is not equivalent to claiming that the physician is not using a morally illicit means. In other words, the claim "the physician does not fulfil his f-intention by means of killing the foetus (fulfilling the c-intention)" does not imply the claim "the physician fulfils the f-intention in a morally licit way." The physician crushes the foetus's head and irreversibly damages its brain. Even if we grant that he did not intend its death, he must have intended crashing its head. That is an encroachment on the physical integrity of the human body, mutilation, which in this case is not justified by any reason. Let us now take a look at the following scenario:

- **Amputation.** A strong diabetes patient's lower limb is gangrenous and after rigorous consideration physicians reach the conclusion that it must be amputated. They inform the patient and on obtaining his informed consent perform the operation.

In a certain respect the amputation is similar to crushing the head: the result of the action is a physical evil (missing limb, crushed head). But there is a major difference: the amputation will not be labelled as mutilation, as it was necessitated by the patient's state of health and he consented to it. Not every physical evil brought about on the human body (missing limbs, organs, deformations of the body) is mutilation: mutilation implies the non-existence of a reason for action (or an accident, e.g. when someone is mutilated by falling down stairs). In the sphere of human action mutilation implies immoral action. The amputation of a lower limb is not a case of mutilation, since it was necessary to save the patient's life. Crushing the head most certainly is mutilation of the foetus, because it was not required by the foetus's state of health. Let us now take a look at another scenario:

- **Mutilation.** Physicians urgently need a healthy heart for their VIP patient. A young man who comes to the hospital for a routine check-up turns out to be a suitable donor. The physicians put him to sleep, take out his heart and transplant it to the recipient.

Let us grant that the physicians' intention need not be to "kill the donor" but merely to "take out his heart." Let us even grant that the physicians connect the donor to a device replacing his heart and disconnect him some time later (they could thus argue that they did not commit *killing* but *letting die*). Extracting the heart from a healthy patient, which is not necessitated by his state of health (e.g. an operation on the heart) is a straightforward example of mutilation, regardless of the fact that the obtained heart will save someone's life. An analogical judgment can be made in the case of craniotomy: crushing the foetus's head is necessary to save the mother's life (as the heart was necessary to save the VIP patient). But the foetus is healthy and vital, crushing its head is not necessitated by its state of health. So it is a case of mutilation and for advocates of the principle of double effect mutilation is a morally illicit way of acting. Here the first condition of the principle of double effect applies: the action itself must be at least morally indifferent. Crushing the head is mutilating the foetus and as such is an instance of morally bad (incorrect) action. There is no point considering whether crushing the head is a means of saving the mother's life, since this applies only to actions that pass the first criterion.

Let us now take a look at other difficult examples. In all cases we will grant that the intention is not to kill a human being.

**Obese man on the bridge.** The c-intention is to push the man off the bridge into the tram's path, the f-intention is to save five human lives. It cannot be claimed that the c-intention consists merely in pushing the man off the bridge: if he dropped down when the tram had passed or outside its course, the action (stopping the tram) would fail. The man is pushed off the bridge so that he collides with the tram, which stops against his massive body. Fulfilling the c-intention is a means to fulfilling the f-intention, waiting for a suitable moment, grasping the man (e.g. by the legs) and throwing him over to the tram's path are means of fulfilling the c-intention. Already over the course of realizing the c-intention the obese man's rights are violated: he is made a means to an end, pushed against his will off the bridge into the tram's path. The collision with the tram need not result in death, but together with the fall it will without doubt cause him serious injuries. So actualizing the c-intention in action is a morally illicit means of fulfilling the f-intention. No problem arises here for proponents of the principle of double effect: it is not applicable to this situation.

**Obese speleologist.** The speleologists claim that their c-intention is to blast the man to pieces and so open up the cave's mouth to save their lives (f-intention). Blasting to pieces, even if it did not result in death (the man could lose all four limbs and still live), is a serious encroachment on bodily integrity, mutilation, and as such illicit. Again no problem arises here for proponents of the principle of double effect: it is not applicable in this case either.

**Terror bomber.** The terror bomber differs from his strategic counterpart in that he wants to disable the enemy (f-intention) by terror (subordinate f-intention). He chooses suitable bombs, a moment when there are most children in school, and drops the bombs on the school. But he could claim that he did not want to kill the children (c-intention), but merely to make them look dead. How could he attain that? Apparently only by causing such injuries that they will die. Although he will claim that their death was merely an unintended consequence of the intention to "make the children look dead," he can nonetheless attain that only by causing them serious injuries (if he merely put the children to sleep, he would not convince anyone that they are dead, i.e., he would not fulfil his end to make the children look dead). So the means of fulfilling the f-intention is morally illicit, it is again a case of mutilation and again no problem arises for proponents of the principle of double effect: they will evaluate the bomber's action as morally unacceptable *ex obiecto*.

In my view this strategy of solving the closeness problem is acceptable, but it is not the only one and in my view not the best one. We can also focus on the question of determining the content of intentions and the rationality of their ascription. As Elizabeth Anscombe notes, intentions are not mental labels accompanied by a linguistic description, which can be *ex post* attached to the action. Thomas Aquinas, Joseph Boyle, John Finnis, Ralph Wedgwood, or Michael Bratman would agree that human actions are actualizations of the corresponding intentions in action and cannot be characterized only based on the agents' verbal description. Intentions are ascribed to agents on the assumption that they are rational agents and their action has some rationally expressible structure (it is a certain rational plan). Bratman's theory of the three roles of intentions is in fact an expression of the rationality of plans: if we intend X, we must try to realize X, X restricts further intentions (and actions) and X is the starting point – in the horizon of practical rationality – to forming further intentions. But ascribing intentions is not enclosed in the subjectivity of rational agents: it always requires reference to extramental reality. Let us recall the example of the thief who claims that he was not stealing (theft was not his c-intention). Let us say that X decides to take his neighbour's watch. X knows very well that the watch does not belong to him, that it belongs to the neighbour (here is a clear reference to the order of reason, which enters the specification of the c-intention). He also cannot be ignorant of the fact that the neighbour has not given the watch to him, that he has not resigned on his particular right of ownership. Nonetheless X makes use of the situation, takes the watch and hides it well. When he has been found out he can defend himself as follows: my intention was to take the watch, but I never once thought of theft, I would never do that. Despite that we can legitimately ascribe the intention to steal to him based on the assumption of basic rationality (the thief knew that he was taking someone else's property, he planned that and realized his plan, whereby his intention to take the watch led up to other intentions and prevented the realization of other possible intentions) and we will correctly characterize his action as theft.

This ascription of intentions is a basic requirement of rationality. If it was not possible, the objective character of actions *qua* human actions would cease to exist and together with it the possibility of their rational and interpersonal interpretation. Let us imagine that over the course of a lecture a student lifts up her hand and when the lecturer asks her to speak she says: "But I did not want to speak, I just wanted to have my hand up." Of course, a student can want to have her hand up, but in the given context raising a hand means requesting the opportunity to speak and it is quite rational to ascribe this intention to her, while the explanation that she was not in fact asking for an opportunity to speak will be regarded as irrational. The thief can also claim that he really did not want to steal, but his claim contradicts what he has done: stole a watch. It is quite rational to ascribe the intention to steal to him, condemn his action as immoral and hand him over to the criminal police for investigation.

Let us now take another look at the individual scenarios.

**Craniotomy.** The physician claims that his intention (c-intention) was not to kill the child, merely to crush its head in order to save the mother's life (f-intention). If we think of him as a rational agent, we can assume some fundamental awareness of the relationship between an action (crushing the head) and its result (death of the foetus). But the physician's situation does not allow us to judge him merely as an "ordinary" rational agent: he has good knowledge of anatomy, physiology, extensive experience from his practice. In this situation he is not a merely rational agent, but an expert rational agent. It is irrational to claim that an "ordinary" person does not know that crushing a foetus's head is a way of killing it and it is *a fortiori* irrational to think that it is not clear to an expert physician. The physician simply knows that his action is a way of killing the foetus and it is quite rational to ascribe the corresponding intention to him, which he fulfils by crushing the head.

**Obese man on the bridge.** In the case of the obese man on the bridge the situation is more complex, because it seems possible to grant that pushing the man into the tram's path is not necessarily killing him. The problem with this proposal consists in that it is irrational and based merely on a vague possibility: the possibility that the man survives the fall off the bridge and survives also the collision with the dashing tram. A murderer who stuck a knife in his victim's skull could argue in a similar fashion: there is a certain possibility that the victim survives, but that itself does not ground the possibility not to ascribe the intention to kill to the murderer. Of course the man on the bridge does not want to kill the obese man in the same way as a murderer wants to kill his victim: but he wants to push him off the bridge into the path of the rapidly approaching tramcar. In such a situation a rational agent would assume that falling off the bridge and colliding with the tram will result in death (it will not result in death only in quite extraordinary cases); it is a rational *ceteris paribus* moral generalization. This justifies us in ascribing the intention to kill to the agent, even if the intention was merely implicit, non-verbalized and necessitated by the conditions of rationality.

**Obese speleologist.** This situation is similar to craniotomy: it is irrational to claim that blasting a human body to pieces is not a way of killing. Every rational agent deliberating the plan of his action knows that placing dynamite to the body of a human being and detonating it will blast him to pieces and kill him. If someone claims that his intention was not to kill the obese speleologist, he understands intentions only as verbal characterizations of his mental states. But intentions in action are mental components of actualized actions and their imputability is not based only on how the agent characterizes them: the character of the action itself is also important. Blasting a human body to pieces with dynamite is killing the man, it is killing realized by a certain means and as such was guided by a corresponding intention.

**Terror bomber.** As in the preceding scenarios the corresponding intention must be characterized not only "from the inside" based on the bomber's statements but also with respect to the action carried out. Dropping bombs on the school is a means of killing children and it is irrational to claim that the bomber in fact does not need the children to be dead, he only needs (and intends) them to look dead. A rational agent knows that if he drops bombs on a school he will cause extensive casualties. Furthermore, the bomber is an expert rational agent with combat experience, he selects bombs that will hit the school most effectively and cause greatest harm (he wants to demoralize the enemy). It is very difficult to claim that he chooses bombs which will merely make the children look dead: there are no such bombs. Bombs kill people, and if someone drops them on people, they are trying to kill them, no matter how they describe their action.

I personally find that the closeness problem is in some respect a pseudoproblem, based on an overly subjectivist conception of intentions. When intentions are interpreted as the controlling elements of human action, their correct description must derive not only from the agents' subjectivity (and the possibility to quite arbitrarily describe their c- and f-intentions), but also from the objective states of affairs related to the order of reason. A thief commits theft (type of action), if he wrongfully and knowingly appropriates the property of another person; he can easily claim that the word "theft" did not appear in his mind at all. A murderer wrongfully takes the life of another person; it is murder even if he claimed that he merely wanted to insert a knife in his victim's heart. The speleologists intentionally kill their stuck colleague, even if they object that they only wanted to blast him to pieces with dynamite.

I do not claim, though, that I have solved the problem of closeness, and I'm aware that there has been an ongoing debate about it without any consensus in sight.[44] However, analogically, as in the case of the Loop scenario, there are and always will be some borderline cases in which the applicability of the principle of double effect will be disputed. As I stated above, I consider this to be a natural part of our moral lives and our theorizing about morality. My aim was, in a way, modest: I tried to show how advocates of the principle of double effect can tackle these problematic cases, and I hope that my efforts were not wholly unsuccessful.

## Conclusion

This last chapter systematically summarized and deepened the understanding of the principle of double effect and presented a defence of the principle against most common objections. To conclude I will now briefly return to the four conditions which together specify the necessary and sufficient conditions authorizing the actualization of an action with good and bad consequences.[45]

**Nature of the act.** The act must be good or at least morally indifferent (independently of its consequences). This condition constitutes a selecting mechanism of applying the core of the principle of double effect (the bad effect must not be intended). It can also be expressed conditionally: if $\varphi$ is an at least morally indifferent act, then the core of the principle of double effect can be applied to $\varphi$. Some versions of the principle of double effect merely state that we usually have stronger reasons not to carry out an action whose bad consequences are intended. This version is stronger, since it assumes that some acts are of their nature (*ex obiecto*) morally illicit regardless of their consequences. These are deeds forbidden by negative moral norms valid always and everywhere (*semper et ad semper*). Individual authors can differ in enumeration and specification of these moral norms and *ipso facto ex obiecto* illicit actions. I personally regard the moral norm forbidding the killing of innocent human beings and morally illicit encroachments on their psychophysical constitution (e.g. mutilation) as essential. Let us take a look at the following scenario:

- **Naval battle.** Over the course of a naval battle a ship with civilians on board is sunk. Lifeboats are launched and most of the crew and passengers climb in them. But the commander of the enemy submarine wants to demoralize the enemy and orders all lifeboats to be shot to pieces with machine guns.

The submarine commander deliberates shooting the boats to pieces (c-intention) to undermine the enemy moral (f-intention). The first condition of the principle of double effect stipulates that it is a case of breaking a moral norm forbidding the killing of innocent human beings, which is why a deliberation based on the principle of double effect does not apply to it. It is not necessary to consider the good and bad effects: from the nature of its c-intention the action is morally illicit. Let us compare that with another scenario:

- **Collision with iceberg.** A pleasure boat collides with an iceberg. The captain has several seconds to decide: either he has watertight partitions closed and saves most passengers, or he does not have them closed and most will die in the ocean's icy waters. If he closes the partitions, several crew members will not reach safety and will drown. Nonetheless, the captain decides to act and has the partitions closed.

In this scenario the captain's c-intention is to have the watertight partitions closed in order to (f-intention) save the passengers and most of the crew. His action is at least morally indifferent, so the principle of double effect can be applied: the good effect is intended (it is the object of the f-intention, or motive of the action), the bad effect (the death of several crew members) is not the object of any of the intentions; it is unintended but foreseen (the captain knows that several crew members will not reach safety in time). But the closeness problem seems to appear here again: if crushing the foetus's head is a way of killing it and bombarding children is also a way of killing them, is not ultimately closing the partition a way of killing the sailors? Is it therefore not correct to claim that the captain killed the crew members (his action was not closing the partitions but killing the sailors)?

I believe the answer is negative. Crushing the foetus's head is killing it. But closing the partition does not constitute killing. If all the sailors reached safety no one would die. But it is difficult to claim that we can crush a foetus's head and nonetheless not kill it. Analogically it is difficult to imagine that we could drop bombs on a school and not kill any children. We will regard the statement "I did not want to kill the children, I wanted them to look dead" as inadequate, since the description "to look dead" comprises that the children really are dead (we merely claim that we did not intend that). But closing the partition does not imply the sailors' death in the same way as crushing a foetus's head or pushing a man in the path of a tram implied death. Here we can effectively apply Bratman's theory of the three roles of intentions: (i) The ship's captain wants to close the partitions and if one of them e.g. got stuck he would take all the steps necessary to enable it to be closed. But he most certainly will not try to detain the sailors where they are so that they would drown. (ii) In the horizon of practical rationality the intention "to close the partitions" leads up to further intentions: the captain orders the respective sailor to set the partition-closing mechanism in motion. At the same time he orders all crew members to show up on board as soon as possible. (iii) Some intentions will be forbidden to the captain (for reasons of consistence of practical rationality): e.g. all intention whose actualization would prevent effective closure of the partitions. But intentions due to which he would succeed in saving as many sailors as possible from the part of the ship that will be hermetically closed off by the partitions will not be forbidden to him.

So the captain's intention cannot be characterized (c-intention) as killing the sailors: their death is a consequence of actualizing the c-intention, but it is an unintended consequence. Of course, someone could claim that the captain's action could be characterized by two descriptions: (i) closing the partitions and (ii) killing the sailors. But even if we agreed with this theory of action individualization, what is morally relevant for most proponents of the principle of double effect is the *ex obiecto* description of the action, from the nature of the c-intention (not from action descriptions). Closing the partition is an actualization of the corresponding c-intention, while the sailors' death is an unintended consequence of the action.

Let us now take a look at the second condition: **The agent's intention.** The agent intends only the good effect. The bad effect can be foreseen, tolerated and admitted, but it must not be intended. We have thoroughly dealt with this condition in the preceding chapters and its key significance ought to be sufficiently clear. David S. Oderberg illustrates it with two examples, which show that he applies the principle of double effect in a way different to what I have proposed. Let us take a look at one of them[46]:

- **Election.** The manager of an election campaign wants to make sure that his candidate is elected and with his consent decides to distribute money among poor electors to make sure that his end is fulfilled.

Oderberg believes that the action (distributing money among the poor) is by nature at least morally indifferent; so the principle of double effect can be applied. The action's bad effect is the election of a corrupting candidate; the good effect is the improvement of the poor electors' financial situation. The good effect is not attained by means of the bad effect, but the bad effect is intended (the manager gives out money to ensure his candidate is elected). That is why Oderberg evaluates the considered action as morally illicit, because it violates the second condition of the principle of double effect. I agree with the author in that the action described in this thought scenario is morally unacceptable, but I disagree with his reasoning. Oderberg claims that the action (distributing money among the poor) is at least morally indifferent. I believe that he erroneously evaluated its nature: although he acknowledges that moral evaluation of human actions depends on *fontes moralitatis*, i.e., on the object, end and circumstances, here he evaluates the action merely *ex obiecto*. The election manager hands out money to ensure that poor electors vote for his candidate. The f-intention here co-specifies the nature of the action *in genere moris*: it is not mere giving money to the poor, but corruption. Corruption is neither morally good not indifferent: so it involves a type of action excluded by the first condition of the principle of double effect, not the second one.

The third condition of the principle of double effect (the bad effect must not be a **means** to attaining the good effect) is contained in the second condition and its significance ought to be clear from this chapter and the preceding ones. Let us therefore now take a look at only one example:

- **Angry wife.** Peter is in hospital, and his friend John decides to visit him. John knows that at Peter's bedside he will meet his wife, and he is also well aware that she does not like him, and his visit will make her very angry. But John wants to cheer Peter up by coming to visit him, not by making his wife angry. That is why he sets out to visit him.

John knows that his action (visiting a friend in hospital) will have two effects: one good (he will make his friend happy), the other one bad (he will make his wife angry). But the good effect is not attained by means of the bad one; the third condition of the principle of double effect is satisfied. The action itself is morally at least indifferent (we would say that it is even good), John does not intend to make Peter's wife angry (the second condition is satisfied) and finally there is a commensurate reason to actualize the action (making an ill friend in hospital happy will be regarded as a stronger reason to action that the fact that his healthy wife will get angry; assuming that the wife's anger will not make the patient too upset).

We now come to the last, fourth condition of the principle of double effect: The good effect must **outweigh** the bad effect. It is often erroneously conceived; e.g. Peter Singer is critical of the principle of double effect, because in his view in applying the last condition it in fact employs a consequentialist comparison of good and bad effects. But the preceding exposition should have made clear that this criticism is quite ungrounded. I understand its structure as follows:

- Proponents of the principle of double effect engage deontological ethics and reject consequentialism.

- But applying the principle of double effect is a case of employing a consequentialist calculation of good and bad effects.
- Therefore proponents of the principle of double effect are inconsistent.

But premise 2 is false, at least for two reasons. Consequentialists mostly refuse to acknowledge that intentions play a significant direct role in evaluating human actions, while for proponents of the principle of double effect intentions (c-intentions and f-intentions) are crucial. Further, applying the principle of double effect in its classical form assumes the existence of actions which are *ex obiecto* illicit: killing an innocent human being, mutilation, corruption, etc. Consequentialists, like Peter Singer and his preference utilitarianism, do not acknowledge the concept of *ex obiecto* illicit actions: whether some action is correct or incorrect does not depend on the nature of the act, but on comparing the relevant consequences with reference to some evaluating key (in Singer's case these are vaguely defined preferences). Furthermore, the fourth condition of the principle of double effect does not comprise only comparing effects (moral arithmetic of the type one life exchanged for two), as the following scenario shows:

- **Closing the partitions**. A ship has run on a rock and is in danger of sinking. The captain must decide whether and which partitions to close to save the lives of most passengers and crew. He can close a partition that will imprison five sailors, or a partition that will imprison three passengers. The captain decides to close the partition that will imprison five sailors; they drown.

The moral arithmetic in this case is clear: five human lives to three. Singer would probably claim that there is only one morally correct action in this situation: to save five human lives at the expense of three. But the situation is more complex: the captain and the sailors are obliged to protect the passengers. The captain and the crew have pledged that and accepted the associated risks. The passengers, on the other hand, have no such general moral obligation to the sailors. Based on that pledge the captain is obliged to protect primarily the passengers, which is why he decides to close the partition that will cut off the sailors' way to safety.

Applying the fourth condition is not easy and it is always necessary to apply knowledge of the particular situation and balance out all the moral factors coming into play. But it is possible to state several general rules specifying it.[47] The **first rule** states that the graver the bad effect of action $\varphi$ is, the graver the reasons for actualizing $\varphi$ must be. Over the course of a stomatological treatment the dentist causes pain, the reasons for his action need not be as strong as the reasons for an action whose consequence is not merely pain, but also the death of human beings. The **second rule** states that if physical evil occurred even without $\varphi$, the reasons for carrying out $\varphi$ are weaker. An example can be hysterectomy: the uterus of a pregnant woman is affected with cancer, and if the operation is not performed, the mother will die together with the foetus. So the foetus would die regardless of whether the physician performs hysterectomy or not. So in applying the fourth condition of the principle of double effect there is not only the moral arithmetic of one life (the foetus) for another (the woman), but also the fact that the foetus would die anyway. The **third rule** specifies that if $\varphi$ leads up to a bad effect that would otherwise not occur, the reasons for the action must be stronger than if the bad state of affairs (physical evil) was independent of $\varphi$ (as in the case of hysterectomy). If the casual passer-by did not pull the lever, the tram would not change direction and would not kill one worker. This bad state of affairs (death of a human being – physical evil) would otherwise not occur, so there must be stronger reasons for the action (in the case of the casual passer-by it is mere moral arithmetic: five lives against one). The **fourth rule** stipulates the relationship between the reasons for action and the probability of the bad effect: if it is merely probable, then the reasons for action can be weaker. The **fifth rule** expresses an important deontological condition: there must be stronger reasons to actualize action $\varphi$, if there is some prior obligation (for the agent) not to actualize $\varphi$. The police are obliged to prevent crime, e.g. burglary. But human life is more valuable, so if fire breaks out in a gold shop, the police will try to save the shop assistant, even though it will mean that they will not prevent the shop being burgled. Finally the last, **sixth rule** specifies that if it is possible to attain the action's end in an alternative way which does not lead up to a bad consequence or leads up to less serious bad consequences, the agent is obliged to choose this alternative action. If it is possible first to save the foetus and only then extract the uterus affected with cancer, the physician ought to choose that.

I have presented several arguments for the principle of double effect. They will certainly not convince consequentialists that consequentialism is wrong; but that was not my goal. They do show, however, that if we accept certain assumptions (the role of intentions in moral evaluation, moral definition of human action by means of c- and f-intentions), then the principle of double effect is an intelligible and rational principle of the admissibility of actions having not only good effects. Since virtually all actions have good and bad effects, the principle of double effect enters practical deliberation in a very broad spectrum of cases and allows us to decide in relatively simple and more difficult situations. But it is not a mathematical principle whose rules of application are precisely specified: as in the whole of ethics, practical experience, prudence, personal maturity and practical wisdom are required to decide in uncertain and difficult situations of human life. In my view the main reason to accept the validity of the principle of double effect is fairly simple: if some action has a bad consequence which is intended, then our will is motivated by evil.[48] Intentions express not only what we intend, but also the degree of our involvement as rational human beings in the production of the relevant effect.[49] Let us recall the example of the two dentists: the normal dentist and the sadistic dentist. Both cause their patients pain: the former unintentionally, the pain is merely foreseen as a consequence of the intervention, whereas the latter causes pain intentionally. Clearly the two are guided by different motives and a different degree of involvement in the production of the negative effect, which is morally relevant. It matters whether someone causes pain intentionally or merely permits it as a necessary component of the consequences of his action. The validity of the principle of double effect is based precisely on this distinction and its moral relevance. Human action is not black and white; virtually every act has good and bad consequences. It is essential that the bad consequences are not the objects of intentions: precisely that is what makes us good and virtuous persons even in uneasy life situations and choices.

## Notes

1 Cf. Tom L. Beauchamp and James F. Childress, *Principles of Biomedical Ethics*. 4th ed. (New York: Oxford University Press, 1994), 207.
2 Ezio di Nucci, *Ethics without Intention* (London: Bloomsbury, 2014), 16–17.
3 Cf. Ezio di Nucci, "*Ethics without Intention*," 27. Davis speaks of "*agent-interpretation*" and "*event-interpretation*," i.e., of interpreting means from the agent's point of view or from the point of view of the events. Cf. Nancy Davis, "The Doctrine of Double Effect: Problems of Interpretation." *Pacific Philosophical Quarterly* 65, no. 2 (1984): 107–123, reprinted in *The Doctrine of Double Effect: Philosophers Debate a Controversial Moral Principle*, ed. P. A. Woodward (Notre Dame, IN: University of Notre Dame Press, 2001), 119–142. In the following I quote from Woodward's collection of texts.
4 Cf. the following chapter *Are intentions irrelevant?*
5 Joseph Boyle and T. A. Cavanaugh reach the same conclusion, cf. Joseph M. Boyle, "Toward Understanding the Principle of Double Effect." *Ethics* 90, no. 4 (1980): 527–538, and Thomas A. Cavanaugh, *Double-Effect Reasoning. Doing Good and Avoiding Evil* (Oxford: Clarendon Press, 2006), 28–31.
6 Cf. Ezio di Nucci, "*Ethics without Intention*," 29–31.
7 Nancy Davis, "The Doctrine of Double Effect," 130.
8 This description of craniotomy and the reason for performing it comes from Tom L. Beauchamp and James F. Childress, "*Principles of Biomedical Ethics*," 207.
9 Nancy Davis, "The Doctrine of Double Effect," 131–132.
10 Elizabeth G. M. Anscombe, "War and Murder," in *Nuclear Weapons: A Catholic Response*, ed. Walter Stein (New York: Sheed and Ward, 1962), 45–62. Reprinted in P. A. Woodward, "*The Doctrine of Double Effect. Philosophers Debate a Controversial Moral Principle*," 247–260. Anscombe ascribes this inadequate understanding of intentions to the influence of Cartesian philosophy and theory of mind. Cf. also David S. Oderberg, *Moral Theory. A Non-Consequentialist Approach* (Oxford: Blackwell, 2000a), 113–126.

11 Nancy Davis, "The Doctrine of Double Effect," 135–137.
12 I discuss these roles of intentions in more detail in the section of this chapter entitled *Bratman and Three Roles of Intentions.*
13 Of course the second physician's final end can be different: to comply with the patient's autonomous request, or his final end can comprise a number of motives: to comply with the patient's request and to relieve his tormenting pain.
14 James Rachels, *The End of Life. Euthanasia and Morality* (Oxford: Oxford University Press, 1990), 93.
15 Ibid., 94.
16 Anne Maclean, *The Elimination of Morality. Reflections on Utilitarianism and Bioethics* (London: Routledge, 1993), 85.
17 Jorge L. A. Garcia, "Intentions in Medical Ethics," in *Human Lives: Critical Essays on Consequentialist Bioethics,* eds. David S. Oderberg and Jacqueline A. Lang (Basingstoke: Macmillan, 1997), 161–181.
18 Thomas M. Scanlon, *Permissibility, Meaning, Blame* (Cambridge, MA: Belknap Press of Harvard University Press, 2008).
19 Ibid., 13.
20 Thomas Nagel, *The View from Nowhere* (New York: Oxford University Press, 1986), 181.
21 Cf. Shelly Kagan, *The Limits of Morality* (Oxford: Clarendon Press, 1989), 167–168.
22 Leonard W. Sumner. *Assisted Death. A Study in Ethics & Law* (New York: Oxford University Press, 2011), 68–69.
23 Frances M. Kamm, "The Doctrines of Double and Triple Effect and Why a Rational Agent Need Not Intend the Means to His End," in *Intricate Ethics,* ed. Frances M. Kamm (New York: Oxford University Press, 2007), 91–129, 95. Chapter four would be a more natural place for this section on F. Kamm, but I wanted to discuss her arguments after I would introduce the distinction between c- and f-intentions.
24 Ezio di Nucci, *"Ethics without Intention,"* 136.
25 Frances M. Kamm, "The Doctrines," 119.
26 Especially in his work *Intention, Plans, and Practical Reason.* Cf. Michael Bratman, *Intention, Plans, and Practical Reason* (Stanford, CA: Center for the Study of Language and Information, 1999). Of course, Bratman does not endorse Aquinas's metaphysics of intentions and theory of the structural moments of the intrinsic human act. However, in this work I am not interested in metaphysics, but in the role intentions play in ethics and in deliberations based on the principle of double effect.
27 Bebhin Donnelly-Lazarov, *A Philosophy of Criminal Attempt. The Subjective Approach.* (Cambridge: Cambridge University Press, 2015), 18.
28 Joseph Shaw, "Intention in Ethics." *Canadian Journal of Philosophy* 36, no. 2 (2006): 187–223.
29 In general it is possible to distinguish among three kinds of intentions with respect to action within a plan: (i) **prior intention**, which relates to future action; (ii) **intention in action**, which is the actualization of the intention in the action it controls (actions can thus be conceived as actualizations of intentions); and finally (iii) **further intention**, which is related to prior intention (it is possible to infer further intentions from a prior intention).
30 As I have already stated, this work is not concerned with the metaphysics of intentions, but with the role intentions play. The metaphysics of intentions would require a separate monograph.
31 Michael Bratman, *"Intention,"* 140–164.

32 Cf. Herbert L. A. Hart, "Intention and Punishment," in *Punishment and Responsibility. Essays in the Philosophy of Law,* ed. Herbert L. A. Hart (Oxford: Oxford University Press, 1975), 113–135.

33 Cf. Philippa Foot, "The Problem of Abortion and the Doctrine of Double Effect." *Oxford Review,* no. 5 (1967): 5–15. Reprinted in Paul Woodward, *The Doctrine of Double Effect: Philosophers Debate a Controversial Moral Principle* (Notre Dame, IN: University of Notre Dame Press, 2001), 143–155, at 145–146. In the following I will refer to Woodward's collection.

34 Ezio di Nucci, *"Ethics without Intention,"* 107–112.

35 Ibid., 107.

36 Thomas A. Cavanaugh, *Double-Effect Reasoning. Doing Good and Avoiding Evil* (Oxford: Clarendon Press, 2006), 112.

37 Jonathan Bennett, *The Act Itself* (Cambridge: Cambridge University Press, 1995).

38 Ibid., 213.

39 Ralph Wedgwood, "Defending Double Effect." *Ratio* 24, no. 4 (September 2011): 384–401. Cf. also Ralph Wedgwood, "Intrinsic Values and Reasons for Action." *Philosophical Issues* 19, no. 1 (2009): 321–342.

40 Ralph Wedgwood, "Defending Double Effect," 386.

41 Ibid., 397.

42 The condition "virtuous" excludes all those who enjoy the bad event, profit on it, etc. In that way it expresses a certain condition of moral objectivity.

43 Christopher Kaczor, *Proportionalism and the Natural Law Tradition* (Washington, DC: The Catholic University of America Press, 2002), 111–113.

44 Dana K. Nelkin and Samuel C. Rickless, "So Close, Yet So Far: Why Solutions to the Closeness Problem for the Doctrine of Double Effect Fall Short." *Noûs* 49, no. 2 (2015): 376–409; Joshua Stuchlik, "The Closeness Problem for Double Effect: A Reply to Nelkin and Rickless." *Journal of Value Inquiry* 51, no. 1 (2017): 69–83.

45 David S. Oderberg, *Moral Theory. A Non-Consequentialist Approach* (Oxford: Blackwell, 2000a), 91–123.

46 Ibid., 91.

47 Ibid., 93–94.

48 Thomas Nagel, *"The View from Nowhere,"* 181.

49 Ralph Wedgwood, "Defending Double Effect," 392.

# 7   Conclusion

In my monograph I aimed to defend the following three theses:

1   It is impossible to speak of one principle of double effect. Various formulations have appeared in history, which are not merely different ways of expressing the same principle. The individual formulations are set in certain ethical contexts, in which they can play and often do play different roles. To speak of "the principle of double effect" is historically inadequate.

2   The first formulation of a deliberation based on the principle of double effect – on balancing the moral admissibility of actualizing an action having good and bad consequences – appears in the work of the Dominican philosopher and theologian, Thomas Aquinas.

3   The principle of double effect in the form I give it in the last chapter of my work is still a controversial moral principle; its assumptions (the ethical requirement of taking into account the intentions of agents in the ethical evaluation of their actions) are especially controversial. If these assumptions are accepted, then the principle of double effect appears to be a rational way of justifying certain actions.

The second chapter was devoted to demonstrating the second thesis. I rigorously analyzed Thomas Aquinas's texts, introduced his conception of moral evaluation of human action and focussed on interpreting the phrases "*in intentione*," "*praeter intentionem*," "*per accidens*" and "*quandoque*." I believe that I have succeeded to show that Aquinas really presented the first version of moral deliberation based on the principle of double effect.

The third and fourth chapters were, like the first one, prevalently historical in character. I selected authors I regard as most important (Tommaso de Vio, Francisco de Vitoria, Domingo de Sta Teresa, Jean Pierre Gury, Peter Knauer and G. L. Hallett) and presented their formulations of the principle of double effect set in their contexts. This historical material served to demonstrate the first thesis of my monograph: it is historically inadequate to speak of *the* principle of double effect.

The individual versions of the principle of double effect differ not only in formulation, but also by being set in certain contexts of moral theories and the roles they play in them.

The fifth and sixth chapters did not serve merely as a historical introduction to the contemporary debate on the validity and applications of the principle of double effect. Over the course of the critical historical exposition in the fifth chapter I had an opportunity to gradually clarify the function of the individual components in formulating the principle of double effect and illustrate its practical application with examples. The sixth chapter focussed on demonstrating the third thesis of my work. Its core consists of three parts: (i) the first one deals with the role of intentions in moral evaluation of human action, (ii) the second one presents Bratman's influential theory of intentions and their three roles, and finally (iii) the third one is devoted to the difficult closeness problem. I believe that I have successfully shown that upon accepting certain assumptions, which I attempt to justify, the principle of double effect is a valid and important moral principle of evaluating human action having good and bad effects.

# Literature

Aquinas, Thomas. *In octo libros Physicorum expo.*

Aquinas, Thomas. *Quaestiones disputatae: De malo.*

Aquinas, Thomas. *Quaestiones disputatae: De veritate.*

Aquinas, Thomas. *Summa contra Gentiles.*

Aquinas, Thomas. *Summa Theologiae.*

Anscombe, Elisabeth G. M. "War and Murder." In: *Nuclear Weapons: A Catholic Response*, edited by Walter Stein, 45–62. New York: Sheed and Ward, 1962.

Anscombe, Elisabeth G. M. *Intention.* 2nd ed. Cambridge, MA: Harvard University, 2000.

Beauchamp, Tom L., and James F. Childress. *Principles of Biomedical Ethics.* 4th ed. New York: Oxford University Press, 1994.

Bennett, Jonathan. *The Act Itself.* Cambridge: Cambridge University Press, 1995.

Boyle, Joseph. "Intentions, Christian Morality, and Bioethics: Puzzles of Double Effect." *Christian Bioethics* 3, no. 2 (January 1997): 87–88.

Boyle, Joseph. "Who Is Entitled to Double Effect?" *Ethics and Medical Decision-Making*, May 2017, 237–256.

Boyle, Joseph M. "Praeter Intentionem in Aquinas." *The Thomist: A Speculative Quarterly Review* 42, no. 4 (1978): 649–665.

Boyle, Joseph M. "Toward Understanding the Principle of Double Effect." *Ethics* 90, no. 4 (1980): 527–538. Reprinted in Woodward, Paul A. *The Doctrine of Double Effect: Philosophers Debate a Controversial Moral Principle.* Notre Dame, IN: University of Notre Dame Press, 2010, 7–20.

Bratman, Michael. *Intention, Plans, and Practical Reason.* Stanford, CA: Center for the Study of Language and Information, 1999.

Brugger, Christian E. "Praeter Intentionem in Aquinas and Issues in Bioethics." In: *Bioethics with Liberty and Justice: Themes in the Work of Joseph M. Boyle*, edited by Christopher Tollefsen, 97–111. Dordrecht: Springer Science Business Media, 2011.

Cathcart, Thomas. *The Tram Problem, or, Would You Throw the Fat Guy off the Bridge? A Philosophical Conundrum.* New York: Oxford University Press, 2008.

Cavanaugh, Thomas A. "Double Effect and the Ethical Significance of Distinct Volitional States." *Christian Bioethics* 3, no. 2 (January 1997): 131–141.

Cavanaugh, Thomas A. *Double-Effect Reasoning: Doing Good and Avoiding Evil.* Oxford: Clarendon Press, 2009.

Coplestone, Frederick. *A History of Philosophy. Vol. III: Late Medieval and Renaissance Philosophy.* New York: Doubleday, 1993.

Davis, Nancy. "The Doctrine of Double Effect: Problems of Interpretation." *Pacific Philosophical Quarterly* 65, no. 2 (1984): 107–23. Reprinted in Woodward, Paul A. *The Doctrine of Double Effect: Philosophers Debate a Controversial Moral Principle.* Notre Dame, IN: University of Notre Dame Press, 2010, 119–142.

De Finance, Joseph. *Éthique Générale.* Roma: Presses de l'Université Grégorienne, 1967.

Di Nucci, Ezzi. *Ethics without Intention.* London: Bloomsbury, 2014.

Donagan, Alan. *The Theory of Morality.* Chicago, IL: University of Chicago Press, 1977.

Donnelly-Lazarov, Bebhinn. *A Philosophy of Criminal Attempt. The Subjective Approach.* Cambridge: Cambridge University Press, 2015.

Driver, Julia. *Consequentialism.* New York: Routledge, 2012.

Edmonds, David. *Would You Kill the Fat Man? The Tram Problem and What Your Answer Tells Us about Right and Wrong.* Princeton, NJ: Princeton University Press, 2014.

Elders, Leo J. *La metafisica dell'essere di san Tommaso d'Aquino in una prospettiva storica.* Vol. 1. *L'essere comune.* Città del Vaticano: Libreria editrice vaticana, 1995.

Finnis, John M. *Fundamentals of Ethics.* Washington, DC: Georgetown University Press, 1983.

Finnis, John M. *Moral Absolutes. Tradition, Revision, and Truth.* Washington, DC: The Catholic University of America Press, 1991.

Finnis, John M. *Natural Law and Natural Rights.* 2nd ed. Oxford: Clarendon, 2011.

Flannery, Kevin L. "John Finnis on Thomas Aquinas on Human Action." In: *Reason, Morality, and Law. The Philosophy of John Finnis,* edited by Keown, John, and Robert P. George, 118–132. Oxford: Oxford University Press, 2013.

Foot, Philippa. "The Problem of Abortion and the Doctrine of Double Effect." *Oxford Review,* 5 (1967): 5–15.

Foot, Philippa. "Morality, Action, and Outcome." In: *Morality and Objectivity: A Tribute to J. L. Mackie,* edited by Honderich, Ted, and J. L. Mackie, 23–38. London: Routledge, 2012.

Garcia, Jorge L. A. "Intentions in Medical Ethics." In: *Human Lives: Critical Essays on Consequentialist Bioethics,* edited by Oderberg, David S., and Jacqueline A. Laing, 161–181. Basingstoke: Macmillan, 1997.

Gómez-Lobo, Alfonso. *Morality and the Human Goods. An Introduction to Natural Law Ethics.* Washington, DC: Georgetown University Press, 2002.

Gury, Jean-Pierre. *Compendium theologiae moralis. Editio decima septima.* Tomus primus. Romae: Typis civilitatis catholicae, 1866.

Hallett, Garth. *Greater Good. The Case for Proportionalism.* Washington, DC: Georgetown University Press, 1995.

Hart, H. L. A. "Intention and Punishment." In: *Punishment and Responsibility. Essays in the Philosophy of Law,* 113–135. Oxford: Oxford University Press, 1975.

Hayen, André. *L'intentionnel selon saint Thomas*. Deuxième édition. Bruges: Desclée de Brouwer, 1954.

Herring, Jonathan. *Criminal Law. The Basics*. London: Routledge, 2010.

Jensen, Steven J. *Good & Evil Actions. A Journey through Saint Thomas Aquinas*. Washington, DC: The Catholic University of America Press, 2010.

Jensen, Steven J. *Knowing the Natural Law. From Precepts and Inclinations to Deriving Oughts*. Washington, DC: The Catholic University of America Press, 2015.

Johnstone, Brian V. "The Meaning of Proportionate Reason in Contemporary Moral Theology." *The Thomist: A Speculative Quarterly Review* 49, no. 2 (1985): 223–247.

Jordan, Mark D. "The Summa's Reform of Moral Teaching." In: *Contemplating Aquinas. On the Varietes of Interpretation*, edited by Fergus Kerr, 41–54. London: SCM Press, 2003.

Kaczor, Christopher. "Double-Effect Reasoning from Jean Pierre Gury to Peter Knauer." *Theological Studies* 59, no. 2 (1998): 297–316.

Kaczor, Christopher. "Moral Absolutism and Ectopic Pregnancy." *The Journal of Medicine and Philosophy* 26, no. 1 (January 2001): 61–74.

Kaczor, Christopher. *Proportionalism and the Natural Law Tradition*. Washington, DC: The Catholic University of America Press, 2002.

Kagan, Shelly. *The Limits of Morality*. Oxford: Clarendon Press, 1989.

Kamm, Frances M. "The Doctrines of Double and Triple Effect and Why a Rational Agent Need Not Intend the Means to His End." In: *Intricate Ethics*, 91–129. New York: Oxford University Press, 2007.

Kamm, Frances M. *The Trolley Problem Mysteries*. New York: Oxford University Press, 2019.

Keenan, James F. "The Function of the Principle of Double Effect." *Theological Studies* 54, no. 2 (1993): 294–315.

Knauer, P. "The Hermeneutic Function of the Principle of Double Effect." *The American Journal of Jurisprudence* 12, no. 1 (January 1967): 132–162.

Lee, Steven P. *Ethics and War: An Introduction*. Cambridge: Cambridge University Press, 2012.

Lessius, Leonardus S. J. *De iustitia et iure. Editio secunda, auctior et castigatior*. Antverpiae: Ex officina plantiniana, 1609.

Luño, Ángel R. *Etica General*. Pamplona: Ediciones Universidad de Navarra, S.A., 1991.

Macauley, Robert C. *Ethics in Palliative Care: A Complete Guide*. New York: Oxford University Press, 2018.

Maclean, Anne. *The Elimination of Morality. Reflections on Utilitarianism and Bioethics*. London: Routledge, 1993.

Mangan, Joseph T. "An Historical Analysis of the Principle of Double Effect." *Theological Studies* 10, no. 1 (1949): 41–61.

Maritain, Jacques. "La loi naturelle ou loi non écrite." In: *OEuvres complètes*. Vol. XVI, edited by Maritain, Jacques, and Raïsa Maritain. Paris, Fribourg: Éditions Universitaires, Éditions Saint-Paul, 1999.

Masek, Lawrence. "Intentions, Motives and the Doctrine of Double Effect." *The Philosophical Quarterly* 60, no. 240 (February 2009): 567–585.

Matthews, Gareth B. "Saint Thomas and the Principle of Double Effect." In: *Aquinas's Moral Theory: Essays in Honor of Norman Kretzmann*, edited by

MacDonald, Scott, and Eleonore Stump, 63–78. Ithaca, NY: Cornell University Press, 2008.

McInerny, Ralph. *Aquinas on Human Action. A Theory of Practice.* Washington, DC: The Catholic University of America Press, 1992.

McInerny, Ralph. "Ethics." In: *The Cambridge Companion to Aquinas,* edited by Kretzmann, Norman, and Eleonore Stump, 196–216. Cambridge: Cambridge University Press, 1993.

McInerny, Ralph. *Ethica Thomistica: The Moral Philosophy of Thomas Aquinas.* Revisited edition. Washington, DC: The Catholic University of America Press, 1997.

Mcintyre, Alison. "Doing Away with Double Effect." *Ethics* 111, no. 2 (2001): 219–255.

Mondin, Battista. *Dizionario enciclopedico del pensiero di San Tommaso d'Aquino.* Bologna: ESD, 1991.

Mulgan, Tim. *The Demands of Consequentialism.* New York: Oxford University Press, 2001.

Mulgan, Tim. *Understanding Utilitarianism.* Stocksfield: Acumen, 2007.

Munson, Ronald. *Intervention and Reflection: Basic Issues in Medical Ethics.* Belmont, CA: Wadsworth, 1979.

Nagel, Thomas. *The View from Nowhere.* New York: Oxford University Press, 1986.

Nathanson, Stephen. *Terrorism and Ethics of War.* Cambridge: Cambridge University Press, 2010.

Nelkin, Dana K., and Samuel C. Rickless. "So Close, Yet so Far: Why Solutions to the Closeness Problem for the Doctrine of Double Effect Fall Short." *Noûs* 49, no. 2 (2015): 376–409.

Oderberg, David S. *Moral Theory. A Non-Consequentialist Approach.* Oxford: Blackwell, 2000a.

Oderberg, David S. *Applied Ethics. A Non-Consequentialist Approach.* Oxford: Blackwell, 2000b.

Oderberg, David S., and Jacqueline A. Laing. *Human Lives: Critical Essays on Consequentialist Bioethics.* Basingstoke: Palgrave Macmillan, 2014.

Osborne, Thomas M. Jr. *Human Action in Thomas Aquinas, John Duns Scotus & William of Ockham.* Washington, DC: The Catholic University of America Press, 2014.

Parenti, Sergio. Legge ed eccezione." *Sacra Doctrina,* no. 1 (2015): 197–291.

Pereira, Luís M., and Ari Saptawijaya. *Programming Machine Ethics.* Dordrecht: Springer, 2016.

Pilsner, Joseph. *The Specification of Human Actions in St. Thomas Aquinas.* Oxford: Oxford University Press, 2006.

Porter, Jean. "Recent Studies in Aquinas's Virtue Ethics." *Journal of Religious Ethics* 26, no. 1 (1998): 191–215.

Rachels, James. *The End of Life.* New York: Oxford University Press, 1990.

Randall, Fiona, and Robin S. Downie. *The Philosophy of Palliative Care: Critique and Reconstruction.* New York: Oxford University Press, 2006.

Salmanticenses, *Cursus theologicus.* Tomus quartus. Lugduni: Joannis Antonii Huguetan, 1697.

Scanlon, Thomas M. *Permissibility, Meaning, Blame.* Cambridge, MA: Belknap Press of Harvard University Press, 2008.

Shafer-Landau, Russ. *Ethical Theory: An Anthology*. 2nd ed. Malden, MA: Wiley-Blackwell, 2013.

Shaw, Joseph. "Intention in Ethics." *Canadian Journal of Philosophy* 36, no. 2 (2006): 187–223.

Singer, Peter. *Practical Ethics*. 2nd ed. Cambridge: Cambridge University Press, 1993.

Smart, J. J. C., and Bernard Williams. *Utilitarianism: for and Against*. New York: Cambridge University Press, 2008.

Smith, Janet E. *Humanae Vitae, a Generation Later*. Washington, DC: Catholic University of America Press, 2010.

Steinhoff, Uwe. *On the Ethics of War and Terrorism*. New York: Oxford University Press, 2007.

Stuchlik, Joshua "The Closeness Problem for Double Effect: A Reply to Nelkin and Rickless." *Journal of Value Inquiry* 51, no. 1 (2017): 69–83.

Stump, Eleonor. *Aquinas*. New York: Routledge, 2005.

Sumner, Leonard W. *Assisted Death. A Study in Ethics & Law*. New York: Oxford University Press, 2011.

Thomson, Judith Jarvis. "Killing, Letting Die, and the Trolley Problem." *Monist* 59, no. 2 (1976): 204–217.

Thomson, Judith Jarvis. "The Trolley Problem." *The Yale Law Journal* 94, no. 6 (1985): 1395–1415.

Timmons, Mark. *Moral Theory. An Introduction*. 2nd ed. Lanham, MD: Rowman & Littlefield Publishers, 2013.

Torrell, Jean-Pierre. *Initiation à Saint Thomas d'Aquin. Sa personne et son oeuvre*. Fribourg: Editiones Universitaires, 1993.

Torrell, Jean-Pierre. *Aquinas's Summa. Background, Structure, & Reception*. Washington, DC: Catholic University of America Press, 2005.

Vidal, Marciano. *Manuale di etica teologica*. Parte seconda. *Morale dell'amore e della sessualità*. Cittadella: Assisi, 1996.

Vitoria, Francisco de, and John P. Doyle. *Reflection on Homicide & Commentary on Summa Theologiae IIa-IIae Q. 64 (Thomas Aquinas)*. Milwaukee, WI: Marquette University Press, 1997.

Wedgwood, Ralph. "Intrinsic Values and Reasons for Action." *Philosophical Issues* 19, no. 1 (2009): 321–342.

Wedgwood, Ralph. "Defending Double Effect." *Ratio* 24, no. 4 (September 2011): 384–401.

Wippel, John F. *The Metaphysical Thought of Thomas Aquinas. From Finite Being to Uncreated Being*. Washington, DC: The Catholic University of America Press, 2000.

Woodward, Paul A. *The Doctrine of Double Effect: Philosophers Debate a Controversial Moral Principle*. Notre Dame, IN: University of Notre Dame Press, 2010.

# Index